RED HOT
FRANKFURTERS
AND ICE COLD
LEMONADE
Tellas Busy Bee
5¢ A Glass
Ice Cold Lemonade
Hot … & … ¢ Each

ONE WAY
BRIGHTON BEACH
BRIGHTON 5TH ST
1/2 PRICE
7:30-8AM EXCEPT SUNDAY
8am-7pm EXCEPT SUNDAY
PAY MUNI METER
CHILDRENS CLOTHES CLEARANCE
KIDS SHIRTS
OPEN
MAGIC CORSET
Lingerie
258
718-332-4141
BRIGHTON
JEWELRY EXPERT
WE BUY GOLD & DIAMONDS
256
ЗОЛОТО
256
254
769-9800
OCEAN VIEW
OPTICAL
CLEARANCE
Rx
OPEN
252
OPEN

TENEMENTS, TOWERS & TRASH

An Unconventional Illustrated History of New York City

JULIA WERTZ

BLACK DOG
& LEVENTHAL
PUBLISHERS
NEW YORK

PARTS OF THIS BOOK FIRST APPEARED IN *NEW YORKER* MAGAZINE AND/OR *HARPER'S* MAGAZINE.

COVER DESIGN BY AMANDA KAIN

BLACK DOG & LEVENTHAL PUBLISHERS
HACHETTE BOOK GROUP
1290 AVENUE OF THE AMERICAS
NEW YORK, NY 10104

WWW.HACHETTEBOOKGROUP.COM
WWW.BLACKDOGANDLEVENTHAL.COM

FIRST EDITION: OCTOBER 2017

BLACK DOG & LEVENTHAL PUBLISHERS IS AN IMPRINT OF HACHETTE BOOKS, A DIVISION OF HACHETTE BOOK GROUP. THE BLACK DOG & LEVENTHAL PUBLISHERS NAME AND LOGO ARE TRADEMARKS OF HACHETTE BOOK GROUP, INC.

PRINT BOOK INTERIOR DESIGN BY OHIOBOY DESIGN CO.

LCCN: 2017933752
ISBNS: 978-0-316-50121-7 (HARDCOVER), 978-0-316-50122-4 (EBOOK)

PRINTED IN CHINA

IM

10 9 8 7 6 5 4 3 2

"THERE ARE ROUGHLY THREE NEW YORKS. THERE IS, FIRST, THE NEW YORK OF THE MAN OR WOMAN WHO WAS BORN HERE, WHO TAKES THE CITY FOR GRANTED AND ACCEPTS ITS SIZE AND ITS TURBULENCE AS NATURAL AND INEVITABLE. SECOND, THERE IS THE NEW YORK OF THE COMMUTER—THE CITY THAT IS DEVOURED BY LOCUSTS EACH DAY AND SPAT OUT EACH NIGHT. THIRD, THERE IS THE NEW YORK OF THE PERSON WHO WAS BORN SOMEWHERE ELSE AND CAME TO NEW YORK IN QUEST OF SOMETHING. OF THESE THREE TREMBLING CITIES THE GREATEST IS THE LAST—THE CITY OF FINAL DESTINATION, THE CITY THAT IS A GOAL. IT IS THIS THIRD CITY THAT ACCOUNTS FOR NEW YORK'S HIGH-STRUNG DISPOSITION, ITS POETICAL DEPORTMENT, ITS DEDICATION TO THE ARTS, AND ITS INCOMPARABLE ACHIEVEMENTS. COMMUTERS GIVE THE CITY ITS TIDAL RESTLESSNESS, NATIVES GIVE IT SOLIDITY AND CONTINUITY, BUT THE SETTLERS GIVE IT PASSION."

-E.B. WHITE, *HERE IS NEW YORK*, 1949

DEAR KIND READER,

THIS IS NOT A TYPICAL HISTORY BOOK, NOR IS IT A USEFUL GUIDE TO NEW YORK CITY. THERE IS NO MENTION OF THE CITY'S NATIVE PEOPLES, THERE ARE NO DRAWINGS OF ELLIS ISLAND OR THE EMPIRE STATE BUILDING. THE STATUE OF LIBERTY MAKES A BRIEF APPEARANCE, BUT ONLY FOR THE SAKE OF A STORY ABOUT GARBAGE. INSTEAD, THIS IS A BOOK ABOUT UNIQUE AND OFTEN FORGOTTEN STORIES FROM THE CITY'S PAST, ACCOMPANIED BY ILLUSTRATIONS OF RANDOM NEIGHBORHOODS AS THEY WERE AND AS THEY ARE. IF YOU'RE EXPECTING A REGULAR HISTORY BOOK OR LOOKING FOR A GUIDE TO THE CITY'S RESTAURANTS OR LANDMARKS, YOU'RE SHIT OUT OF LUCK. BUT IF YOU'RE SICK OF THOSE BOOKS AND WANT A LESS CONVENTIONAL TAKE ON NEW YORK CITY, WELL, HERE IT IS.

I GREW UP ON THE WEST COAST IN A SMALL NORTHERN CALIFORNIA TOWN, WHERE I NEVER QUITE FIT IN. I SPENT MY EARLY TWENTIES IN SAN FRANCISCO, WHERE I FIT MUCH BETTER, BUT IT WASN'T UNTIL I DISCOVERED NEW YORK CITY WHEN I FELT LIKE I FOUND THE PLACE I WAS SUPPOSED TO BE. THE FRENZIED, NEUROTIC PACE OF THE EAST COAST FELT COMFORTABLE AND FAMILIAR, SO I SETTLED IN. I ONLY INTENDED TO STAY IN THE CITY FOR TWO YEARS, MAYBE FIVE TOPS, BUT BEFORE I KNEW IT, I'D BEEN THERE FOR A DECADE.

MY YEARS IN NEW YORK WERE FRACTURED. I SPENT THE FIRST FEW WORKING ON AUTOBIOGRAPHICAL COMICS AND DRINKING TOO MUCH BY MYSELF IN MY APARTMENT. THEN I PULLED IT TOGETHER, QUIT COMICS, AND SPENT A COUPLE OF YEARS EXPLORING, PHOTOGRAPHING, AND RESEARCHING ABANDONED BUILDINGS. THAT LED ME TO THE DISCOVERY OF PLACES LIKE BOTTLE BEACH, HARLEM'S PS 186, CREEDMOOR PSYCHIATRIC CENTER, SEAVIEW TUBERCULOSIS HOSPITAL, AND OTHER ABANDONED SPOTS IN THE FIVE BOROUGHS. NOT ALL OF THESE PLACES MADE IT INTO THIS BOOK (TO SEE THOSE PLACES, GO TO ADVENTUREBIBLESCHOOL.COM), SINCE I WANTED TO FOCUS MORE ON COMICS AND ILLUSTRATION, BUT THEY HELPED SHAPE THE WAY I SAW HISTORIC AND MODERN NEW YORK.

DURING MY LAST YEARS IN THE CITY, I SPENT ALL MY TIME DRAWING BUILDINGS, RESEARCHING AND WRITING, AND WANDERING THROUGH DIFFERENT NEIGHBORHOODS. I'D ALWAYS LOVED LONG WALKS, BUT IT WASN'T UNTIL I STARTED OBSESSIVELY DRAWING NYC WHEN I STARTED TO REALLY SEE IT—THE ARCHITECTURE, THE PEOPLE, THE HISTORY—AND TO REALLY LOVE IT. THE NEW YORKER, HARPER'S MAGAZINE AND THE NEW YORK TIMES BEGAN PUBLISHING MY HISTORY COMICS AND ILLUSTRATIONS, AND I FELT LIKE I'D FINALLY MADE IT, I WAS A REAL NEW YORKER. AND THEN, JUST LIKE THAT, IT ALL FELL APART.

IN 2016, I WAS ILLEGALLY EVICTED FROM MY GREENPOINT STUDIO, WHERE I'D BEEN LIVING FOR THE LAST NINE YEARS. I WAS JUST ONE OF MANY VICTIMS OF THE WIDESPREAD GREED THAT IS CONSUMING NEW YORK'S REAL ESTATE MARKET. I COULD HAVE STAYED, CITING NUMEROUS HOUSING RIGHTS, BUT MY LANDLORD HAD BECOME A TYRANT WHO FREQUENTLY YELLED AT AND BERATED HIS TENANTS, AND I COULDN'T LIVE LIKE THAT ANYMORE; IT WAS TIME TO GO. I BRIEFLY CONSIDERED MOVING TO A NEW APARTMENT IN THE CITY, BUT I KNEW THAT AS A FREELANCER WITH A VERY MODEST AND UNSTABLE INCOME, ANY PLACE I MIGHT WANT TO LIVE WOULD BE SNAPPED UP BY MORE FINANCIALLY STABLE PEOPLE. AND I JUST COULDN'T FACE THE FRESH NIGHTMARE THAT IS APARTMENT HUNTING IN NYC.

I RELUCTANTLY PACKED UP MY STUFF AND MOVED BACK HOME TO CALIFORNIA. LIVING IN MY MOM'S GARAGE ATTIC IN MY MID-30'S FACILITATED A BIT OF AN EXISTENTIAL CRISIS, WHICH WAS EXACERBATED BY HAVING TO WORK ON THIS BOOK EVERY SINGLE DAY. IT WAS AN ABSOLUTE FUCKING TORTURE DRAWING AND WRITING ABOUT A CITY I NO LONGER LIVED IN BUT DESPERATELY MISSED. MY LOVE FOR NYC, WHICH WAS STRONG WHEN I WAS A RESIDENT, SEEMED TO GROW EVEN MORE IN ITS ABSENCE, BECAUSE TIME IS A CRUEL MISTRESS. EVER SINCE I LEFT, I'VE NEVER STOPPED DAYDREAMING ABOUT THE CITY AND SCHEMING OF WAYS TO GET BACK TO IT. I'M NOT SURE I EVER WILL, BUT I DO KNOW THAT I'LL NEVER LOVE ANOTHER CITY THE WAY I LOVED NEW YORK.

AND SO, KIND READER, YOU NOW KNOW A BIT OF MY BACKSTORY, WHICH SHOULD INFORM SOMEOF THE COMICS IN THIS BOOK IN WHICH MY CHARACTER MAKES AN APPEARANCE. BUT FOR THE MOST PART, I'VE STAYED OUT OF IT, LETTING NYC BE THE MAIN PROTAGONIST. WHILE WORKING ON THIS BOOK, I OFTEN WONDERED IF IT WAS POSSIBLE TO MAKE A GOOD HISTORY BOOK THAT DOESN'T INCLUDE ICONIC LANDMARKS AND POPULAR ATTRACTIONS. I'M NOT REALLY SURE, BUT I DID IT ANYWAYS, BECAUSE ULTIMATELY, I MADE THIS BOOK FOR MYSELF. THIS IS MY NEW YORK.

-JULIA WERTZ, 2017

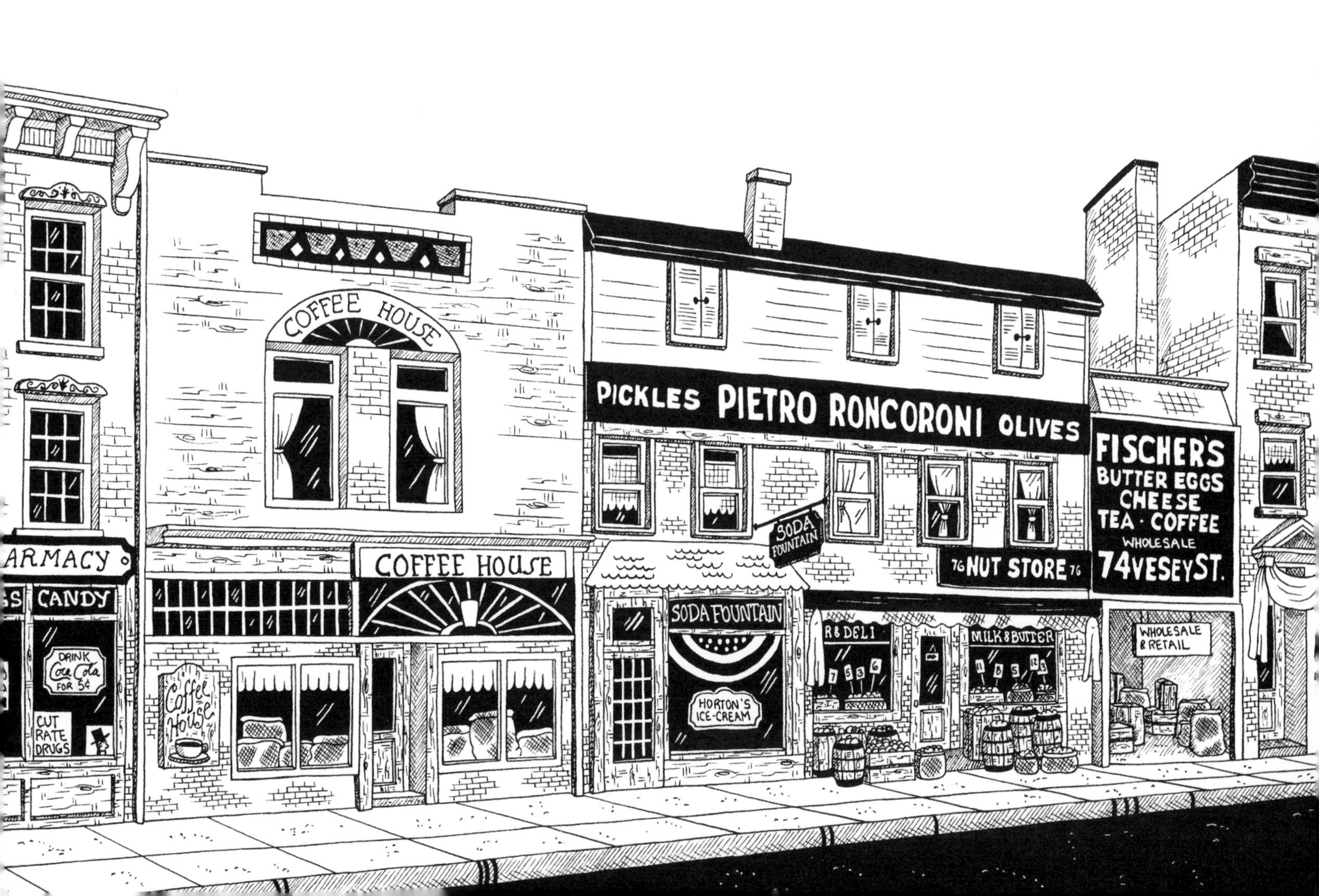

MY RELATIONSHIP WITH NEW YORK CITY

A RANDOM MORNING:
IT'S SO NICE OUT! I SHOULD QUIT DRAWING AND GO FOR A LONG WALK IN THE CITY!

UGH, WHY AM I WALKING ACROSS THE BRIDGE IN THE BLISTERING SUN ON THE HOTTEST DAY?
PROBABLY BECAUSE I'M CRAZY AND I HATE MYSELF.

ARG! I HATE WHEN PEOPLE LINE UP THREE ACROSS AND THEN WALK SLOW! IT'S SO RUDE!! HOW DO THEY NOT SEE THE CHAOS THEY'RE CREATING IN THEIR LEISURELY WAKE? BUNCHA SAVAGES...

YAK! BUBBLES AGAIN? I DON'T MEAN TO BE A WET BLANKET BUT I REALLY DON'T APPRECIATE HAVING TO DODGE AIRBORNE SOAP WHILST WALKING DOWN THE STREET.

NOPE, I'M NOT WAITING AN HOUR IN LINE AT A BAGEL STORE, THAT'S A LINE I REFUSE TO CROSS. ALTHOUGH ONCE I DID WAIT IN LINE FOR 40 MINUTES FOR A COOKIE, AND IT WAS WORTH IT, BUT NEVER AGAIN!

BLEH, WHY IS EVERYTHING SO FUCKING PRECIOUS THESE DAYS? ENOUGH WITH THIS ALREADY!
WINDOW TEXT VERBATIM. THERE WERE ALSO REAL AUTUMN LEAVES SCATTERED ABOUT THE TABLES INSIDE. OUTSIDE THERE WAS A CHALKBOARD ON WHICH WAS WRITTEN, "A CUPCAKE IS HAPPINESS WITH ICING." DISGUSTING.
GLUTEN FREE - DAIRY FREE
REFINED SUGAR FREE
SOY FREE – PEANUT FREE
ALLERGY FRIENDLY
ORGANIC – ARTISAN
GOODNESS

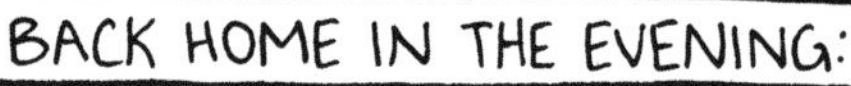

BARF! IS THAT A RAT EATING A DEAD PIGEON? IS THAT AN ACTUAL THING I'M SEEING, OR SOMETHING MY BRAIN IS FABRICATING TO PERPETUATE THE NOTION THAT NYC IS JUST A PILE OF TRASH BUILT ON TOP OF GARBAGE? OH, IT'S EATING FRIED CHICKEN, PHEW!

HEY BABY, CAN I GET A SMILE? YOU'D BE PRETTIER IF YOU SMILED.
I CANNOT SCOWL ANY HARDER...

BACK HOME IN THE EVENING:
AH, WHAT A LOVELY DAY IN THE CITY!

CONTENTS

AFTER THE NEW YORK WORLD'S FAIR

THE STRUCTURAL REMAINS OF THE 1964-'65 NEW YORK WORLD'S FAIR ARE ONE OF THE WORST-KEPT "SECRETS" IN THE CITY'S HISTORY.

A BETTER-KEPT SECRET IS THE ONE OF THE UNIQUE LAMPPOSTS THAT LINED THE WALKWAYS OF THE FAIR DURING ITS TWO-YEAR TENURE IN QUEENS.

THE 1964-'65 NEW YORK WORLD'S FAIR WAS THE SECOND WORLD'S FAIR TO BE HELD IN FLUSHING MEADOWS. THE PREVIOUS FAIR WAS HELD IN 1939-'40. THE TRADITION OF WORLD FAIRS BEGAN UNOFFICIALLY IN FRANCE, IN 1844, AND OFFICIALLY IN LONDON IN 1851. MANY COUNTRIES PARTICIPATED, BUILDING TEMPORARY EXPOSITIONS TO INTRODUCE THE WORLD TO VARIOUS CULTURES, TRADITIONS, AND TECHNOLOGICAL ADVANCES.

THE FAIR'S THEME WAS DEDICATED TO...
"...MAN'S ACHIEVEMENT ON A SHRINKING GLOBE IN AN EXPANDING UNIVERSE."
OOF, THAT'S A MOUTHFUL OF NONSENSE. LET'S GO WITH "PEACE THROUGH UNDERSTANDING."
ROBERT MOSES, THE CONTROVERSIAL "MASTER BUILDER" OF NEW YORK.

THE FAIR'S ROOTS WERE OF A MORALLY DUBIOUS NATURE, REVOLVING MOSTLY AROUND CORPORATION-SUPPORTED CONSUMERISM DISGUISED AS "CULTURAL EXPERIENCE." THE FAIR WAS THE WORK OF A GROUP OF NEW YORK BUSINESSMEN, OSTENSIBLY IN AN ATTEMPT TO PROFIT OFF THEIR OWN CHILDHOOD MEMORIES.

LIFE HAS GROWN TIRESOME AND STALE. PERHAPS I'LL BUY A CHEVELLE OR A BARRACUDA, SPICE THINGS UP A LITTLE.

REMEMBER THE GENERAL MOTORS EXPO AT THE 1939 WORLD'S FAIR? THAT WAS A GRAND OLD TIME. SAY, WHY DON'T WE HOST ANOTHER WORLD'S FAIR. GET SOME OF THAT CORPORATE SPONSORSHIP AND EXPO RENTAL MONEY!

I MEAN, GIVE OUR CHILDREN AND GRANDCHILDREN THE SAME WONDERFUL, WORLDLY EXPERIENCE WE HAD.

FIFTY EIGHT COUNTRIES PARTICIPATED IN THE FAIR, SPREAD OUT ACROSS 650 ACRES IN FLUSHING MEADOWS CORONA PARK.

ACTUAL WORLD'S FAIR POSTCARDS

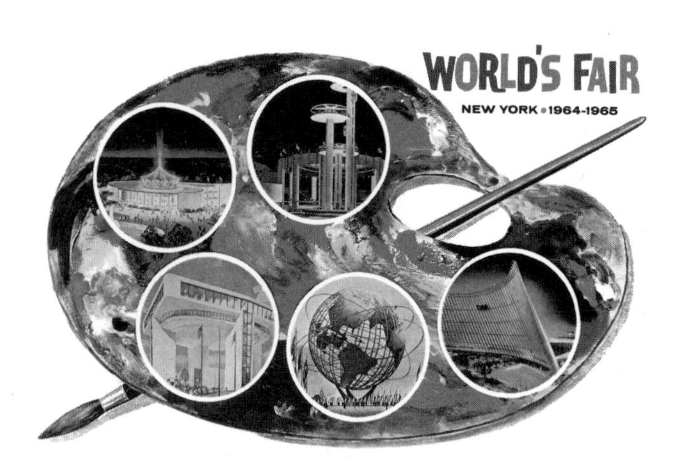

ALTHOUGH ATTENDED BY 50 MILLION PEOPLE, THE FAIR FELL SHORT OF THE NECESSARY 70 MILLION VISITORS NEEDED TO MAKE A PROFIT. IT WAS CONSIDERED A FINANCIAL FAILURE.

ONE OF THE ONLY AMUSEMENTS TO MAKE MONEY WAS *LES POUPÉES DE PARIS* (*THE DOLLS OF PARIS*), AN ADULTS-ONLY PUPPET MUSICAL.
IT'S NOT WHAT IT LOOKS LIKE, LOUISE, THEY'RE PUPPETS! *PUPPETS*, LOUISE!!
THAT'S EVEN WORSE, BOB!
SPECTACULAR
PHIL SILVERS
Brilliant
MILTON BERLE
PEARL BAILEY
SMASH HIT
SID & MARTY on stage KROFFTS
Les Poupées de Paris

THE FAIR CLOSED AMID ALLEGATIONS OF FINANCIAL MISMANAGEMENT AND INSUFFICIENT ATTENDANCE, AND THE DEATH KNELL OF BEING LABELED BORING.
I TOLD YOU NO ONE WOULD COME ALL THE WAY OUT TO QUEENS FOR A SUNDAY AMUSEMENT. WE SHOULD HAVE PUT IT IN MANHATTAN!
PERHAPS. DEFINITELY NOT BROOKLYN. NO ONE WILL EVER WANT TO GO TO THAT GARBAGE BOROUGH.

THE FAIR WAS DISMANTLED AND ABANDONED, AND THE REMAINING STRUCTURES FELL INTO DISREPAIR FOR MANY DECADES.

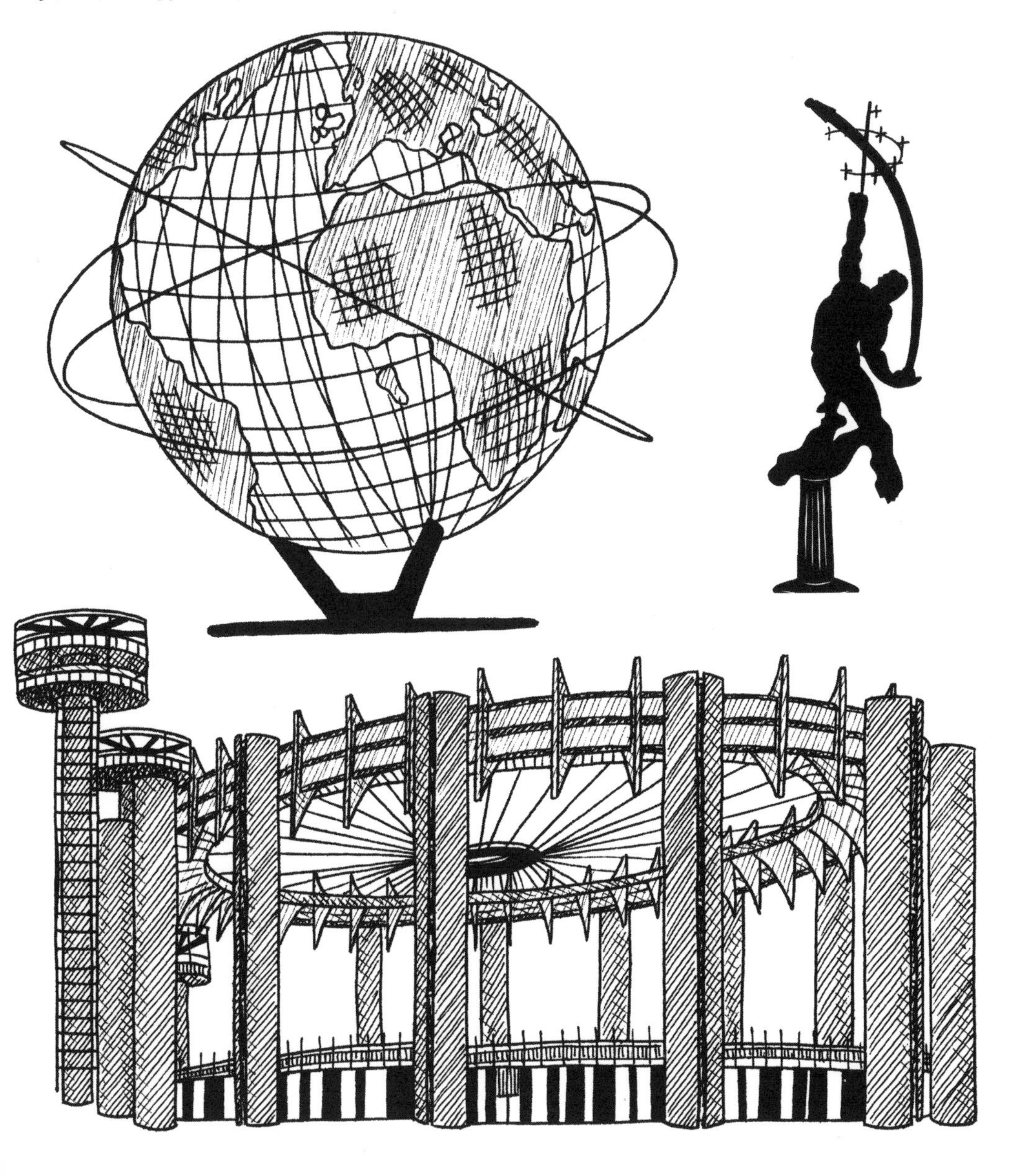

SOME STATUES AND EXHIBITS WERE TRANSFERRED TO OTHER LOCATIONS IN NEW YORK CITY, BUT NONE TRAVELED AS FAR AND WIDE AS THE WORLD'S FAIR LAMPPOSTS.

OPINIONS OF THE POSTS' DESIGN VARIED. SOME FAIR ATTENDEES THOUGHT THEY WERE AN ENCHANTING CREATIVE ACHIEVEMENT, WHILE OTHERS THOUGHT THEY WERE JUST UGLY AS FUCK.

GOOD HEAVENS! THOSE THINGS ARE UGLY AS FUCK!

NO, THEY'RE... UNIQUE...

WHEN THE FAIR ENDED, THE LAMPPOSTS WERE TAKEN DOWN. MOST WERE HAULED TO THE SCRAPYARD, WHILE THE REMAINING FEW HUNDRED WERE SHIPPED OFF TO NEIGHBORING TOWNS AND STATES. SOME EVEN MADE IT AS FAR AS OKLAHOMA.
VILLA VOSILLA RESORT, TANNERSVILLE, NEW YORK
ORANGE COUNTY FAIR, MIDDLETOWN, NEW YORK

MOST OF THEM ENDED UP AT TOWN FAIRS, HOTELS, AND RESORTS.
OH MY GOD, LOOK AT THOSE HIDEOUS LAMPPOSTS. THEY SHOULD HAVE FIRED THEIR DESIGNER.
OH, I KNOW, THEY'RE UGLY AS FUCK.

20 LAMPPOSTS FOUND A NEW HOME IN THE POCONOS, IN PENNSYLVANIA. THEY WERE INSTALLED ON THE GROUNDS OF PENN HILLS, AN INFAMOUSLY CAMPY HONEYMOON RESORT.

I LOVE YOU, DOLLFACE, BUT THIS HEART-SHAPED JACUZZI IS LITERALLY COMING BETWEEN US.

YEAH, AND BONING ON THE HEART-SHAPED BED HAS TURNED OUT TO BE RATHER CHALLENGING. IT'S AN IMPRACTICAL SHAPE.

I SET ABOUT RESEARCHING THE LAMPPOSTS.
OUT OF THE ORIGINAL 1,800 LAMPPOSTS, ONLY AN ESTIMATED 200 REMAIN.
BUILT BY WESTINGHOUSE.
CAME IN COLORS LIKE RED, YELLOW, VIOLET, CORAL, OLIVE GREEN, AND CHARTREUSE, ACCORDING TO RENDERINGS AND FAIR BROCHURES.
THERE WERE 76 MODULAR CONFIGURATIONS, RANGING FROM 4 TO 18 CUBES PER POST.
THE PLEXIGLAS CUBES WERE 16X16 INCHES.

I WROTE A BLOG POST ON PENN HILLS ON MY EXPLORING SITE ADVENTUREBIBLESCHOOL.COM THAT I FIGURED NO ONE WOULD EVER READ. I THOUGHT NOTHING OF IT FOR OVER A YEAR, UNTIL I RECEIVED THIS EMAIL:

HI, JULIA, I JUST READ YOUR HILARIOUS TAKEDOWN OF THE PENN HILLS RESORT IN ANALOMINK, PA. I'M WRITING BECAUSE YOU WERE HOPING SOMEONE WOULD SAVE THE WORLD'S FAIR LAMPPOSTS AND—I DID. I HAVE SAFELY REMOVED ALL 20 THAT WERE ON-SITE AND THEY ARE SECURE NOW AND AWAITING RESTORATION. KEEP UP THE GOOD WORK! -DAVID TURNER

DAVID TURNER AND HIS FIANCÉ,* AARON HILL, MANAGED TO REMOVE AND SAVE ALL 20 LAMPPOSTS. THEY PLAN TO HAVE THEM FULLY RESTORED AND INSTALLED AT THEIR PRIVATE AIRPORT, THE FLYING DOLLAR.

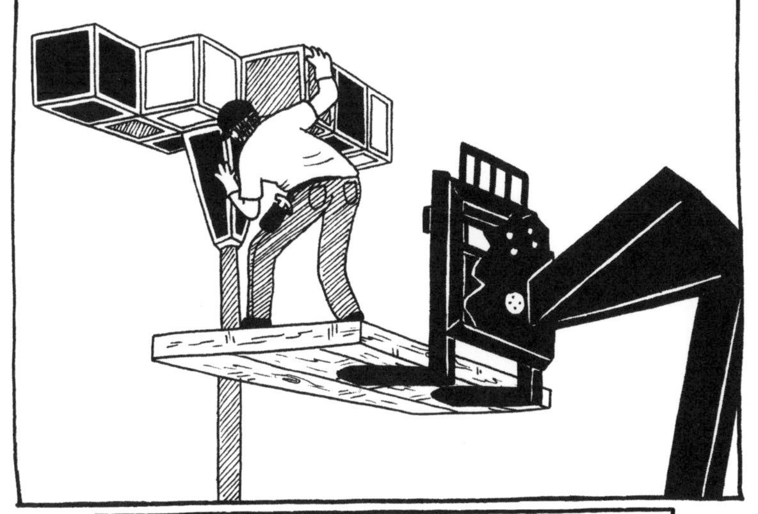

*AARON, WILL YOU MARRY ME? –DAVID

SO IN THE NEAR FUTURE, YOU WILL BE ABLE TO TRAVEL TO PENNSYLVANIA TO SEE A BIT OF UNIQUE AND UNEXPECTED NEW YORK CITY HISTORY.

ADDENDUM: THE MARRIAGE PROPOSAL THAT APPEARS ON THE SECOND TO LAST PANEL IS REAL. AFTER A FEW WEEKS OF CORRESPONDENCE WITH DAVID ABOUT THE LAMPPOSTS, HE CAME UP WITH THE IDEA TO SNEAK THE PROPOSAL INTO THE COMIC SO AARON WOULD SEE IT WHEN THE COMIC WAS PUBLISHED. I'M NOT A TERRIBLY ROMANTIC PERSON, BUT I LOVED THIS IDEA, SO I DID IT, DESPITE EDITORIAL QUESTIONING. THE PIECE CAME OUT, AND DAVID SAID YES. FOR THE CERMONY, THEY ARE PLANNING TO MAKE A COOLER OUT OF ONE OF THE HILARIOUS HEART-SHAPED HOT TUBS THEY ALSO GOT FROM PENN HILLS WHEN THEY ACQUIRED THE LAMPPOSTS. TO VISIT THEIR AIRPORT, CHECK OUT FLYINGDOLLAR.COM. AND IF YOU GO, TELL THEM I SAID HI!

THE NEW YORK STATE PAVILION, THE "TENT OF TOMORROW," AND THE THREE OBSERVATION TOWERS.

INSIDE THE PAVILION BEFORE THE 2015 RESTORATION.

INSIDE THE PAVILION DURING THE RESTORATION.

THE UNISPHERE, WHICH HAS A 120-FOOT DIAMETER. IT REPRESENTED "GLOBAL INTERDEPENDENCE."

THE PAVILION AND OBSERVATION TOWERS.

THE OBSERVATION TOWERS, WHICH WERE ACCESSIBLE VIA THE "SKY STREAK CAPSULE" ELEVATOR. THE TALLEST TOWER IS 226 FEET.

THE ROCKET THROWER, BY DONALD DE LUE.

GREENPOINT THEN & NOW

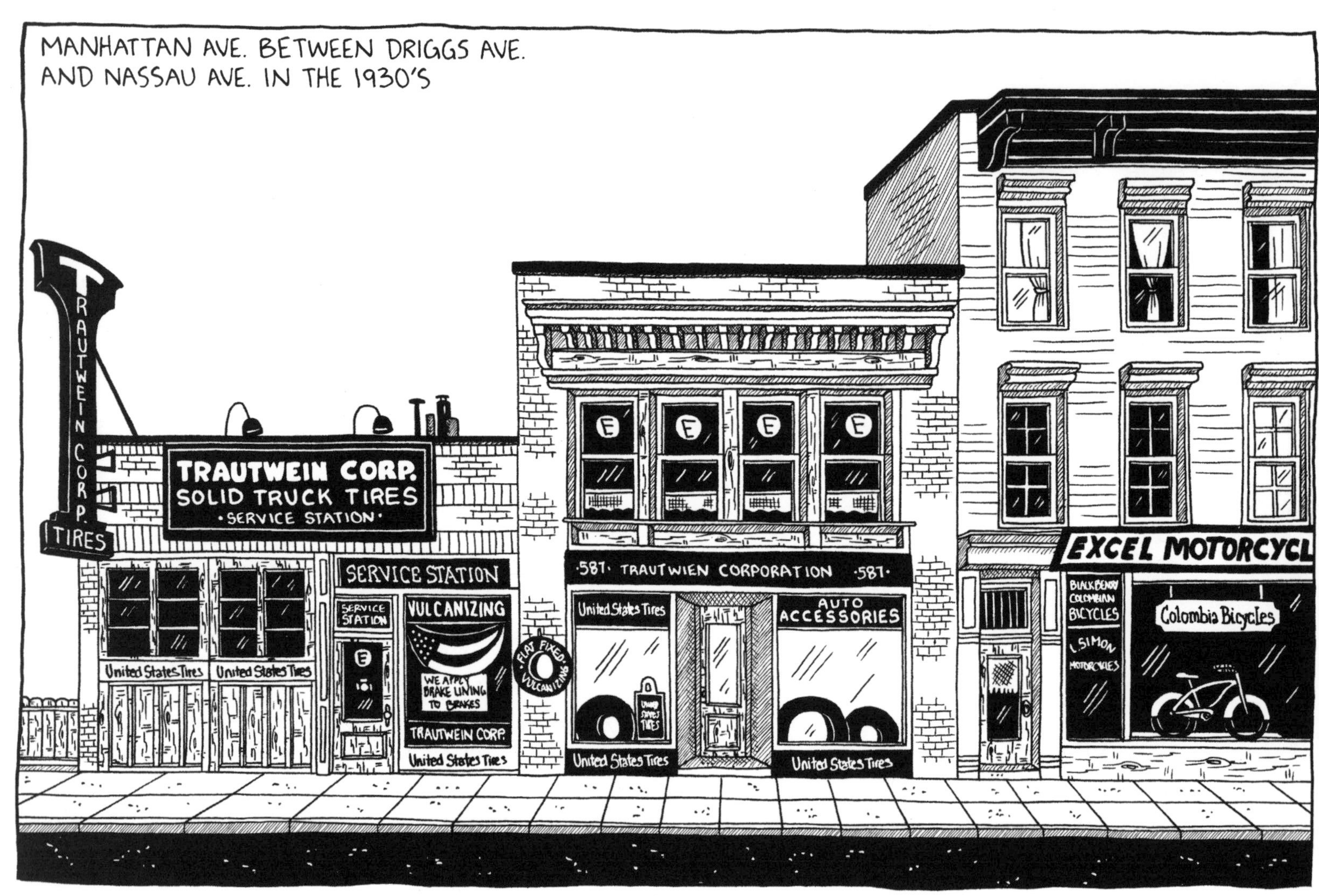

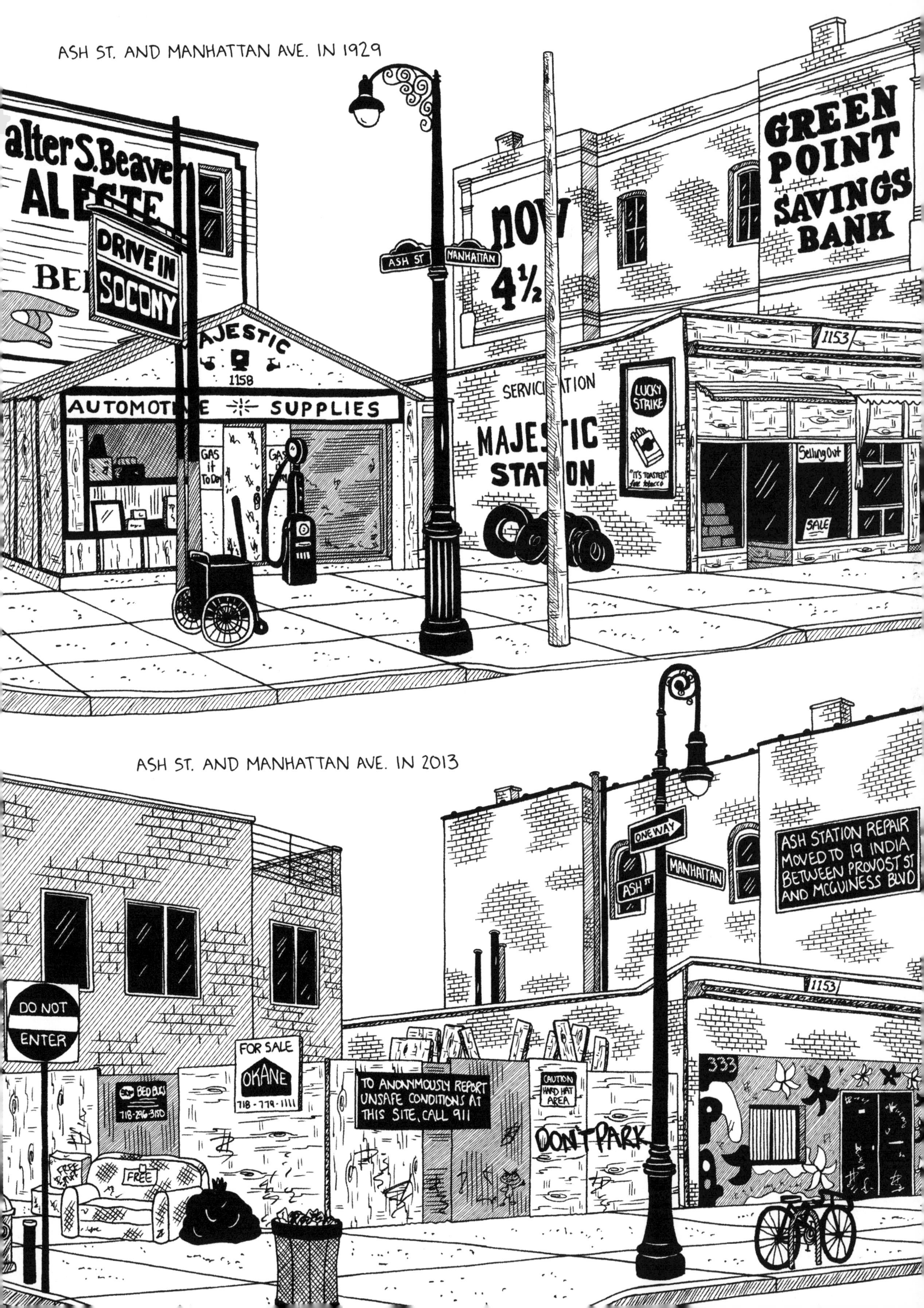
ASH ST. AND MANHATTAN AVE. IN 1929
alter S. Beaver
DRIVE IN SOCONY
MAJESTIC
1158
AUTOMOTIVE SUPPLIES
GAS it To Day
ASH ST
MANHATTAN
NOW 4½
GREEN POINT SAVINGS BANK
SERVICE STATION
MAJESTIC STATION
LUCKY STRIKE
"IT'S TOASTED!"
1153
Selling Out
SALE
ASH ST. AND MANHATTAN AVE. IN 2013
ONE WAY
MANHATTAN
ASH ST
ASH STATION REPAIR MOVED TO 19 INDIA BETWEEN PROVOST ST AND MCGUINESS BLVD
1153
DO NOT ENTER
BED BUG
718-296-3150
FOR SALE
OKANE
718-779-1111
TO ANONYMOUSLY REPORT UNSAFE CONDITIONS AT THIS SITE, CALL 911
CAUTION HARD HAT AREA
DON'T PARK
FREE
333

MANHATTAN AVE. AND NORMAN AVE. IN THE 1930'S

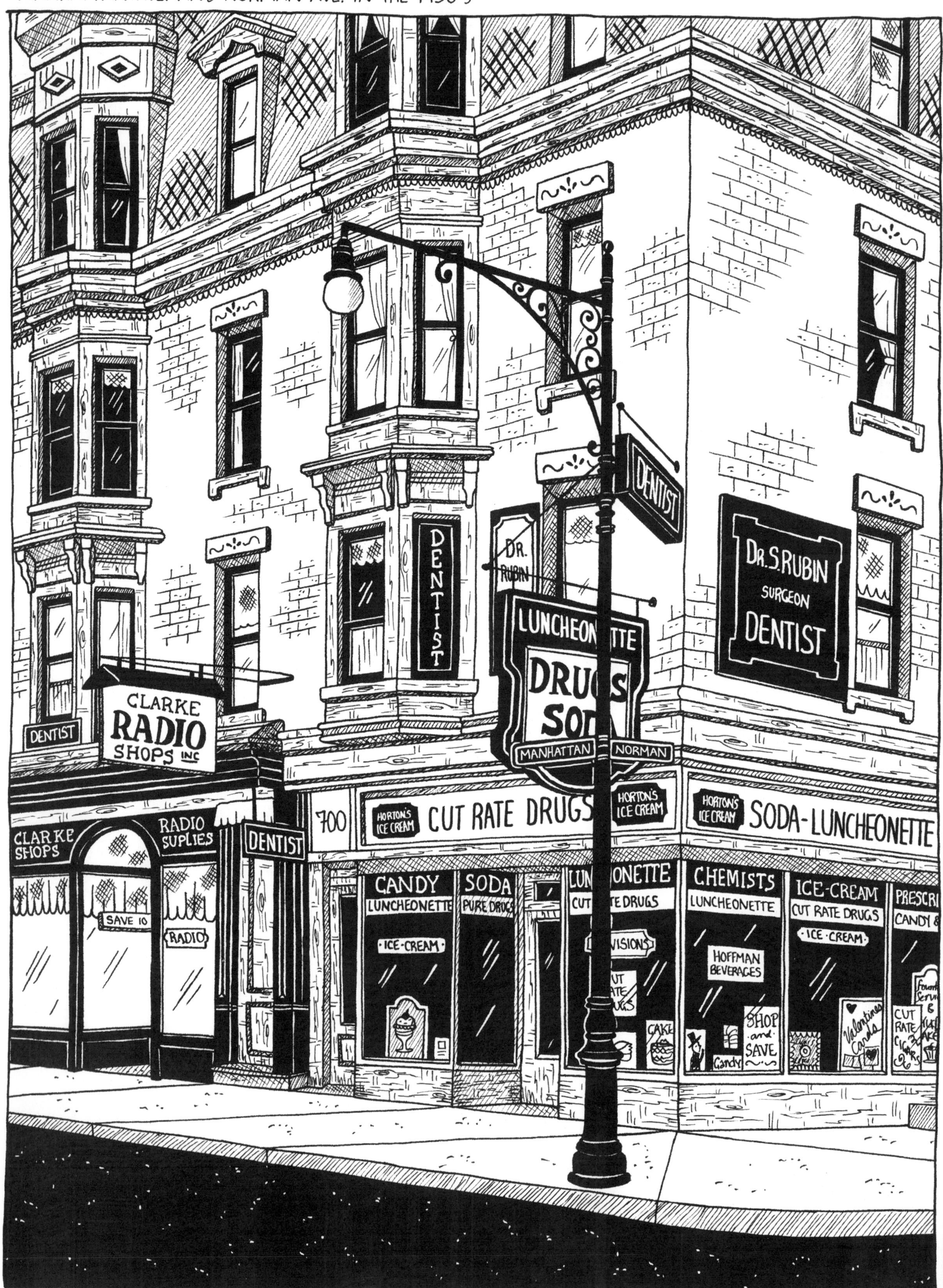

MANHATTAN AVE. AND NORMAN AVE. IN 2016

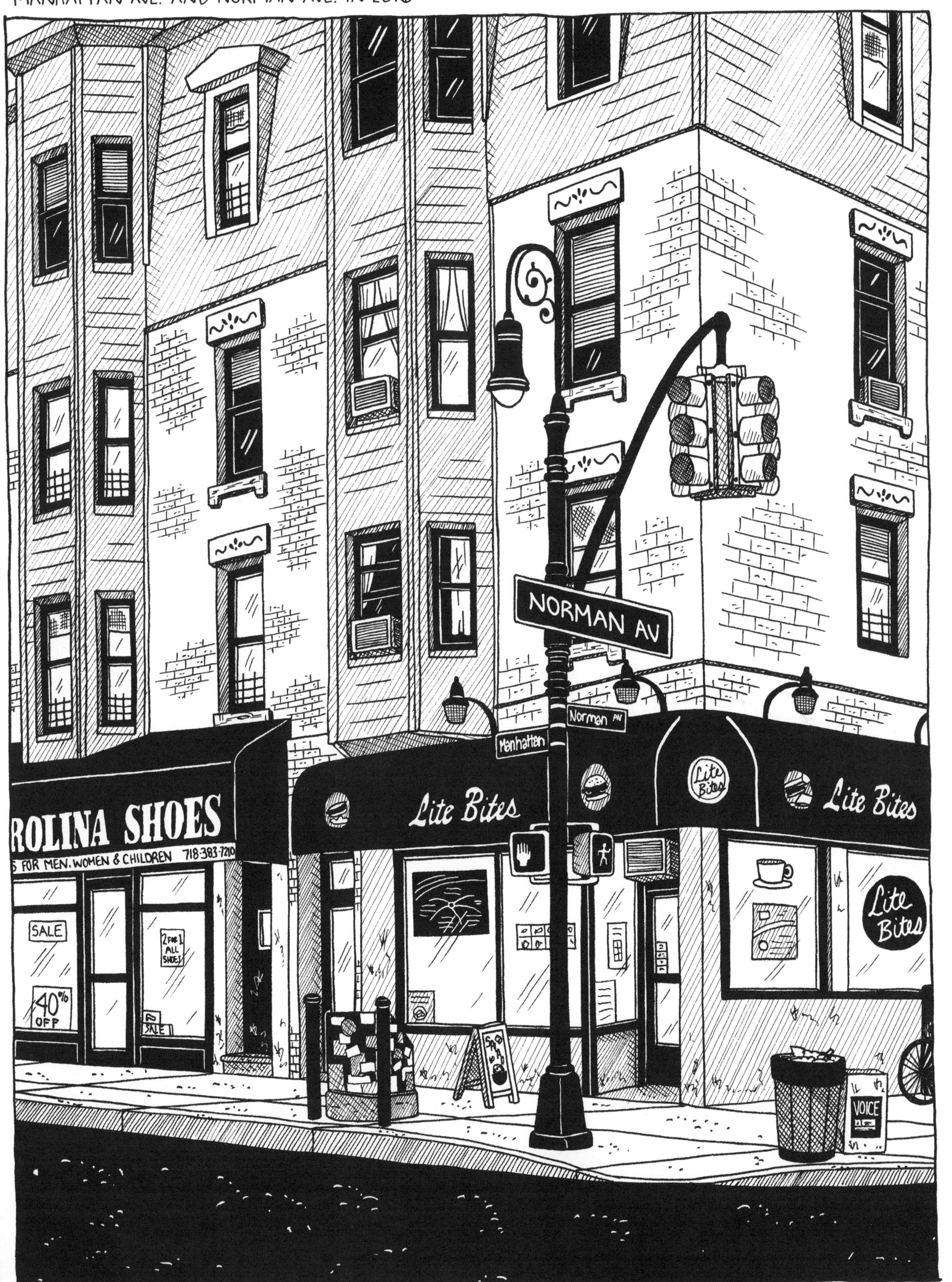

HURON ST. AND MANHATTAN AVE. IN THE 1930'S

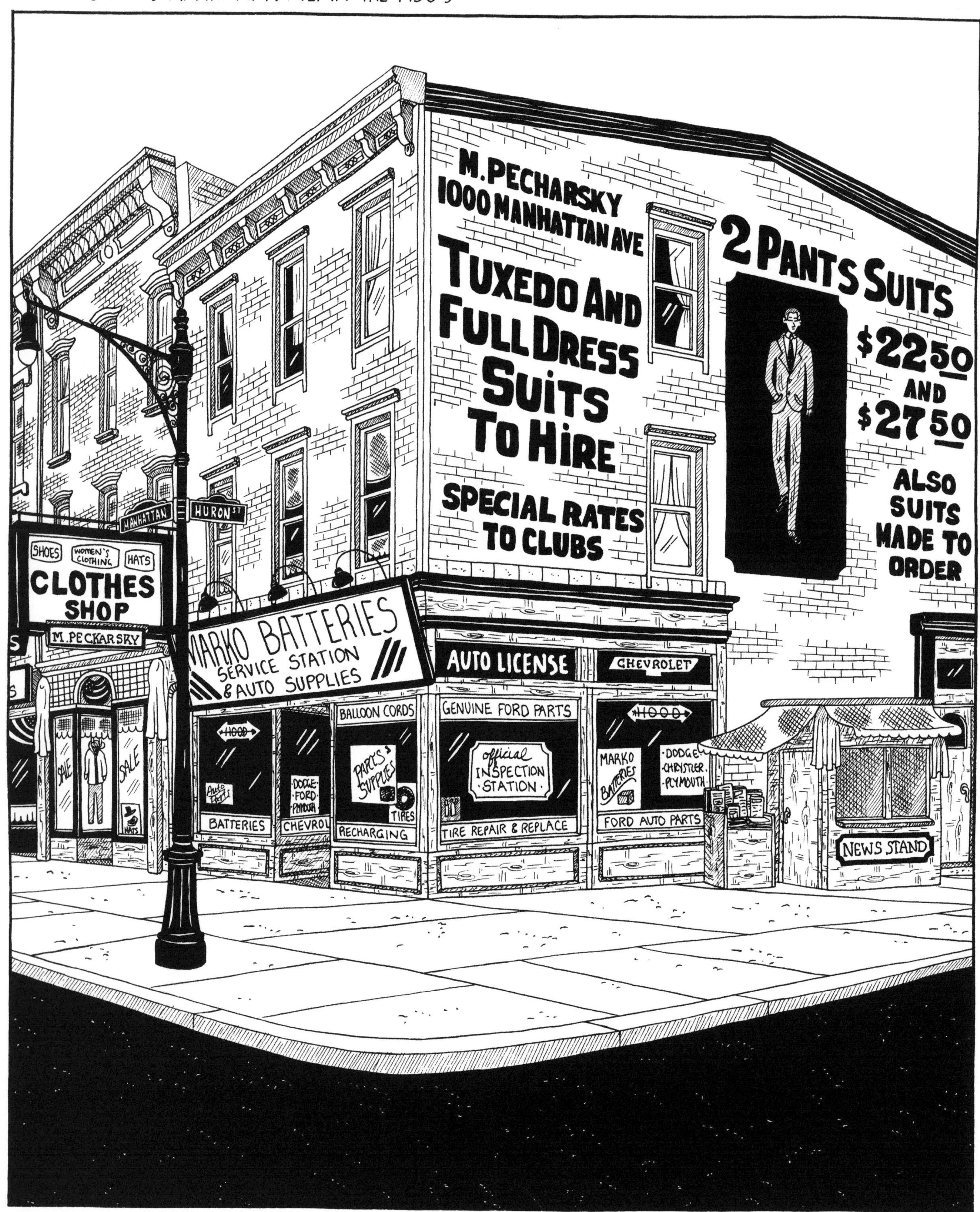

HURON ST. AND MANHATTAN AVE. IN 2016

THE GREAT PINBALL PROHIBITION

ALONG MANHATTAN AVENUE IN GREENPOINT, BROOKLYN, IS A SMALL, SEEMINGLY INNOCUOUS WATCH REPAIR SHOP.

IT IS ACTUALLY THE FRONT TO A CLANDESTINE YET EXPANSIVE PINBALL LAUNDROMAT.

WHILE PATRONS LAUNDER THEIR CLOTHES AND PLAY *THEATRE OF MAGIC*, MOST ARE UNAWARE THAT, FOR OVER THREE DECADES, PINBALL WAS ILLEGAL IN NEW YORK CITY.

IT ALL STARTED IN THE 1930'S, WHEN FIORELLO LA GUARDIA BECAME NEW YORK CITY'S MAYOR ON A PLATFORM OF ENDING ORGANIZED CRIME. FIRST, HE REMOVED ALL MAFIA-RUN SLOT MACHINES...

OUT!!! OUT WITH THE SCOURGE OF HUMANITY!!

...ONLY TO SEE THEM REPLACED BY PINBALL MACHINES.
WHAT THE HOLY HELL??!!

LA GUARDIA TURNED HIS ABOLITION EFFORTS TO PINBALL, CLAIMING THAT THE GAME ENCOURAGED DELINQUENCY AND ANTISOCIAL BEHAVIORS SUCH AS GAMBLING, LOITERING, AND BEING LATE FOR DINNER.

LISTEN HERE, CAPTAIN COMMISSIONER CHIEF, PINBALL IS NOT THE MERE TRIFLE OF AMUSEMENT IT APPEARS TO BE! IT IS A GAME OF CHANCE, AND ANY GAME THAT RELIES ON CHANCE RATHER THAN SKILL QUALIFIES AS GAMBLING!
BUT THERE IS NO PAYBACK IN PINBA...
YOU HEARD ME!! PINBALL IS A CRIME!!!

LA GUARDIA APPEALED TO THE PUBLIC FOR SUPPORT.

PINBALL IS A RACKET DOMINATED BY INTERESTS HEAVILY TAINTED WITH CRIMINALITY...
IT ROBS THE POCKETS OF SCHOOLCHILDREN IN THE FORM OF NICKELS AND DIMES GIVEN TO THEM AS LUNCH MONEY!*

HEY, MAURICE, YOU CLEAN OUT THE *BAFFLE BALL* YET?

I'M SO HUNGRY BUT I SPENT MY LAST HA'PENNY PLAYING *THE HUMPTY DUMPTY*!

*DIRECT QUOTE VIA SUPREME COURT AFFIDAVIT.

IN 1941, HIS VENDETTA AGAINST PINBALL GOT THE BOOST IT NEEDED FOLLOWING THE ATTACK ON PEARL HARBOR.

FURTHERMORE, PINBALL MACHINES ARE MADE OF PRECIOUS METALS THAT WE NEED TO FIGHT THE WAR!*

*AS PARAPHRASED BY *THE NEW YORK TIMES*

FUCK YEAH, NAILED IT!

*DIRECT QUOTE UNAVAILABLE. BEST GUESS MADE.

HIS MISSION WAS A SUCCESS AND BY EARLY 1942, THE PINBALL PROHIBITION WAS OFFICIALLY UNDER WAY. POLICE RAIDED NEW YORK CITY'S BOROUGHS, CONFISCATING THOUSANDS OF PINBALL MACHINES.

WHERE ARE THEY, WILLIAM?

WHERE ARE WHAT? I AM BUT A HUMBLE SODA-STORE CLERK.

EGG CREAM?

MANY OF THE MACHINES WERE TURNED OVER TO THE MILITARY FOR SCRAP METAL, WHICH WAS USED TO MAKE BOMBS.

PINBALL SEIZURES PUSHED BY POLICE

2,326 Machines Collected in City and Summonses for

PINBALL MACHINES TO HELP WIN WAR

2,450 of Those Seized by the Police Junked to Produce 10 Tons of Scrap Metal

SALVAGE DRIVE A

NOT ALL PINBALL MACHINES MET SUCH A DUBIOUSLY NOBLE FATE. TO MAKE A POINT, LA GUARDIA MADE A SPECTACLE OF HAVING PINBALL MACHINES SMASHED WITH A SLEDGEHAMMER IN FRONT OF THE PRESS.

PRESS PHOTO OF WEIRDLY SUBDUED POLICE CHIEF DESTROYING THE CYCLONE.

NICE JOB, SUPERINTENDENT SHERIFF SIR.
NOW WHAT DO WE DO WITH THEM?
WE DO WHAT THE MAFIA DOES...
DUMP 'EM IN THE HUDSON.

THE WAR ON PINBALL RAGED ON FOR DECADES. BUT, AS WITH ALL BANNED THINGS, IT DID NOT DISAPPEAR, IT SIMPLY WENT UNDERGROUND.

PSST, WHADDA YA GOT?
I GOTS JUGGLE BALL, SEA BREEZE, HAWAIIAN BEAUTY...
YOU GOT BALLYHOO?
NAW, BUT I GOT POOSH-M-UP JR.

AS SOON AS THE BAN WAS LIFTED IN 1978, PINBALL MADE A PUBLIC RESURGENCE. EVEN TODAY, THE GROUP PINBALL NEW YORK CITY HOSTS LEAGUES AND TOURNAMENTS, AND BUSINESS IS GOOD AT SUNSHINE LAUNDROMAT.

FOR MANY OF US, PINBALL REMAINS ONLY IN THE BACK OF OUR MINDS AS A PASTIME TO BE PLAYED AT LAUNDROMATS, IN BARS, OR IN THE NICHE ECONOMY OF ARCADES. BUT ITS HISTORY REMAINS, LANGUISHING IN A WATERY GRAVE AT THE BOTTOM OF THE HUDSON.

BALLYHOO

EAST VILLAGE THEN & NOW

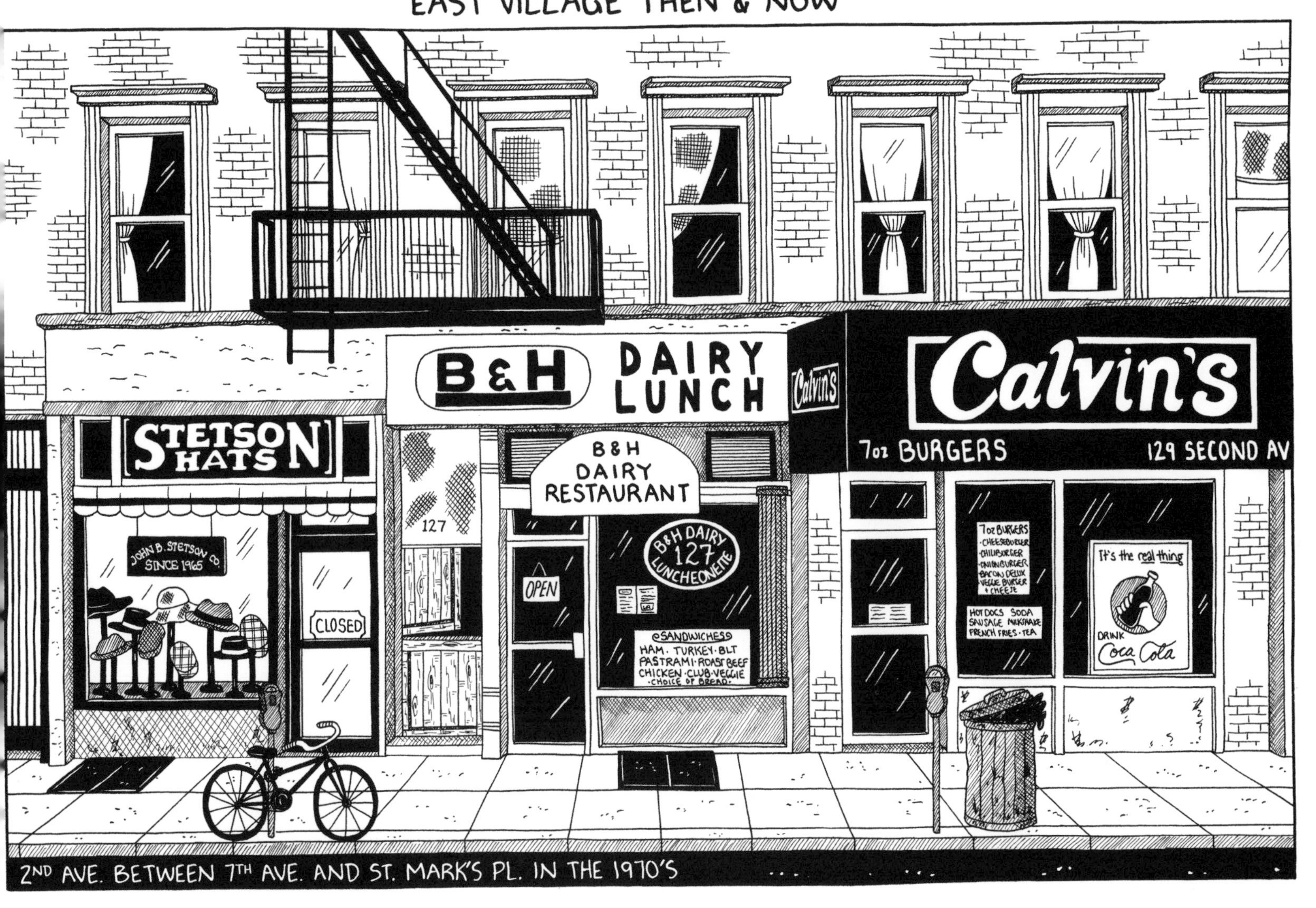

2ND AVE. BETWEEN 7TH AVE. AND ST. MARK'S PL. IN THE 1970'S

2ND AVE. BETWEEN 7TH AVE. AND ST. MARK'S PL. IN 2011

2ND AVE. BETWEEN 4TH AND 5TH ST. IN 1924

ESKY'S
ESS SUITS
OH
BENJAMIN STEIN
MARRIAGE PERFORMER
·DENTIST·
DOCTOR BERNSTEIN
SUITS & JACK
OPTIMO
CIGARS
~ RETAIL & WHOLESALE ~
ORANGE FLOWER
5¢ CIGAR 5¢
Muriel Cigarettes
LUCKIES TASTE BETTER
COLOMBIAN JAMAICA
Fine Cigars
3/6 EACH
WILLS
GOLD FLAKE
CIGARETTES

2ND AVE. BETWEEN 4TH AND 5TH ST. IN 2014

NOMAD
NOMAD
78
80
A

ST. MARKS CINEMA OPENED IN 1914 AS THE ASTOR THEATRE. BY THE 1920'S, IT WAS THE ST. MARKS THEATRE. IN THE 70'S AND 80'S, IT OPERATED AS A SECOND-RUN MOVIE HOUSE. THE THEATER CLOSED IN THE 80'S AND WAS TEMPORARILY REPLACED BY A GAP CLOTHING STORE.

133 2ND AVE. IN THE 1930'S

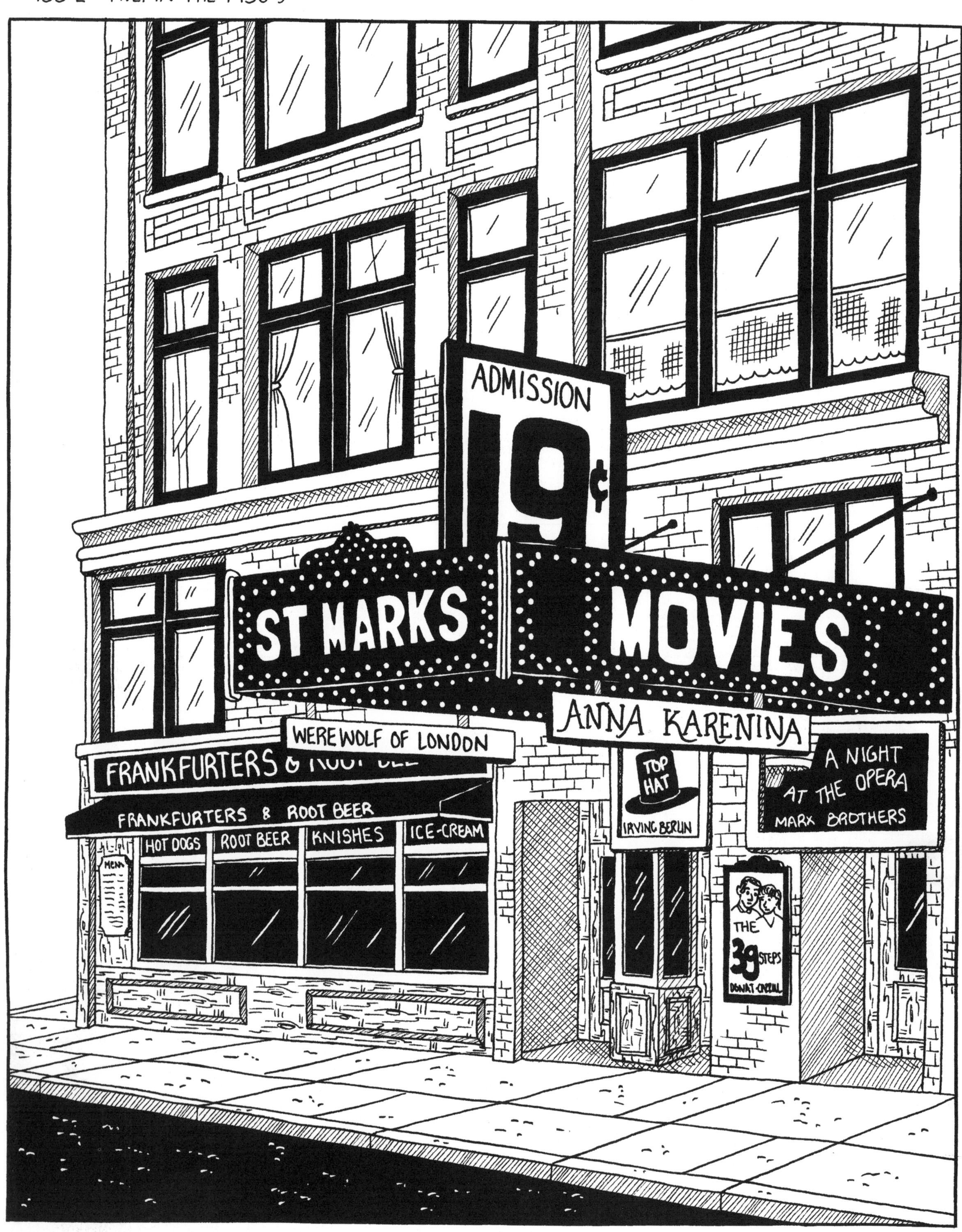

After the Gap closed, the location saw numerous businesses come and go. Since this 2011 illustration, Roastown became Eastside Bakery and then DF Mavens Frozen Desserts. Cohen's became Verizon, but in 2016, the store was empty.

133 2nd Ave. in 2011

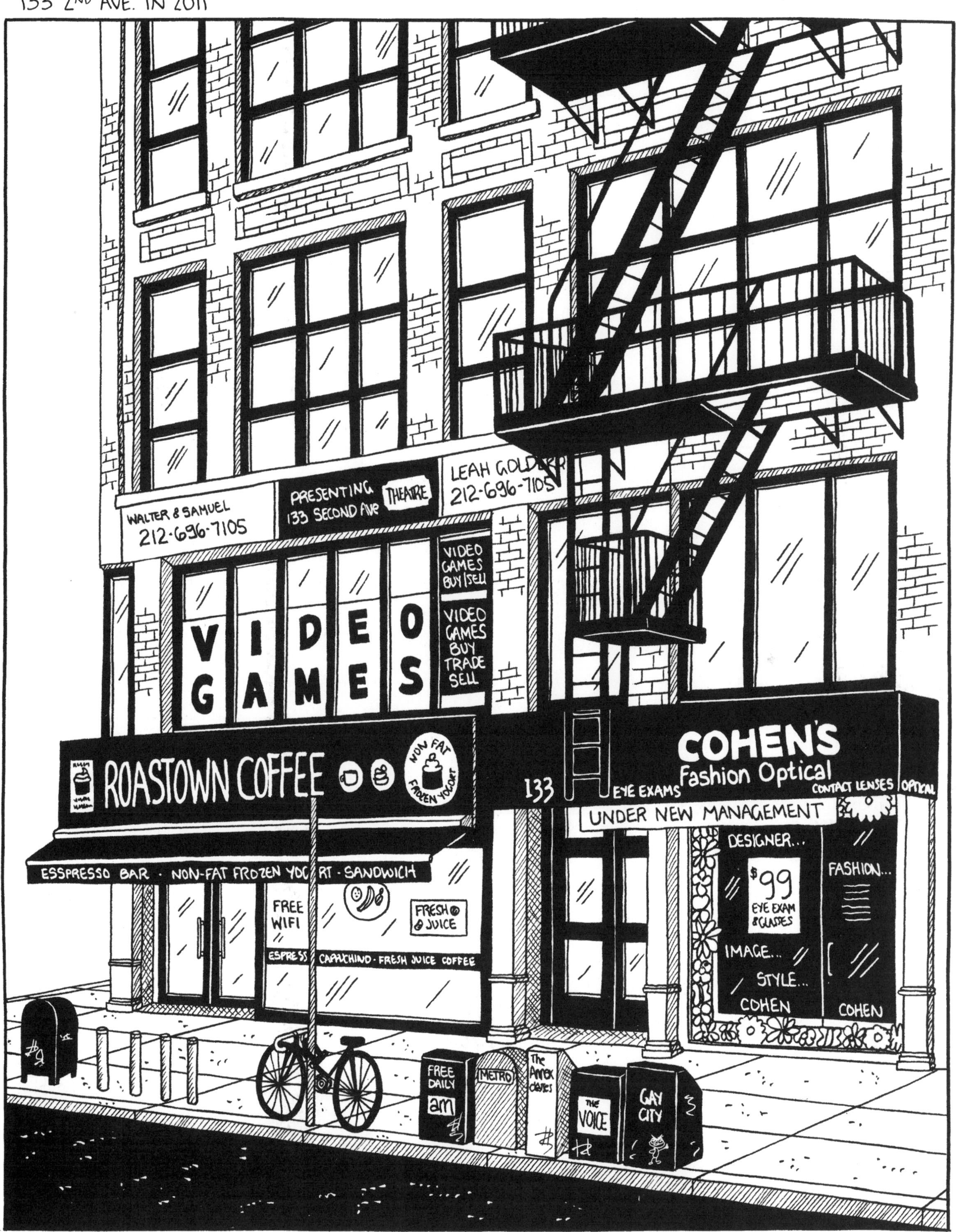

THE HESS SPITE TRIANGLE

THE SMALLEST AND ANGRIEST PIECE OF MANHATTAN REAL ESTATE

THE RAPIDLY EXPANDING SUBWAY DISRUPTED MANY OF THE CITY'S RESIDENCES AND BUILDINGS, SOME OF WHICH WERE CLEARED TO MAKE WAY FOR THE NEW ABOVEGROUND LINES. ONE OF THE MOST FAMOUS CASES WAS THAT OF DAVID HESS, OWNER OF THE VOORHIS, A FIVE-STORY APARTMENT BUILDING.

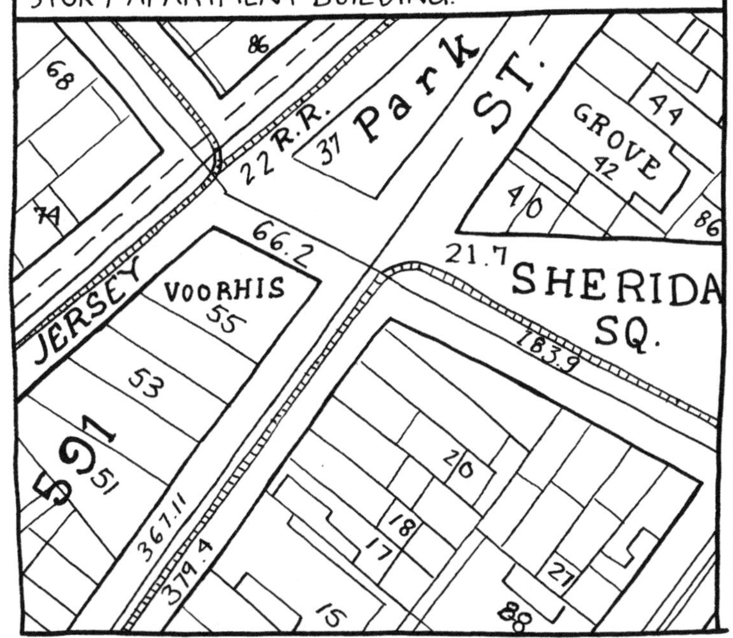

IN 1910, THE CITY PROPOSED A NEW LINE ALONG 7TH AVENUE IN GREENWICH VILLAGE. THE STREET NEEDED WIDENING, SO ANY STRUCTURES ALONG THE ROADSIDE HAD TO BE DEMOLISHED. THE VOORHIS WAS ONE OF THEM.

THEY WANT TO DEMOLISH MY BUILDING SO PEOPLE CAN GO WILLY-NILLY FROM TIMES SQUARE TO THE FERRY?

OH HELL NO!

MAP OF PROPOSED DEMOLITION AREAS.

HESS ULTIMATELY LOST THE FIGHT, AND HIS BUILDING WAS GONE BY 1914.

BUT NOT ALL WAS LOST. HESS'S HEIRS DISCOVERED A SMALL DISCREPANCY IN THE CITY'S LAND SURVEY, WHICH HAD MISSED A TINY PIECE OF HESS'S PROPERTY ON THEIR MAP OF THE LAND TO BE TAKEN OVER BY THE CITY.

I FOUND IT! UNCLE DAVID'S LAND!

YES! WE'RE RICH!!! FILTHY, FILTHY RICH!

OH, WAIT, HANG ON...

THE PLOT OF LAND MEASURED ONLY 27½ INCHES X 27½ INCHES X 25½ INCHES. ADDING INSULT TO INJURY, THE CITY REQUESTED THAT THE HESS FAMILY DONATE THE LAND TO THE CITY.
WE WERE HOPING THE FAMILY WOULD JUST *GIVE* THE LAND TO THE CITY, AND END THIS NONSENSE.
FIRST THEY TOOK UNCLE DAVID'S BUILDING AND NOW THEY WANT HIS WEE PLOT O' LAND?!
FUCK THAT.

IN 1922, THE FAMILY HAD A MOSAIC EMBEDDED ON THE SMALL PLOT, WHICH HAD BEEN PAVED OVER. THE MOSAIC WAS INSCRIBED WITH A BITTER PRONOUNCEMENT OF DEFIANT OWNERSHIP OF THE LAND, LEADING PEOPLE TO REFER TO IT AS THE "SPITE TRIANGLE." THE MOSAIC CAN STILL BE SEEN IN FRONT OF VILLAGE CIGARS, WHICH HAS BEEN THERE SINCE 1938 WHEN THE HESS FAMILY SOLD THE LAND FOR ONE THOUSAND DOLLARS.

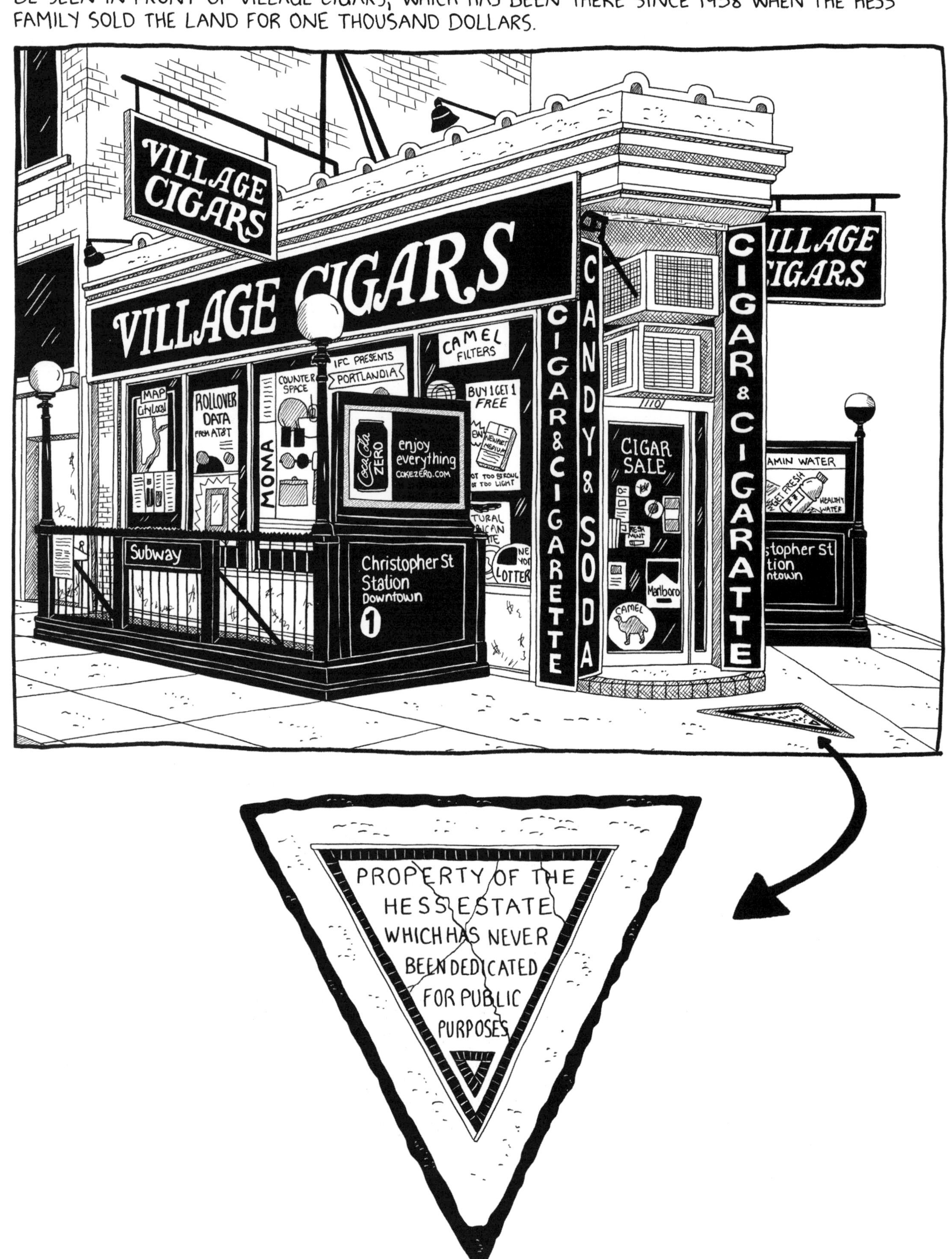

GREENWICH VILLAGE
& THE WEST VILLAGE
THEN & NOW
225 W.4TH ST. IN 1937
7ave South
RIKER'S
BUY MERCHANDISE AND SERVICE FROM THESE CONCERNS
·ICE-CREAM AND BUTTER·
·TODAY FARMS·
PLUMBING AND REPAIRING
·JACK LICHTENBERGER·
·BREAD AND ROLLS·
·GOTTFRIED BAKING COMPANY·
·KITCHEN OVENS·SINKS·REFRIGERATORS·TABLES
·NY GRADE RESTAURANT EQUIPTMENT·
·AIR CONDITIONING·
·YORK ICE MACHINERY CORPORATION·
·MILK AND ICE CREAM DISPENSARY·
·LYON'S SANITARY VAN COMPANY·
·PASTERIES AND PIES·
·ROLFMAN'S BAKERY & CO·
·COFFEE·
·RIKER'S SPECIAL BLEND·
·LUNCH·
·DINNER·
Riker's
Riker's
NO BETTER FOOD AT ANY PRICE
Sandwiches · Soda · Ice Cream
BREAKFA
LUNCH
DINNER
Riker's Cafe
225 W.4TH ST. IN 2016
ONE WAY
ONE WAY
7 AV SOUTH
8-9:30 TUES FRI
1 HOUR PARKING EXCEPT SUN
RIVIERA
THE RIVIERA CAFE

THE WAVERLY THEATRE OPENED IN 1931. ORIGINALLY A CHURCH, IT WAS CONVERTED INTO A MOVIE THEATER IN 1937. THE ART HOUSE VENUE WAS POPULAR FOR SHOWING FOREIGN, RETROSPECTIVE, AND ARTY FILMS. IT WAS THE ORIGINAL HOME TO THE WEEKLY MIDNIGHT SCREENING OF *THE ROCKY HORROR PICTURE SHOW*, AN AUDIENCE PARTICIPATION EVENT THAT BECAME POPULAR WITH NERDS NATIONWIDE, AND STILL CONTINUES TODAY. THE WAVERLY CLOSED IN 2001.

IN 2005, THE IFC CENTER TOOK OVER THE FORMER WAVERLY THEATRE. ITS OPENING NIGHT WAS MET WITH CONTROVERSY, AS THE THEATER HAD EMPLOYED ONLY NON-UNION PROJECTIONISTS, PROMPTING PICKETING USING THE PRO-UNION INFLATABLE RAT. THE UNION RAT IS A COMMON SYMBOL OF PROTEST AGAINST NON-UNION HIRING. HISTORICALLY, WHEN WORKERS BREAK A UNION STRIKE, THEY'RE CALLED RATS AND/OR SCABS, HENCE THE INFLATABLE RAT'S NICKNAME "SCABBY THE RAT." CURRENTLY, THE IFC HAS FIVE SCREENS ON WHICH IT SHOWS MOSTLY ART-HOUSE AND DOCUMENTARY FILMS, AND THE OCCASIONAL MAINSTREAM MOVIE.

IN THE EARLY 1900'S, THESE TWO BUILDINGS ON THE CORNER OF MACDOUGAL ST. AND MINETTA LN. WERE HOME TO THE NAPOLEON RESTAURANT AND A HORSE-DRAWN CARRIAGE HOUSE/STABLE. DURING THIS TIME, GREENWICH VILLAGE WAS A BUDDING ARTISTS COMMUNITY, NON-INCIDENTALLY DUE TO THE NUMBER OF HIDDEN SPEAKEASIES THE AREA HAD DURING PROHIBITION. MUSIC AND ART WERE STARTING TO DEFINE THE NEIGHBORHOOD, WHICH WOULD SOON SEE A RASH OF NEW CAFES AND CLUBS OPEN ALONG ITS IDYLLIC STREETS.

MACDOUGAL ST. AND MINETTA LN. IN THE 1920'S

CAFE WHA? IS A LIVE MUSIC CLUB THAT HAS BEEN OPEN SINCE 1959. MUSICIANS SUCH AS JIMI HENDRIX, THE VELVET UNDERGROUND, BOB DYLAN, AND MANY MORE HAVE PLAYED THERE. COMEDIANS RICHARD PRYOR, LENNY BRUCE, JOAN RIVERS, AND OTHERS ALSO GOT THEIR START AT THE CLUB. ABOVE CAFE WHA? IS THE PLAYERS THEATRE, AN OFF-BROADWAY VENUE AND REHEARSAL STUDIO.

NEXT DOOR, THE OLIVE TREE CAFE & BAR SITS ABOVE THE COMEDY CELLAR, ONE OF THE CITY'S MOST POPULAR PLACES TO SEE STAND-UP COMEDY. OPEN SINCE 1982, THE COMEDY CELLAR WAS IMMORTALIZED BY LOUIS C.K., WHO FREQUENTLY FILMED HIS TV SHOW IN THE VENUE. SO MANY FAMOUS COMEDIANS HAVE PERFORMED AND/OR STARTED THERE THAT A LIST OF NAMES WOULD BE SUPERFLUOUS.

MACDOUGAL ST. AND MINETTA LN. IN 2016

C.O. BIGELOW APOTHECARY: NEW YORK CITY'S OLDEST PHARMACY

COMEDIAN LOUIS C.K. ONCE JOKED THAT THE SLOGAN FOR CVS DRUGSTORE SHOULD BE, "CVS: SOMETIMES YOU GOTTA COME IN HERE." IT'S A BEGRUDGING SENTIMENT THAT SUCCINCTLY SUMS UP HOW MOST PEOPLE FEEL ABOUT MODERN PHARMACIES. BUT GOING TO C.O BIGELOW IN THE WEST VILLAGE IS AN ENTIRELY DIFFERENT AND DELIGHTFUL EXPERIENCE THAT MAKES ME GENUINELY LOOK FORWARD TO BUYING DANDRUFF SHAMPOO AND ADULT ACNE TREATMENTS.

C.O. BIGELOW APOTHECARY OPENED AS THE VILLAGE APOTHECARY SHOPPE IN 1838 IN GREENWICH VILLAGE. IT IS THE OLDEST STILL-OPERATING APOTHECARY IN AMERICA. CURRENTLY, 3RD-GENERATION PHARMACIST IAN GINSBERG RUNS THE 6TH AVE. STORE WITH HIS SON, ALEC. C.O. BIGELOW APOTHECARIES, IN PARTNERSHIP WITH L BRANDS, EXPANDED TO NINE LOCATIONS NATIONWIDE, BUT ALL WERE CLOSED (EXCEPT THE ORIGINAL NYC STORE) BY 2009.

THE VILLAGE APOTHECARY SHOPPE WAS ORIGINALLY FOUNDED BY DR. GALEN HUNTER, WHO SOLD IT TO HIS CO-WORKER CLARENCE OTIS BIGELOW IN 1880, SETTING OFF A TRADITION OF PASSING THE STORE FROM EMPLOYEE TO EMPLOYEE, AS EVIDENCED BY A BRASS PLAQUE ON THE STORE'S GRANDFATHER CLOCK. THE FIRST LOCATION OF THE APOTHECARY WAS AT 102 6TH AVE., WHERE DR. HUNTER HAD ONLY THREE EMPLOYEES. WHEN CLARENCE BIGELOW TOOK OVER, HE EXPANDED THE STORE AND HIRED MORE HELP. IN 1902, A LARGE, ORNATE BUILDING WAS ERECTED TWO DOORS DOWN AT 106-108 6TH AVE. IT WAS RENUMBERED SOMETIME IN THE 1930'S, MAKING THE ADDRESS 414 6TH AVE., WHERE THE PHARMACY IS STILL LOCATED TODAY.

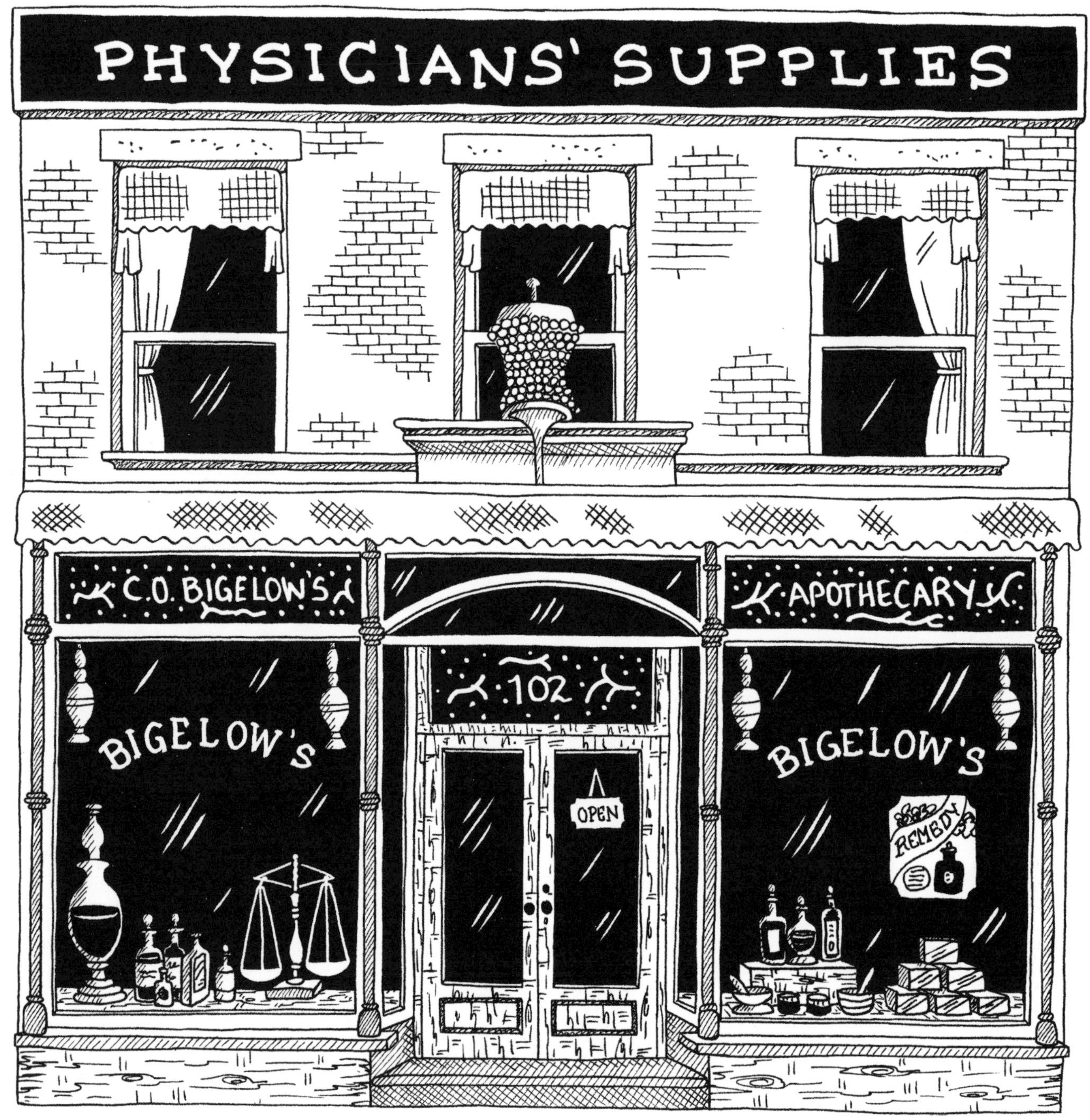

BIGELOW APOTHECARY'S FIRST LOCATION AT 102 6TH AVE. WEST VILLAGE, MANHATTAN

THROUGHOUT ITS NEARLY 180 YEARS IN OPERATION, BIGELOW HAS HAD NUMEROUS FAMOUS CLIENTS, INCLUDING MARK TWAIN, THOMAS EDISON, ELEANOR ROOSEVELT, SUSAN SARANDON, CALVIN KLEIN, ELVIS COSTELLO, THE PUNK BAND NEW YORK DOLLS, CHRISTINA RICCI, JENNIFER JASON LEIGH, LIV TYLER, AND WORLD-FAMOUS CARTOONIST JULIA WERTZ. THAT LAST ONE IS SUSPECT, BUT OLD HANDWRITTEN STORE LEDGERS ARE EVIDENCE OF BIGELOW'S MORE FAMOUS CLIENTS. ONE LEDGER SHOWS THAT SAMUEL CLEMENS (A.K.A. MARK TWAIN) PURCHASED 39 CENTS' WORTH OF NONSPECIFIC PRODUCTS IN 1906. IN THE 1920'S, BIGELOW OPENED A SODA FOUNTAIN INSIDE THE STORE, WHICH WAS FREQUENTED BY JOHN WATERS.

THE 1902 INCARNATION OF C.O. BIGELOW APOTHECARY IN ITS CURRENT 6TH AVE. BUILDING. THIS IS JUST THE STOREFRONT, BUT AS YOU CAN SEE, IT WAS IN THE SAME BUILDING THAT BIGELOW OCCUPIES TODAY.

INSIDE, THE PHARMACY IS LITTERED WITH ARTIFACTS FROM ITS EARLY DAYS, INCLUDING ANTIQUE APOTHECARY BOTTLES, SCALES, REGISTERS, OAK CABINETS AND PRESCRIPTION DRAWERS, CHANDELIERS, AND EVEN A SLIDING WOODEN LADDER TO ACCESS HIGH CUPBOARDS. OWNER IAN GINSBERG EVEN HAS AN ANTIQUE OPIUM BOTTLE IN THE APOTHECARY'S PRIVATE COLLECTION.

ARCHITECTURAL DETAILS, SUCH AS THE CEILING MOLDING AND TILE FLOOR, REMAIN REMARKABLY INTACT. BIGELOW EVEN STILL SELLS SOME OF ITS ORIGINAL FORMULA PRODUCTS, SUCH AS THE LEMON BODY CREAM, FORMULATED IN 1870. FOR MANY DECADES, DR. GALEN'S ROSE WONDER COLD CREAM WAS A BESTSELLER, HOWEVER IT IS NO LONGER AVAILABLE.

ADDENDUM: C.O. BIGELOW APOTHECARY IS SPECIAL TO ME FOR A PERSONAL REASON AS WELL. IT WAS THE FIRST PLACE I USED THE "I'M FROM *THE NEW YORKER*" CARD, AND IT WORKED! I WAS IN THE STORE A FEW YEARS AGO, TAKING REFERENCE PHOTOS FOR ILLUSTRATIONS, WHEN AN EMPLOYEE TOLD ME PHOTOS WEREN'T ALLOWED. I EXPLAINED I WAS A CARTOONIST WORKING FOR *THE NEW YORKER* (WHERE SOME OF THESE COMICS ORIGINALLY APPEARED) AND THE EMPLOYEE WENT TO TALK TO HER MANAGER. SHE RETURNED WITH SAID MANAGER, WHO NOT ONLY LET ME TAKE MORE PHOTOS, BUT ALSO EXPLAINED SOME OF THE INTERIOR ARCHITECTURE AND ANTIQUE RELICS. I STRUGGLED TO PAY ATTENTION, STILL DRUNK WITH MY NEWFOUND POWER AND THE REALIZATION THAT, AFTER A DECADE OF MAKING COMICS IN NYC, I WAS FINALLY LEGIT. (I IMMEDIATELY BEGAN TRYING TO ABUSE THAT POWER, WITH A FAILED ATTEMPT TO GAIN LEGAL ACCESS TO NORTH BROTHER ISLAND. I'M STILL TRYING, SO IF YOU HAVE A BOAT, CONTACT ME!) THIS PIECE WAS FACT-CHECKED BY STORE OWNER IAN GINSBERG. IF YOU FIND CONFLICTING INFORMATION ON THE INTERNET, THAT INFORMATION IS WRONG. THANKS, IAN!

HISTORIC APOTHECARIES THEN & NOW

1209 LEXINGTON AVE. IN 2016
WARBY PARKER
PRESCRIPTIONS
1209
E. 82nd ST
LEXINGTON
ONE WAY
ONE WAY
3 HOUR EXPRESS SERVICE

109 3RD AVE. IN THE 1940'S. KIEHL'S HAS BEEN OPEN SINCE 1851.
PHARMACY
PHARMACY
KIEHL PHARMACY
SINCE 1851
KIEHL PHARMACY
OPEN
KIEHL PHARMACY

109 3RD AVE. IN 2016
KIEHL'S SINCE 1851
KIEHL'S
SINCE 1851
OPEN
KIEHL'S
SINCE 1851
KIEHL'S
VITAMIN C SERUM
KIEHL'S
VIT C
RICKY'S

FROM HORSES TO ELECTRIC CARS:
A HISTORY OF STREET CLEANING IN NEW YORK CITY

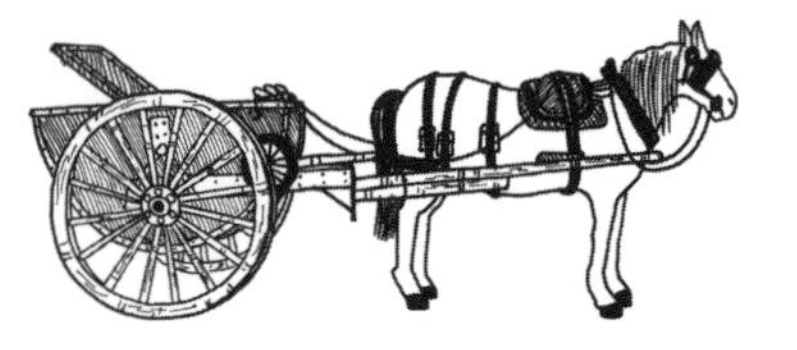

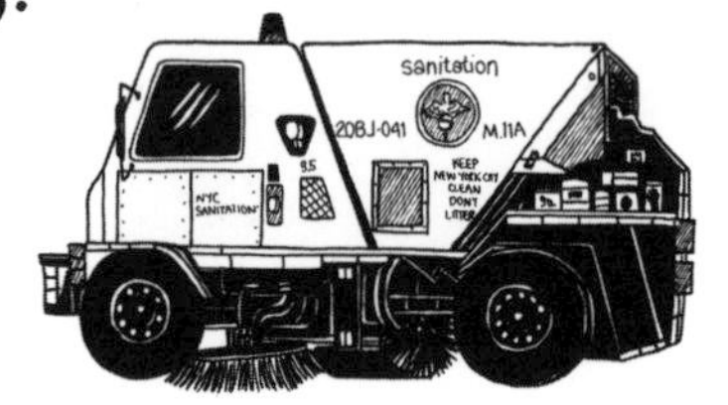

IF YOU'RE ONE OF THE FEW (DISPUTABLY) LUCKY PEOPLE TO OWN A CAR IN NEW YORK CITY, YOU'RE PROBABLY WELL VERSED IN THE INTRICATE AND INFURIATING RULES OF DAILY STREET CLEANING.

IF I MOVE MY CAR AT 9:20 TOMORROW MORNING TO AN 8:00 TUESDAY, I'LL BE GOOD UNTIL THURSDAY, BUT THEN I SHOULD TRY TO MOVE IT WEDNESDAY AT 10:50 INTO A FRIDAY 9:30. OR I CAN GO DOWN A FEW BLOCKS INTO THE 1:30. THEN ON FRIDAY, I CAN MOVE IT AT 9:20 INTO THE 8:00 SPOT AND I'LL BE GOOD UNTIL TUESDAY!
I'M SO GLAD I DON'T HAVE TO DEAL WITH THAT RACKET. I PARK IN A MONITORED GARAGE.
WELL LA-DI-DAH, DADDY WARBUCKS. I HAVE TO PARK ON THE STREET LIKE A COMMONER.
IF YOU'RE A CAR OWNER, AT LEAST ONCE (IF NOT MULTIPLE TIMES) YOU'VE AWOKEN TO THIS AWFUL REALIZATION:
OH FUCK! I FORGOT TO MOVE MY CAR THIS MORNING! UGH, THERE GOES $65 DOWN THE DRAIN. AGAIN.

THE PROCESS OF STREET CLEANING HAS BEEN ANNOYING NEW YORKERS SINCE 1881, WITH THE CREATION OF THE DEPARTMENT OF STREET CLEANING. THROUGHOUT MOST OF THE 1800'S, THE CITY WAS A LITERAL CESSPOOL OF FILTH. WITH NO OFFICIAL SYSTEM TO DISPOSE OF REFUSE, TRASH PILED UP ON THE SIDEWALKS AND STREETS, WHERE IT ROTTED AND FESTERED IN THE HEAT, SPREADING DISEASES LIKE CHOLERA, TYPHUS, TYPHOID, AND YELLOW FEVER.

PRIOR TO THE FORMATION OF AN OFFICIAL GOVERNMENT DEPARTMENT, STREET CLEANING HAD BEEN A PRIVATE AFFAIR, DONE BY HAND WITH A BROOM AND BUCKET, OR BY A HORSE AND CART DRIVEN BY RESIDENTS, STORE OWNERS OR PRIVATELY PAID COLLECTORS.
THE VERY FIRST PATENTED STREET-SWEEPING APPARATUS, DESIGNED BY C.S. BISHOP IN 1849.
WHEN THE DEPARTMENT OF STREET CLEANING FIRST BEGAN OPERATIONS, IT WAS PLAGUED BY CORRUPTION AND FINANCIAL MISMANAGEMENT.
THAT'S AN AWFUL HANDSOME TIMEPIECE YOU'VE GOT THERE, GUV'NA.
WHY THANK YOU, ARTHUR. "MAY THE STREETS FILL WITH GARBAGE, AND MY POCKETS FILL WITH GOLD!" I ALWAYS SAY.
EXCEPT NOT OUT LOUD. FORGET WHAT I JUST SAID.

SOME MID-TO-LATE 1800'S DESIGNS FOR STREET CLEANING CARTS

"WE LIVE IN THE GREATEST CITY IN THE WORLD. LET'S MAKE IT THE CLEANEST AND HEALTHIEST."
THE HAND-SWEEPER
VARIOUS HORSE-DRAWN CARTS*

*IN A SPECTACULAR EXAMPLE OF IRONY, HORSE-DRAWN CARTS CREATED A SECONDARY PROBLEM OF ABUNDANT PILES OF HORSE SHIT DROPPED ON THE NEWLY SWEPT STREET.

WITH THE FORMING OF AN OFFICIAL STREET CLEANING COMMITTEE, CLEANERS WORKED REGULAR 9- TO 10-HOUR DAYS, AND WERE THE LOWEST PAID CIVIL SERVANTS.
WELL, AT LEAST WE'RE NOT NIGHT-SOIL COLLECTORS.*
THEY MAKE PRETTY GOOD MONEY THOUGH.
YEAH, BUT THEY NEVER GET LAID.
*MEN WHO COLLECTED AND SOLD HUMAN WASTE FROM THE OUTDOOR PRIVIES.

IN THE LATE 1800'S,* 75% OF THE CITY'S WASTE, INCLUDING STREET GARBAGE, WAS CARTED OFF AND DUMPED INTO THE ATLANTIC.
*OCEAN DUMPING WAS NOT HALTED UNTIL 1934.

IN NOVEMBER OF 1914, THE CITY HELD A WEEKLONG STREET CLEANING EXHIBITION, WHICH WAS ATTENDED BY OVER 27,000 PEOPLE. EXHIBITORS SHOWED OFF NEW AND INNOVATIVE TRASH-DISPOSAL METHODS, WHILE CIVILIANS ATTENDED IN HOPES OF GETTING A UNION JOB WITH STEADY PAY AND REGULAR HOURS. AT THAT TIME, THERE WAS NO GOVERNMENT POLICY TO PROTECT WORKERS, SO UNION JOBS WERE EXTREMELY COMPETITIVE.

FOR INFORMATION ASK SWEEPER OR DRIVER

APPLY AT MUNICIPAL CIVIL SERVICE COMMISSION ROOM 1400

THE STREET-CLEANING DEPARTMENT offers men as DRIVERS and SWEEPERS

1. STEADY EMPLOYMENT
2. GOOD PAY
3. PROMOTION
4. MEDICAL ATTENTION
5. PENSION

THE EXPO HELD LECTURES AND DEBATES ON THE FUTURE OF GARBAGE DISPOSAL IN THE CITY.
GENTLEMEN, I KNOW THIS IS A RADICAL PROPOSITION, BUT SINCE WE ALREADY REUSE TRASH LIKE ASH AND COAL, WHAT IF WE SOMEHOW CLEANED THE OTHER GARBAGE AND THEN REUSED IT AS IF IT WERE NEW?
THAT'S DISGUSTING, CLARENCE.
PREPOSTEROUS! THAT IDEA WILL NEVER CATCH ON, YOU FOOL.

SIDE NOTE: ALTHOUGH NEW YORKERS REUSED ASH AND COAL THROUGHOUT HISTORY, THEY DID NOT BEGIN OFFICIALLY RECYCLING GLASS, PLASTIC, METAL, AND PAPER UNTIL 1989, WHEN THE CITY PASSED A LAW MANDATING RECYCLING BINS BE GIVEN TO EVERY HOUSE, TO BE PICKED UP BY THE CITY ALONG WITH REGULAR TRASH. DURING WARTIME, RECYCLING METALS FOR BOMBS WAS POPULAR, BUT THE REPURPOSING OF OTHER MATERIALS WAS DONE AT INDEPENDENT DISCRETION. IN THE 1970'S, THE CONCEPT OF MASS RECYCLING GAINED TRACTION, WITH VARIOUS TOWNS AND CITIES DEALING WITH THE ISSUE THEIR OWN WAY. HOWEVER, IT WASN'T UNTIL 1989 WHEN RECYCLING BECAME MANDATORY IN NEW YORK CITY.

THAT YEAR, A MORE COMPREHENSIVE PLAN FOR STREET CLEANING WAS PUT INTO ACTION. HORSES AND CARTS WERE REPLACED BY MOTOR-DRIVEN TRACTORS, WITH AN EMPHASIS ON LEAK-PROOF COMPARTMENTS FOR TRASH STORAGE, TO KEEP GARBAGE FROM FLYING OUT WILLY-NILLY LIKE IT DID FROM THE WOODEN CARTS. ELECTRIC AND GAS STREET SWEEPERS BECAME A FAIRLY LUCRATIVE INDUSTRY, AS BUSINESSES COMPETED FOR GOVERNMENT CONTRACTS.

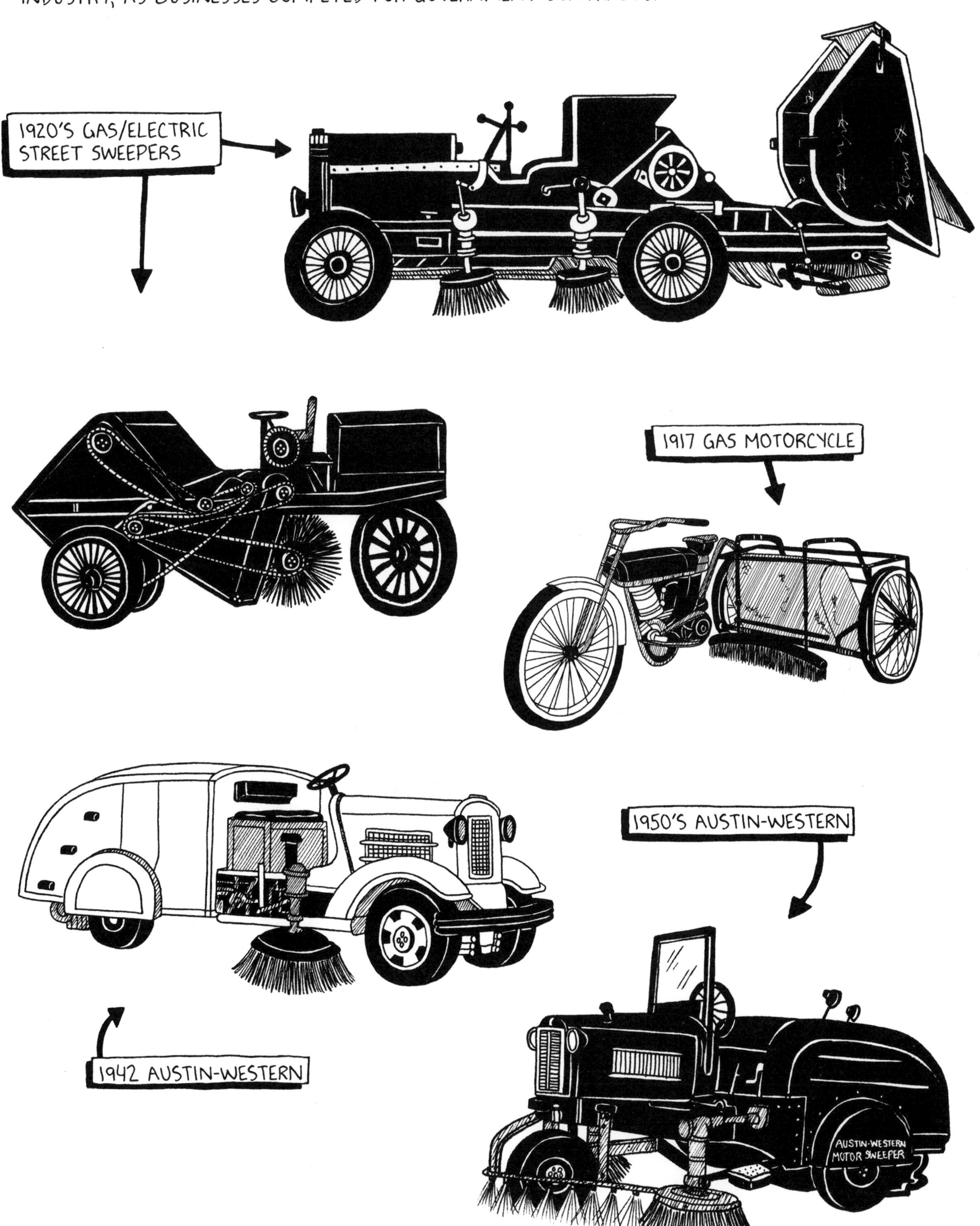

IN 1929, THE DEPARTMENT OF STREET CLEANING BECAME THE DEPARTMENT OF SANITATION, AS IT IS STILL KNOWN TODAY. THROUGHOUT THE REST OF THE 20TH CENTURY, STREET CLEANING BECAME MORE EFFICIENT AND ORGANIZED. LABOR UNIONS CREATED FAIR PAY AND REGULAR HOURS FOR SANITATION WORKERS, AND TRASH WAS DEPOSITED IN LANDFILLS, RECYCLING PLANTS, AND SCRAP YARDS. (SIDE NOTE: WHILE RECYCLING AND GARBAGE FACILITIES HAVE BEEN CHANGED BY TECHNOLOGY, SCRAP YARDS OFTEN LOOK THE SAME AS THEY DID 100 YEARS AGO. BELOW IS A MODERN SCRAP YARD IN EAST WILLIAMSBURG.)

STREET CLEANING VEHICLES FROM THE MID-1900'S TO MODERN DAY

INSIDE THE ALLIANZ 4000

THE TRUCK RUNS ON A COMBINATION OF DIESEL AND LITHIUM-ION BATTERIES, WHICH REDUCES EMISSIONS AND SAVES HELLA MONEY.

THE MAIN COMPARTMENT—THE HOPPER—HOLDS 5.6 CUBIC YARDS OF WHATEVER SHIT YOU THREW IN THE STREET.

WHEN THE HOPPER IS FULL, IT LIFTS, TILTS, AND DUMPS ITS CONTENTS INTO THE APPROPRIATE WASTE DISPOSAL FACILITY.

SIDE ROLLER BRUSHES SWEEP DEBRIS INTO A MANAGEABLE PILE THAT GETS PICKED UP BY...

...THE VERTICAL CONVEYOR BELT, WHICH LIFTS AND DEPOSITS THE TRASH INTO THE HOPPER.

THE TANK HOLDS 250 GALLONS OF WATER. 7 GALLONS AN HOUR ARE SPRAYED ONTO THE STREET WHILE DRIVING.

TODAY, STREET CLEANERS MAKE FAIR WAGES AND HAVE STEADY, UNIONIZED HOURS WITH BENEFITS, PAID HOLIDAYS, AND OVERTIME. DURING WINTER, WHEN STREET CLEANING IS PERIODICALLY SUSPENDED DUE TO BAD WEATHER, THE STREET CLEANERS OPERATE THE SNOWPLOWS. OVERALL, IT'S A PRETTY GOOD GIG, EVEN IF IT IS ONE OF ALL NEW YORKERS' FAVORITE THINGS TO COMPLAIN ABOUT. ACCORDING TO THE DEPARTMENT OF SANITATION, AS OF 2014, THE STREETS OF NEW YORK CITY ARE THE CLEANEST THEY'VE EVER BEEN. SUPPOSEDLY.

TIMES SQUARE THEN & NOW

EVERYONE KNOWS THAT TIMES SQUARE IN THE 1960'S THROUGH THE 1990'S WAS A FETID GARBAGE-COVERED SHITHOLE FULL OF STRIP CLUBS, PORN THEATERS, AND SEEDY CHARACTERS. IT WAS GREAT. WHILE THE CLEANUP AND REAPPROPRIATION OF THE AREA IS A FREQUENT COMPLAINT FROM LONG TERM RESIDENTS WHO REMEMBER THE GOOD OLD DAYS, IF YOU LOOK CLOSELY IN SOME AREAS, YOU'LL SEE THAT NOT EVERYTHING HAS CHANGED, AND SORDID POCKETS CAN STILL BE FOUND.

8TH AVE. BETWEEN W.42ND ST. AND W.43RD ST. IN THE 1990'S

8TH AVE. BETWEEN W.43ND ST. AND W.43RD ST. IN 2014

BROADWAY BETWEEN W.48TH ST. AND W.49TH ST. IN THE 1970'S

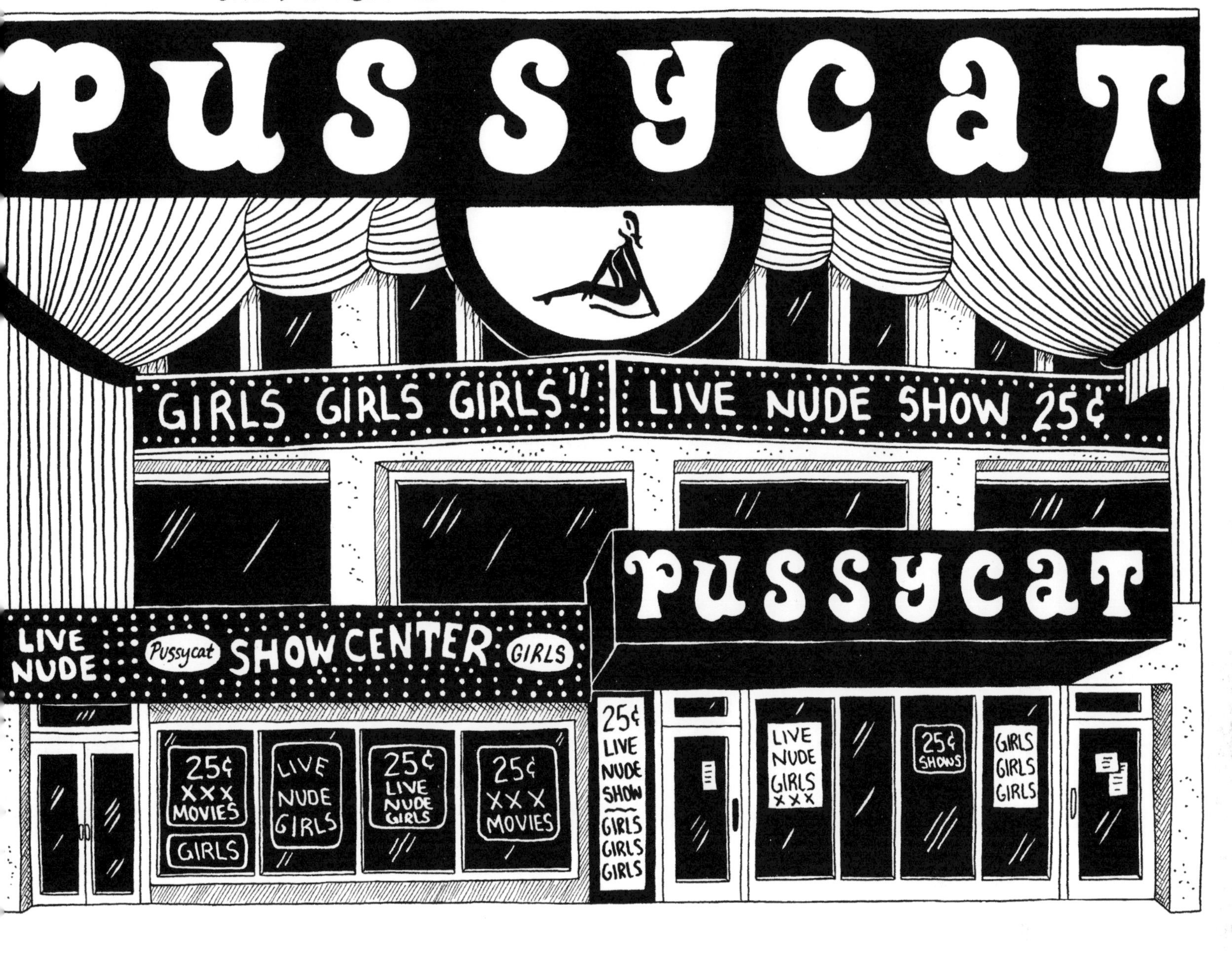

BROADWAY BETWEEN W.48TH ST. AND W.49TH ST. IN 2016

223 W. 42ND ST. IN 1964

APOLLO

Home of Distinguished
FOREIGN
FILMS
65¢
PER
MOVIE

42 ND STREET Apollo

MORAL DECAY EROTICALLY REVEALED!
MAI ZETTERLING'S BOLD SHOCKER
"LOVING COUPLES"
GUNNEL LINDBLOM HARRIET ANDERSSON
"GATE OF FLESH"

HOME
OF
FOREIGN
HITS

RT HILL
JOEL McCREA
TALL ST

65¢
Loving Couples
MOVIE TIMES
GATE of FLESH
SEIJUN SUZUKI
GATE of FLESH

DESERT
HELL
BARBAR
BRIAN K
RICHARD
JOHNNY

THE
TALL
STRANGER

LO
65¢
PER
MOVIE

ANK
BLOOD
BANK
OPEN

223 W. 42ND ST. IN 2014
OLD IDEAS WO
LEONAR
COHEN
APRIL
6 & 7
RADIO C
ticketma
LEONARD
THE NEW VICTORY THEATER
A
THE NEW VICTORY THEATER
THE
Whale
NEW VICTORY THEATE
TRUMP EATS FARTS
P

BROADWAY AND W. 42ND ST. IN 1909
A NEW AMERICAN PLAY
THE INTRUDER
THOMAS BUCHANAN
AUTHOR OF "WOMAN'S WAY"
BIJOU THEATRE
Manhattan Beach
IS BEING SOLD BY
in lots and plots
at Private Sale
31 Nassau St. on Property
A GREAT PLAY
MR. ZANGWILL!
WALKER WHITESIDE
"THE MELTING POT"
COMEDY THEATRE
THE NEW THEATRE
THE CLIMAX
THE DOLLAR-MARK WALLACK'S
$UCCE$$
UNITED CIGARS
TRIP TO
TWICE DA
ALHAMBRA
COLONIAL
TELESTERS
NAT K. WILLS
POOL
CAFE
BILLIARDS
SODA
Fountain
CANDY
CIGARS UNITED CIGARS
E. 42ND ST
GAR STORES CO.
BLACK CROW
Quality Cigars
Coffee
Murad Cigarettes
Quality Cigars

BROADWAY AND W.42ND ST. IN 2014
T··Mobile·
WE'LL PAY
YOUR EARLY
TERMINATION
FEES
T··Mobile·
TASTES SO MUCH
LIKE COKE
WE SHOULD SUE OURSELVES
Coca-Cola zero
Resort World
CASINO
NEW YORK CITY
IN QUEENS NEXT TO JFK AIRPORT JAMAICA
NEWSIES
A MUSICAL WORTH SINGING ABOUT!
★★★★
AN EXHILARATING JOLT OF ENERGY!
HIGH ENERGY WINNER!
IT'S THE TALK OF THE TOWN!!
THE PERFECT MUSICAL FOR OUR TIMES!
NEWSIES
CASIO TRYX
CASIO
BEST BUY
BROADWAY
W. 42 ND
Subway
LOFT
LOFT
LOFT
LOFT
LOFT
SHOE SALE
60% off
SUNDAY SALE
20%-60%
VOICE
am

1540 BROADWAY IN 1915

ZIEGFELD FOLLIES
NEW AMSTERDAM THEATRE
LYRICS BY
GENE BUCK
MUSIC BY
DAVE STAMPER
THE BIRTH OF A NATION
THE LADDER OF ROSES
HIP-HIP HOORAY
AT THE
New York
HIPPODROME
DRINK
Coca-Cola
SIX BOTTLES
in this new handy container
CHIROPODIST
MENS SMART CLOTHES
MEN'S SMART CLOTHES
Mann
Essary
OPEN
MEN'S SMART CLOTHES

1540 BROADWAY IN 2015

1540 B

M·A·C

WEST
SIDE
STORY

WICKED
THE UNTOLD STORY OF THE WITCHES OF OZ

BROADWAY THEATRE

DISNEY

GE

NON

LE

JERSEY BOYS

ROADWAY
WATCH
TUES 24
HAMILTON
AN AMERICAN MUSICAL
Call ticketmaster
(212) 307-4100
FOREVER
FOREVER 21
SALE
SHARED LANE
$25
$30
50-70% OFF T-SHIRTS
U.S. POLO ASSN.
SINCE 1890
FALL SALE
JERSEY BOYS

MADAME RESTELL: THE DESPISED ABORTIONIST OF 5TH AVENUE

OFTEN OMITTED FROM LISTS OF INFLUENTIAL WOMEN OF NEW YORK, MADAME RESTELL WAS AN INFAMOUS AND LARGELY DESPISED FIGURE. RESTELL'S WORK AS AN ABORTIONIST WOULD HAVE BEEN COMPLETELY ACCEPTABLE IN A DIFFERENT ERA, BUT IN THE 1800'S, ABORTION WAS ILLEGAL AND CONSIDERED HIGHLY IMMORAL. IT DIDN'T HELP THAT SHE WAS SUPPOSEDLY A TOTAL FUCKING BITCH.

MADAME RESTELL WAS BORN ANN TROW IN ENGLAND IN 1812. SHE WORKED AS A MAID BEFORE EMIGRATING TO NEW YORK IN 1831, WHERE SHE MARRIED CHARLES LOHMAN, AND BECAME ANN LOHMAN. IN THE CITY, HER BROTHER'S JOB AT A PHARMACY SPARKED HER INTEREST IN WOMEN'S HEALTH ISSUES. LOHMAN, UNDER THE MONIKER MADAME RESTELL, CREATED VARIOUS BIRTH CONTROL PRODUCTS RANGING FROM POWDERS TO PILLS TO TINCTURES, WHICH SHE SOLD FROM HER HOME THROUGH THE POST. (PRIOR TO THE FDA, UNTESTED AND UNPROVEN HOME REMEDIES WERE LEGAL TO ADVERTISE AND SELL AS LEGITIMATE MEDICAL CURES.)

A CERTAIN CURE FOR MARRIED ladies, with or without medicine, by MDM. RESTELL, Professor of Midwifery, over 20 years practice. Her infallible French Female Pills. No.1 price $1 or No. 2, specially prepared for married ladies, price $5, which never fail, are safe and healthy. Sold only at her office, No 1 East 52d-st, first door from 5th av. and at Druggists. 183 Greenwich st. or sent by mail. Caution-All others are counterfeits.

A CLASSIFIED NEWSPAPER AD FOR MADAME RESTELL'S "FRENCH FEMALE PILLS," A SCIENTIFICALLY UNPROVEN FORM OF BIRTH CONTROL IN THE 1800'S

AS HER MEDICINE BUSINESS BOOMED, RESTELL BEGAN PERFORMING ABORTIONS IN HER HOME. SINCE NO ONE ELSE WAS PROVIDING THE SERVICE SO OPENLY, RESTELL DOMINATED THE MOSTLY NONEXISTENT AND HIGHLY ILLEGAL MARKET. SHE PERFORMED ABORTIONS ON MANY WEALTHY NEW YORK SOCIALITES, EARNING HERSELF A TENTATIVE PLACE IN HIGH SOCIETY. EVERYONE HATED HER, BUT THEY TOLERATED HER BECAUSE SHE HELD SECRETS THAT COULD DISGRACE PROMINENT FAMILIES AND MAR POLITICAL RELATIONSHIPS.

ALTHOUGH RESTELL DID NOT OVERTLY ADVERTISE ABORTIONS IN HER NEWSPAPER ADS, THE BLATANT MENTION OF BIRTH CONTROL FLUSTERED MANY NEWSPAPERS. THEY CONSTANTLY HARPED ON HER "IMMORAL AND EVIL" BUSINESS, HELPED FABRICATE HER SORDID REPUTATION, AND LABELED HER "THE WICKEDEST WOMAN IN NEW YORK." ALL OF THAT SEEMS REALLY UNFAIR, NO MATTER HOW UNPLEASANT SHE MAY HAVE BEEN.

NATIONAL POLICE GAZETTE

VOL 9 NO. 27 - $2 A YEAR · NEW YORK, SATURDAY, MARCH 13, 1847 · FOUR CENTS A NUMBER.

THE FEMALE ABORTIONIST

1847 COVER OF THE NATIONAL POLICE GAZETTE, A PENNY-PRESS PAPER THAT REFUSED TO RUN RESTELL'S ADS AND FREQUENTLY DENOUNCED HER EFFORTS IN THEIR CONDEMNING ARTICLES

MADAME RESTELL RETAINED DAMNING INFORMATION ABOUT MANY IMPORTANT PEOPLE, WHICH SHE REPORTEDLY USED AS THREATS TO PROTECT HER BUSINESS. IT MADE HER DESPISED BY THE CITY'S ELITE, EVEN AS SHE YEARNED TO BE ONE OF THEM. IN RETALIATION, THE VERY WEALTHY RESTELL BUILT A HUGE MANSION ON 5TH AVENUE, MUCH TO THE CHAGRIN OF THE WEALTHY FAMILIES THAT LIVED IN THE AREA. THE MANSION WAS SUPPOSEDLY A BIG "FUCK YOU" TO THE CATHOLIC CHURCH —ONE OF HER BIGGEST AND MOST PERSISTENT ADVERSARIES— WHICH WAS JUST ONE BLOCK AWAY.

RESTELL WAS UNDER CONSTANT SCRUTINY BY THE LAW, WHICH EVENTUALLY CAUGHT UP WITH HER IN 1847, FOLLOWING THE DEATH OF ONE OF HER PATIENTS. THE DEATH WAS COMPLICATED AND SENSATIONAL, AND RESTELL SPENT A YEAR IN JAIL FOR THE CRIME. HER SENTENCE WAS SHORTENED BY CONTRADICTORY TESTIMONY. MORE CASES WOULD FOLLOW, AND IN 1878, RESTELL WAS ARRESTED AGAIN AFTER POLITICIAN ANTHONY COMSTOCK POSED AS A CUSTOMER TO ENTRAP HER.

MARY ROGERS, KNOWN AS THE "BEAUTIFUL CIGAR GIRL," WAS THE CENTRAL FIGURE OF RESTELL'S CASE, AS ONE THEORY HAD HER DEATH CAUSED BY A BOTCHED ABORTION. ROGERS'S DEATH WAS NEVER SOLVED.

SHORTLY AFTER HER ARREST, RESTELL WAS DISCOVERED DEAD IN HER BATHTUB BY A MAID. SHE HAD PUT ON ALL HER JEWELRY AND SLIT HER THROAT. EVEN THOUGH RESTELL NEVER GOT THE ACCEPTANCE SHE YEARNED FOR FROM THE CITY'S ELITE, HER FINANCES FIRMLY AFFIXED HER AS ONE OF THEM. AT THE TIME OF HER OPULENT SUICIDE, SHE HAD AMASSED A FORTUNE THAT TODAY WOULD BE WORTH ABOUT $13 MILLION. DESPITE HER PURPORTED REPUTATION, RESTELL DESERVES A PROMINENT PLACE ON THE LIST OF HISTORIC FEMINISTS. SHE RISKED A LOT TO PROVIDE AN ILLEGAL BUT IMPERATIVE SERVICE THAT WE NOW CONSIDER A BASIC HUMAN RIGHT.

SHE WAS BURIED NEXT TO HER HUSBAND IN SLEEPY HOLLOW, NEW YORK.

A BIASED GUIDE TO NEW YORK CITY'S INDEPENDENT BOOKSTORES

IN TODAY'S DIGITALLY DOMINATED CULTURE, BRICK-AND-MORTAR BOOKSTORES ARE A DYING INDUSTRY. OR SO SAYS THE INTERNET AND CONVERSATIONAL RUMBLINGS. HOWEVER, A DEEPER LOOK INTO NEW YORK CITY'S REMAINING BOOKSTORES TELLS A DIFFERENT STORY THAT IS BOTH DARKER AND MORE HOPEFUL THAN THE GENERAL CONSENSUS WOULD HAVE YOU BELIEVE.

IN THE EARLY 2000'S, ONLINE RETAIL GIANT AMAZON THREATENED TO PUT BOOKSTORES OUT OF BUSINESS BY UNDERCUTTING PRICES AND BECOMING A DIRECT SELLER MIDDLEMAN. IN SOME CITIES, AMAZON SUCCEEDED, FORCING MANY INDIE AND CORPORATE BOOKSTORES TO CLOSE. IN 2011, WHEN BORDERS FILED FOR BANKRUPTCY, IT APPEARED THAT THE CLOCK HAD BEGUN TICKING FOR THE SURVIVING STORES.

BUT IN NEW YORK CITY, WE UNDERESTIMATED OURSELVES. AS IT TURNED OUT, THE FEAR OF LOSING OUR BOOKSTORES DROVE US TO START BUYING MORE BOOKS FROM LOCAL SHOPS. THIS FEAR, COUPLED WITH A RISING BACKLASH AGAINST DIGITAL BOOKS, PREVENTED A NUMBER OF BOOKSTORES FROM GOING UNDER.

DESPITE THE SURPRISING AND UPLIFTING TURN OF EVENTS, NOT ALL BOOKSTORES SURVIVED THE DIGITAL REVOLUTION AND ITS SUBSEQUENT SO-CALLED "DEATH OF PRINT." BELOVED STORES SUCH AS PARK SLOPE'S BERGEN STREET COMICS AND COBBLE HILL'S COMMUNITY BOOK STORE RECENTLY CLOSED, CITING SLUMPING SALES AND RISING RENTS. BUT FOR THE SAKE OF OPTIMISM, AND MY LOVE OF BOOKS, THIS SECTION FOCUSES ON A HANDFUL OF THE CITY'S CURRENTLY THRIVING INDIE BOOKSTORES.*

*THERE WAS NO WAY I COULD INCLUDE ALL OF THE INDEPENDENT BOOKSTORES OF NEW YORK CITY IN THIS PIECE, WHICH IS A GOOD THING, BUT I'M LEFT WITH A SEVERELY ABRIDGED LIST THAT OMITS SOME WONDERFUL SHOPS. FORCED TO CHERRY-PICK, I SELECTED SOME STORES FOR THEIR HISTORY, AND OTHERS FOR MY PERSONAL CONNECTION TO THEM AFTER A DECADE OF MAKING BOOKS AND DOING EVENTS IN BOOKSTORES ACROSS THE CITY. A FEW OF THEM I HAVE NO CONNECTION TO, NOR ARE THEY OF ANY HISTORICAL SIGNIFICANCE, BUT I'M COMFORTED BY THEIR STEADFAST PRESENCE IN A-EVER-CHANGING CITY.**

** SOME BOOKSTORES CLOSED DURING THE YEARS I WAS MAKING THIS BOOK; THEY'RE NOTED ACCORDINGLY.

RIZZOLI BOOKSTORE
31 W.57TH ST.
MIDTOWN, MANHATTAN

RIZZOLI BOOKSTORE WAS OPENED IN 1964 BY ANGELO RIZZOLI AT 712 5TH AVENUE. ITS OPULENT BUILDING AND EXTENSIVE COLLECTION OF FOREIGN AND ILLUSTRATED BOOKS ATTRACTED HORDES OF CUSTOMERS. BY THE 70'S AND 80'S, RIZZOLI HAD FRANCHISED AND OPENED STORES THROUGHOUT THE UNITED STATES. IN 1985, THE 57TH STREET LOCATION OPENED, BUT WAS FOLLOWED BY THE CLOSURE OF THE FIRST STORE A FEW YEARS LATER. BY 2001, THE NATIONAL RIZZOLI BOOKSTORES HAD CLOSED, LEAVING ONLY THE FLAGSHIP STORE. IN 2014, RIZZOLI WAS FORCED OUT WHEN THEIR LEASE EXPIRED, DESPITE PROTESTS FROM HISTORICAL PRESERVATIONISTS WHO WANTED TO SAVE THE BUILDING, AS IT WAS MARKED FOR DEMOLITION. EVERYONE ON THE GOOD SIDE LOST, AND THREE HISTORIC BUILDINGS WERE RAZED TO MAKE WAY FOR A SHITTY CONDO TOWER. BUT RIZZOLI DIDN'T GO AWAY; THEY REOPENED A YEAR LATER AT 1133 BROADWAY.

GREENLIGHT BOOKSTORE, 686 FULTON ST. FORT GREENE, BROOKLYN

IN 2008, THE FORT GREENE ASSOCIATION ANNOUNCED THE RESULTS OF THEIR SURVEY OF LOCAL RESIDENTS, WHO CLAIMED THE NUMBER ONE THING THE AREA LACKED WAS A BOOKSTORE. THE TIMING WAS PERFECT FOR REBECCA FITTING AND JESSICA STOCKTON BAGNULO TO JUMP IN, AND WITH OVERWHELMING COMMUNITY SUPPORT, LOANS, AND COMPETITION MONEY, THEY SUCCEEDED IN OPENING GREENLIGHT BOOKSTORE IN 2009. GREENLIGHT IS ON MY LIST BECAUSE IT'S SUCH A GREAT EXAMPLE OF WHAT A COMMUNITY CAN ACHIEVE WHEN PEOPLE PARTICIPATE AND HELP EACH OTHER OUT INSTEAD OF NOT GIVING ANY FUCKS WHEN A CELL PHONE STORE TAKES OVER THE LOCAL BAKERY. GREENLIGHT WAS AN INSTANT SUCCESS, AND IN 2015, THEY ANNOUNCED PLANS TO OPEN A SECOND LOCATION IN PROSPECT LEFFERTS GARDENS.

← SPOONBILL & SUGARTOWN, BOOKSELLERS, 218 BEDFORD AVE. WILLIAMSBURG, BROOKLYN

SPOONBILL & SUGARTOWN, OPEN SINCE 1999, MAKES MY LIST AS A FAVOR TO MY FRIEND/NEIGHBOR, WHO HAS SPENT HUNDREDS, IF NOT THOUSANDS, OF DOLLARS BUYING ART BOOKS THERE OVER THE LAST 15 YEARS. THE STORE OFFERS USED, NEW, AND RARE BOOKS, BUT THEIR EXTENSIVE ART BOOK SECTION IS WHAT REALLY STANDS OUT. HOWEVER, ART BOOKS AREN'T REALLY MY THING, SO BOLGER, THIS ONE'S FOR YOU.

STRAND BOOKSTORE, 828 BROADWAY UNION SQUARE, MANHATTAN →

STRAND BOOKSTORE, MORE COMMONLY REFERRED TO AS JUST THE STRAND, IS ARGUABLY BEST KNOWN FOR ITS SIZABLE ART BOOKS COLLECTION AND $2 OUTDOOR BOOK BINS. THE STRAND SELLS BOTH NEW AND USED BOOKS, SO YOU CAN PRETTY MUCH FIND ANYTHING THERE. THE ONLY DOWNSIDE TO THE MASSIVE BOOKSTORE IS ITS PROXIMITY TO UNION SQUARE, WHICH MEANS IT'S ALWAYS BUSTLING WITH TOURISTS, BUT AT LEAST THAT MAKES FOR GOOD PEOPLE WATCHING.

THE STRAND OPENED IN 1927 ON WHAT WAS THEN KNOWN AS "BOOK ROW," A SIX BLOCK STRETCH OF 4TH AVENUE THAT WAS HOME TO NEARLY 50 BOOKSTORES. IN THE LATE 1950'S, THE STORE RELOCATED TO ITS CURRENT LOCATION ON BROADWAY. WHEN I FIRST MOVED TO THE CITY, I SPENT COUNTLESS HOURS COMBING THROUGH THE DOLLAR BINS TO RESTOCK MY SHELVES AND BOY DID I BUY SOME SHIT, BUT I HAVE FOND MEMORIES OF THAT WASTED TIME.

WORD, 126 FRANKLIN ST. GREENPOINT, BROOKLYN

WORD IS MY FAVORITE BOOKSTORE IN NYC. THEY HAVE A GREAT SELECTION OF NEW BOOKS ACCOMPANIED BY AMUSING STAFF AND LOCAL WRITERS' SUGGESTIONS, PLUS SOME HARD-TO-GET BOOKS ABOUT GREENPOINT. I GOT A BUNCH OF STUFF THERE WHILE DOING RESEARCH FOR THIS BOOK. THE DOWNSTAIRS HAS A COZY, UNPRETENTIOUS EVENTS AREA THAT WAS ONE OF MY FAVORITE PLACES TO DO READINGS. SOMETIMES I USED WORD TO VET TINDER DATES, JUST TO SEE HOW THEY HANDLED THEMSELVES IN A BOOKSTORE, WHICH, NOW THAT I THINK ABOUT IT, IS PROBABLY THE LAST THING SOMEONE FROM TINDER WANTS TO DO. I SUSPECT I MIGHT BE A TERRIBLE DATE.

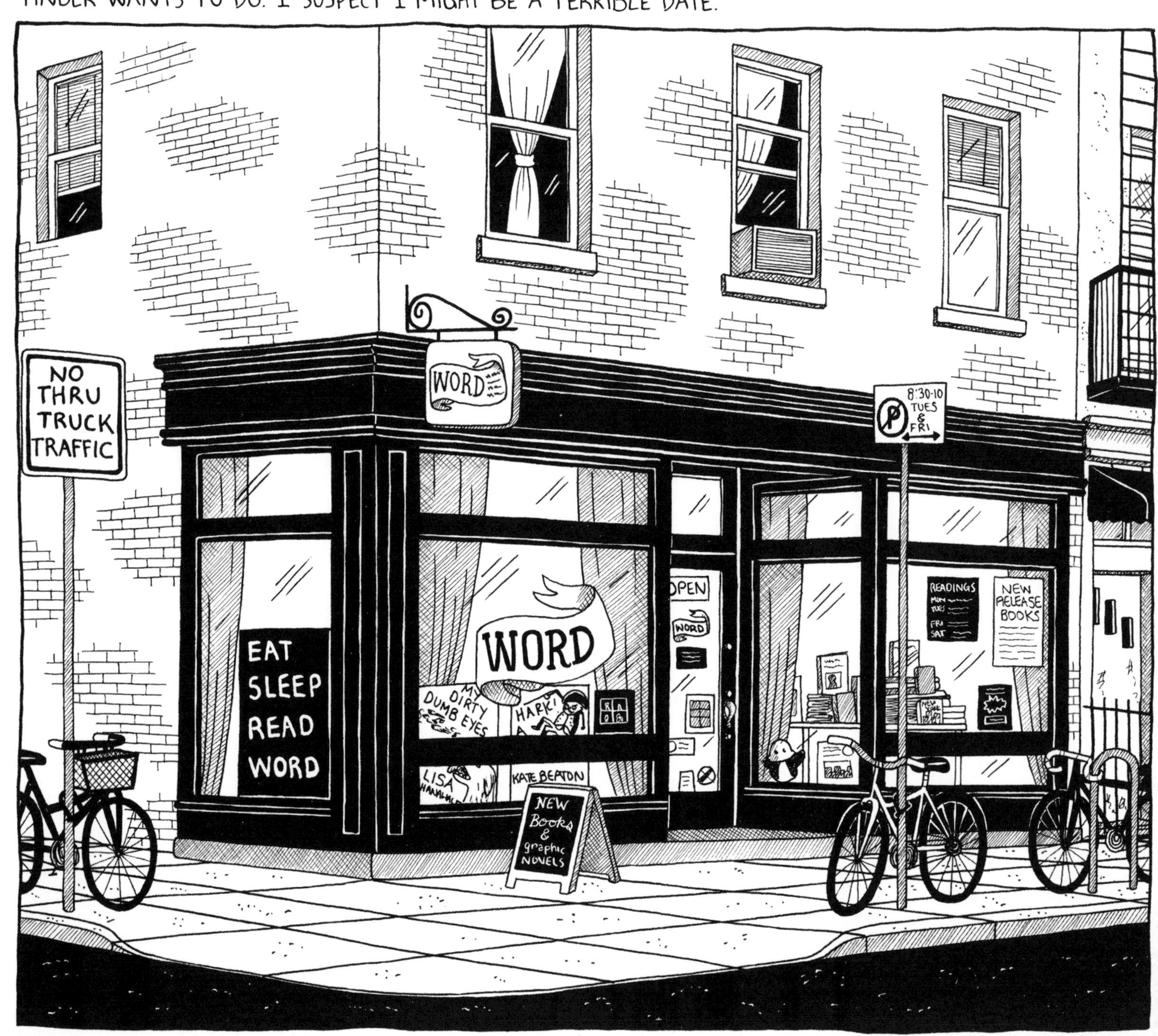

STRAND
ONE WAY
ONE WAY
BROADWAY
E. 12TH ST
AND BOOKSTORE
OLD RARE NEW
LIBRARIES BOUGHT
STRAND BOOKSTO
STRAND GIFT CARD
ATM
Back to School STRAND STYLE
TOP SHELF
VODKA
$2
$1
GAY CITY

THREE LIVES & COMPANY
154 W.10TH ST.
WEST VILLAGE, MANHATTAN

THREE LIVES & COMPANY HAS BEEN OPEN SINCE 1978 AND IS A LYNCHPIN OF NEW YORK LITERARY CULTURE, WHATEVER THAT IS. I'LL LET WRITER MICHAEL CUNNINGHAM EXPLAIN WHY THE BOOKSTORE IS SO BELOVED, AS HE'S QUOTED SAYING THREE LIVES "IS ONE OF THE GREATEST BOOKSTORES ON THE FACE OF THE EARTH. EVERY SINGLE PERSON WHO WORKS THERE IS INCREDIBLY KNOWLEDGEABLE AND WELL READ AND FULL OF SOUL. YOU CAN WALK IN AND ASK ANYBODY, REALLY, WHAT THEY'VE READ LATELY AND THEY'LL TELL YOU SOMETHING—VERY LIKELY SOMETHING YOU'VE NEVER HEARD OF. [BUT] IT'S ALWAYS GOING TO BE SOMETHING INTERESTING AND FABULOUS."

BOOK THUG NATION, 100 N.3RD ST. WILLIAMSBURG, BROOKLYN

ONE OF THE NEWER BOOKSTORES ON MY LIST, BOOK THUG NATION OPENED IN 2009. CO-OWNER AARON COMETBUS IS A LEGENDARY ZINE WRITER WHO HAS BEEN MAKING AND PUBLISHING HIS ZINE, COMETBUS, SINCE 1981. I STARTED READING COMETBUS IN THE 90'S AS A TEENAGER, AND HAD THE DISTINCT PLEASURE OF BEING INTERVIEWED FOR THE ZINE IN 2016. BOOK THUG NATION WAS STARTED BY FOUR INDEPENDENT BOOKSELLERS WHO SOLD BOOKS ON THE STREET AT ASTOR PLACE FOR SIX YEARS BEFORE OPENING THE BRICK-AND-MORTAR BOOKSTORE. THE SHOP SELLS USED BOOKS AND HAS AN IMPRESSIVE FANZINE AND COMICS SECTION. YOU MAY EVEN FIND SOME OF MY OLD ZINES THERE.

ALABASTER BOOKSHOP, 122 4TH AVE.
EAST VILLAGE, MANHATTAN

JUST BLOCKS AWAY FROM THE STRAND, ALABASTER BOOKSHOP IS THE ONLY BOOK-STORE ON WHAT USED TO BE KNOWN AS BOOK ROW. ALTHOUGH IT WAS TOO LATE TO BE PART OF THE ROW (IT OPENED IN 1997) ALABASTER HAS MANAGED TO REMAIN OPEN DESPITE ITS CLOSE PROXIMITY TO THE STRAND. OWNER STEVE CROWLEY KEEPS THE STORE OVERFLOWING WITH USED BOOKS, AND THE WHOLE PLACE JUST HAS THAT COZY STUCK-IN-TIME FEELING THAT LARGER BOOK-STORES CAN'T COMPETE WITH.

THE COMMUNITY BOOKSTORE, 212 COURT ST. COBBLE HILL, BROOKLYN

THE COMMUNITY BOOKSTORE WAS ONE OF THOSE PLACES YOU COULDN'T BELIEVE STILL EXISTED IN THE CITY, UNTIL IT DIDN'T EXIST ANYMORE. THE COBBLE HILL SHOP WAS BELOVED FOR ITS FLOOR-TO-CEILING STACKS OF BOOKS, AND OWNER JOHN SCIOLI, WHO RAN THE STORE FROM AROUND 5PM-MIDNIGHT, DESPITE CONFLICTING SIGNAGE. THE SHOP OPENED IN 1985, HAVING BEEN PREVIOUSLY LOCATED IN PARK SLOPE AND BROOKLYN HEIGHTS. SCIOLI, AN INCREASINLY RELUCTANT SHOP OWNER, TOLD *THE NEW YORK TIMES*, "I TRIED TO GO OUT OF BUSINESS TWO OR THREE TIMES. I CAN'T BELIEVE PEOPLE STILL PUT UP WITH THIS PLACE. BUT NO MATTER WHAT I DID, PEOPLE JUST KEPT BUYING BOOKS." FINALLY, IN 2016, SCIOLI SOLD THE BUILDING HE BOUGHT FOR HALF A MILLION FOR $5.5 MILLION. HE PROMPLTY CLOSED UP SHOP AND RETIRED.

EAST VILLAGE BOOKS
99 ST. MARKS PL.
EAST VILLAGE, MANHATTAN

WHEN FIRST ASCENDING INTO EAST VILLAGE BOOKS, THE STORE LOOKS CHAOTIC AND CRAMPED, PACKED WITH THOUSANDS OF BOOKS, CDS, AND RECORDS, BUT THE DEEPER YOU GO, YOU BEGIN TO REALIZE THE CHAOS IS IN FACT ORDERLY. THE STORE HAS A CUTE LITTLE GARDEN OUT BACK AND DOLLAR BOOK RACKS. OPEN SINCE 1999, THE STORE SPECIALIZES IN PURCHASING ESTATE LIBRARIES, BUT YOU CAN SELL THEM ANYTHING FROM OBSCURE, FOREIGN TEXTBOOKS TO UNDERGROUND COMICS. YOU COULD PROBABLY SELL THEM THIS BOOK IF YOU WERE SO INCLINED. I'D BE OKAY WITH THAT!

THE CORNER BOOKSTORE
1313 MADISON AVE.
UPPER EAST SIDE, MANHATTAN

THE CORNER BOOKSTORE, ON THE CORNER OF MADISON AVE. AND 93RD ST., OPENED IN 1978. WHILE IT HAS ALL TYPES OF BOOKS, IT SPECIALIZES IN OUT-OF-PRINT AND COLLECTIBLE BOOKS. BUT THE CORNER BOOKSTORE MAKES MY LIST FOR A NONLITERARY REASON. THE OWNERS, WHO PURCHASED THE BUILDING IN 1976, TOOK GREAT CARE TO RESTORE THE INTERIOR, WHICH HOUSED A PHARMACY FOR THE PREVIOUS 50 YEARS. THEY PEELED OFF LAYERS OF PAINT TO REVEAL THE ORIGINAL TIN CEILING, WOOD CABINETS, AND TERRAZZO FLOOR THAT CAN BE SEEN IN THE STORE TODAY.

ARGOSY BOOKSTORE, 116 E.59TH ST. MIDTOWN, MANHATTAN →

ARGOSY BOOKSTORE MAKES MY LIST FOR A NUMBER OF REASONS, THE FIRST BEING THAT IT'S THE OLDEST SURVIVING INDEPENDENT BOOKSTORE IN THE CITY. OPENED IN 1925 BY LOUIS COHEN, THE STORE HAS BEEN FAMILY OWNED AND OPERATED FOR THREE GENERATIONS. THEIR COLLECTION OF OLD, RARE, OUT-OF-PRINT AND ANTIQUARIAN BOOKS IS SO BIG, IT FILLS SIX FLOORS IN MANHATTAN AND A WAREHOUSE IN BROOKLYN.

BESIDES ITS HISTORICAL SIGNIFICANCE, THE STORE CATERS TO SOME OF MY MORE SPECIFIC INTERESTS IN A WAY OTHER BOOKSTORES DON'T. IT'S HOME TO THE ARGOSY GALLERY, AN AMAZING COLLECTION OF ANTIQUE MAPS AND PRINTS OF NEW YORK CITY. LAST TIME I VISITED THE GALLERY, I HAD TO BE FORCIBLY REMOVED BY AN IMPATIENT FRIEND WHO WAS UNDERSTANDABLY TIRED OF HEARING ME TALK ABOUT MAPS. THEY ALSO HAVE A GREAT SCIENCE AND MEDICAL HISTORY SECTION, MY FAVORITE GENRE OF LITERATURE, WHICH IS OFTEN LACKING IN OTHER BOOKSTORES THAT JUST STACK SOME MARY ROACH BOOKS NEXT TO OLIVER SACKS AND CALL IT A DAY. I'M A FAN OF BOTH WRITERS, BUT THE GENRE DESERVES A LOT MORE ATTENTION THAN THAT, AND ARGOSY GIVES IT SUCH ATTENTION.

DESERT ISLAND, 540 METROPOLITAN AVE. WILLIAMSBURG, BROOKLYN

WHEN DESERT ISLAND OPENED IN 2008, I ASKED OWNER GABE FOWLER FOR A JOB. I DIDN'T GET ONE, SINCE AT THE TIME HE RAN THE STORE ALONE, BUT WE DID BECOME FRIENDS AND I'VE HAD MANY BOOK RELEASE PARTIES THERE. DESERT ISLAND IS A COMIC BOOK STORE THAT SPECIALIZES IN INDEPENDENT AND ART COMICS, AND HAS A NOTICEABLE (AND PERSONALLY APPRECIATED) LACK OF SUPERHERO BULLSHIT. THE MOST UNIQUE ASPECT OF THE STORE IS THE ELABORATE, PERPETUALLY CHANGING WINDOW DISPLAY, CREATED BY CARTOONISTS AND ARTISTS OF GABE'S CHOOSING. MY FAVORITE ONE (NOT PICTURED) WAS DONE BY LISA HANAWALT. FOWLER ALSO PUBLISHES A FREE COMIC NEWSPAPER CALLED *SMOKE SIGNAL* THAT CAN BE FOUND AT DESERT ISLAND AND OTHER LOCATION SHOPS.

IN 2008, SHORTLY AFTER DESERT ISLAND OPENED, I WAS RIDING MY BIKE HOME FROM MY DINER JOB WHEN A SURPRISE RAINSTORM HIT. I WAS CLOSE TO THE STORE, SO I RAN FOR COVER AND MADE IT JUST AS GABE WAS LOCKING UP. HE LET ME IN, AND WE HUNG OUT AND DRANK BEER AND TALKED COMICS UNTIL THE RAIN LET UP. IT'S ONE OF MY FAVORITE NYC MEMORIES.

IT SHOULD ALSO BE NOTED THAT GABE CREATED AND RUNS COMIC ARTS BROOKLYN, OR CAB, AN INDIE COMICS FESTIVAL HELD ONCE A YEAR IN NOVEMBER AT OUR LADY OF MOUNT CARMEL CHURCH IN WILLIAMSBURG. THE ANNUAL ONE-DAY SHOW IS ALWAYS PACKED, AND RELATED READINGS AND EVENTS HAPPEN ALL WEEK LONG ALL AROUND THE CITY.

ARGOSY BOOK STORE
ARGOSY BOOK STORE
ARGOSY GALLERY
EARLY AMERICAN PAINTINGS
fine Old Maps & Prints
SUITS
ARGOSY
ARGOSY BOOKSTO
ARGOSY
OLD & NEW BOOKS PRINTS PAINTINGS MAPS

UNNAMEABLE BOOKS
600 VANDERBILT AVE.
PROSPECT HEIGHTS, BROOKLYN

ORIGINALLY, UNNAMEABLE WAS CALLED ADAM BOOKS (AFTER OWNER ADAM TOBIN) AND LOCATE ON BERGEN STREET. FACING A RENT HIKE AND A LAWSUIT THREAT OVER THE STORE'S NAME FROM TEXTBOOK DISTRIBUTOR ADAMS BOOKS COMPANY TOBIN RELOCATED TO VANDERBILT AVE IN 2009, AND RENAMED HIS STORE UNNAMEABLE BOOKS. ALTHOUGH UNNAMEABLE DOES CARRY POPULAR TITLES, TOBIN MAKES SURE TO STOCK HIS STORE WITH LOCAL AND SMALL PRESS TITLES AS WELL, WHICH AS A ONCE LOCAL, SMALL-PRESS CARTOONIST, I REALLY APPRECIATE.

BOOKCOURT, 163 COURT ST.
COBBLE HILL, BROOKLYN

BOOKCOURT OPENED IN 1981 AND LASTED UNTIL 2016, SELLING A WIDE VARIETY OF NEW BOOKS AND HOSTING LITERARY EVENTS. I ENJOYED THEIR EXTENSIVE NYC AND CHILDREN'S BOOK SECTIONS. BOOKCOURT'S OWNERS HENRY ZOOK AND MARY GANNETT WORKED AT THEIR STORE FOR 35 YEARS BEFORE DECIDING TO SELL THE BUILDING AND RETIRE IN 2016. IN RESPONSE TO BOOK-COURT CLOSING, AUTHOR EMMA STRAUB AND HER HUSBAND OPENED THEIR OWN BOOKSTORE A FEW DOORS DOWN.

MERCER STREET BOOKS & RECORDS
206 MERCER ST.
GREENWICH VILLAGE, MANHATTAN

FOR OVER 25 YEARS, MERCER STREET BOOKS & RECORDS HAS BEEN QUIETLY SELLING NEW, USED, AND OUT-OF-PRINT BOOKS AND VINYL RECORDS. BUT THIS SHOP MAKES MY LIST FOR MORE SENTIMENTAL REASONS. DURING MY SECOND YEAR IN NYC, I WALKED PAST MERCER STREET BOOKS ALMOST DAILY ON THE WAY TO MY CAFE JOB UP THE STREET. IT WAS JUST AS I WAS REALLY STARTING TO LIKE THE CITY AFTER A ROUGH YEAR, SO, YOU KNOW, IT WAS A TIME.

BLUESTOCKINGS, 172 ALLEN ST. LOWER EAST SIDE, MANHATTAN

BLUESTOCKINGS WAS OPENED BY KATHRYN WELSH IN 1999 WITH THE ORIGINAL NAME "BLUESTOCKINGS WOMEN'S BOOKSTORE." IT WAS A COMMUNITY SPACE, EVENTS VENUE, AND BOOKSTORE FOR WOMEN. A MANAGEMENT CHANGE IN 2003 SAW THE STORE'S MISSION STATEMENT ANGLE MORE TOWARD SOCIAL ACTIVISM, BUT THE STORE STILL RETAINS ITS STRONG FEMINIST ANGLE. THE STORE HOSTS READINGS, SHOWS, WORKSHOPS, AND OTHER EVENTS ALMOST EVERY NIGHT, AND OFFERS A WEALTH OF LGBT RESOURCES AND INFORMATION. IT'S REALLY AMAZING THE BLUESTOCKINGS COLLECTIVE HAS KEPT THE STORE GOING THIS LONG IN THE CURRENT REAL ESTATE ECONOMY. THEY OPERATE ON A BREAK-EVEN MODEL, SO EVERY DOLLAR SPENT HERE REALLY COUNTS.

ROCKETSHIP GRAPHIC NOVELS & COMICS
208 SMITH ST.
COBBLE HILL, BROOKLYN

ROCKETSHIP WAS THE FIRST COMIC BOOK STORE I WENT TO WHEN I MOVED TO BROOKLYN, AND THE FIRST PLACE I DID AN EVENT AT IN NEW YORK. I SPENT MANY EVENINGS THERE, GETTING TO KNOW OTHER LOCAL CARTOONISTS WHO WOULD BECOME GOOD FRIENDS OVER THE NEXT DECADE. FOR A WHILE, MY ART HUNG ON THE WALL. ROCKETSHIP'S CLOSURE IN 2010 HIT HARD, BUT AT LEAST BERGEN STREET COMICS* AND DESERT ISLAND STEPPED IN TO EASE THE BLOW.

*BERGEN STREET COMICS CLOSED IN 2015.

McNALLY JACKSON, 52 PRINCE ST. NOLITA, MANHATTAN

ONE OF THE LARGEST AND MOST POPULAR INDEPENDENT BOOKSTORES, McNALLY JACKSON NOT ONLY HAS A HUGE ECLECTIC SELECTION OF BOOKS, BUT ALSO PRINTS ITS OWN BOOKS. OWNER SARAH McNALLY BOUGHT FOR THE STORE A PRINT-ON-DEMAND BOOKMAKER CALLED ESPRESSO BOOK MACHINE, WHICH IS USED TO PRINT AROUND 700 SELF-PUBLISHED WORKS A MONTH. ALTHOUGH I DON'T HAVE FINANCIAL STATS ON THE BOOKMAKER'S OUTPUT, IT'S SAFE TO ASSUME IT'S MOSTLY A LABOR OF LOVE. THEY ALSO USE THE BOOKMAKER TO REPRINT OLD, OUT-OF-PRINT BOOKS THAT ARE HARD TO FIND, MAKING IT AN INCREDIBLY UNIQUE EFFORT FOR A BOOKSTORE.

HOUSING WORKS BOOKSTORE CAFE, 126 CROSBY ST. SOHO, MANHATTAN

HOUSING WORKS IS A NONPROFIT CHARITY THAT RUNS MULTIPLE THRIFT SHOPS AND ONE OF THE BEST BOOKSTORES IN THE CITY. BESIDES HAVING A HUGE SELECTION OF USED BOOKS, THE STORE HAS A CAFE WITH SEATING, AND HOSTS WORKSHOPS, READINGS, AND EVENTS ALMOST DAILY. I DID A FEW READINGS THERE, THE MOST MEMORABLE BEING IN 2014 WHEN I HAD TO START MY SET BY APOLOGIZING TO THE GENTLEMAN ON WHOM I OPENED THE BATHROOM DOOR, SCREAMED IN HIS FACE, SLAMMED THE DOOR, AND RAN AWAY.

THE BOOKSTORE OPENED IN THE MID-90'S AND IS RUN BY VOLUNTEERS. 100 PERCENT OF ITS PROFITS GO TO ITS CHARITY, WHICH PRIMARILY FOCUSED ON AIDS DURING ITS EARLY YEARS, BUT EXPANDED INTO OTHER AREAS. THE STORE GETS ITS BOOKS FROM DONATIONS, SO NEXT TIME YOU'RE CLEANING YOUR APARTMENT, INSTEAD OF DUMPING YOUR SHIT ON THE CURB FOR SOME CHUCKLEHEAD TO RIFLE THROUGH AND SCOFF AT, TAKE IT TO HOUSING WORKS! YOU'LL GET A TAX DEDUCTION AND THAT SWEET FEELING YOU GET FROM HELPING OTHERS WITH MINIMAL EFFORT EXERTED.

COMMUNITY BOOKSTORE, 143 7TH AVE. PARK SLOPE, BROOKLYN

COMMUNITY BOOKSTORE —OPEN SINCE 1971— IS PERHAPS MOST FAMOUS FOR BEING THE HOME OF "TINY," THE STORE'S RESIDENT CAT. TINY WAS ONCE JOINED BY ANOTHER CAT, SIR MARJORIE LAMBSHANK III, WHO PASSED AWAY A FEW YEARS AGO. BESIDES THE CATS, COMMUNITY BOOKSTORE IS A LOCAL FAVORITE FOR ITS VARIED SELECTION AND CUTE BACKYARD WHERE YOU CAN SIT AND READ. BUT IF YOU DO THAT, MAKE SURE TO BUY SOMETHING OR ELSE YOU'LL BE THAT ASSHOLE WHO USES THEIR LAPTOP AT A CAFE FOR HOURS AND ONLY ORDERS WATER. THAT'S FINE TO DO AT BARNES & NOBLE, BUT NOT AT INDEPENDENT BOOKSTORES.

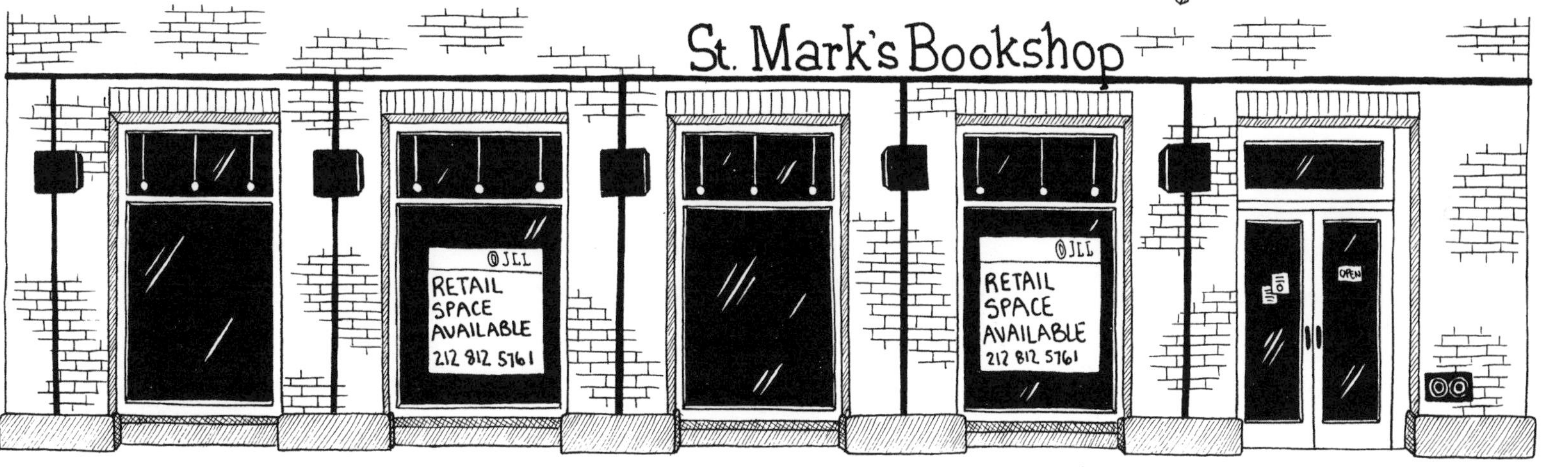

ST. MARK'S BOOKSHOP, 136 E.3RD ST. EAST VILLAGE, MANHATTAN

ST. MARK'S BOOKSHOP WAS A NEIGHBORHOOD STAPLE THAT OPENED IN 1977. KNOWN FOR ITS EXTENSIVE ART BOOKS AND ECLECTIC MAGAZINE SECTION, ST. MARK'S HAD STOCK RANGING FROM BESTSELLING NOVELS TO SELF-PUBLISHED ZINES. LAST YEAR, THE SHOP WAS SERVED AN EVICTION NOTICE DUE TO UNPAID RENT, FINANCIAL DISPUTES, AND TAX TROUBLE. ALMOST 45,000 PEOPLE SIGNED A PETITION TO LANDMARK AND SAVE THE STORE, BUT IT CLOSED ITS DOORS IN 2016.

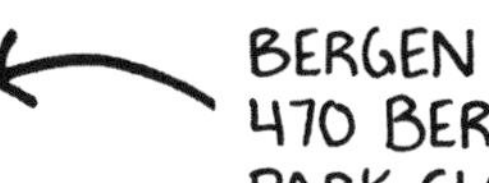

BERGEN STREET COMICS
470 BERGEN ST.
PARK SLOPE, BROOKLYN

BERGEN STREET COMICS ONLY LASTED SIX YEARS, BUT THEY WERE A GREAT SIX YEARS. WITH AN EVEN MIX OF SUPERHERO AND INDIE COMICS, THE STORE APPEALED TO ALL COMICS FANS, AND HELPED SUPPORT LOCAL AND NATIONAL CARTOONISTS WITH READINGS AND EVENTS. OWNERS TOM AND AMY ADAMS OPENED THE STORE IN 2009, FILLING A MUCH NEEDED COMICS VOID IN THE NEIGHBORHOOD. ONCE I DID A READING THERE AND WAS GIVEN A KNITTED DOLL OF MYSELF, WHICH SOUNDS CREEPY BUT I WAS INTO IT. WITH THE CLOSURE OF BERGEN STREET COMICS, DESERT ISLAND BECAME BROOKLYN'S MAIN INDIE COMICS STORE.

MUSIC VENUES OF THE 1970'S THEN & NOW

CBGB & OMFUG WAS ONE OF NEW YORK CITY'S MOST NOTORIOUS MUSIC VENUES. STUDIO 54 WAS ITS CLOSEST CONTENDER, BUT THAT PLACE JUST SOUNDED LIKE A FUCKING NIGHTMARE. THE CLUB'S NAME IS AN ACRONYM FOR "COUNTRY, BLUEGRASS, BLUES, AND OTHER MUSIC FOR UPLIFTING GOURMANDIZERS." HILLY KRISTAL, OWNER OF CBGB, SAID A GOURMANDIZER WAS "A VORACIOUS EATER OF... MUSIC." KRISTAL RAN THE DIVE BAR "HILLY'S ON THE BOWERY" BEFORE CLOSING AND REOPENING AS CBGB IN 1973.

FOUR DECADES OF CBGB & OMFUG AT 315 BOWERY IN MANHATTAN

1940'S

FB
PALACE HOTEL
COFFEE
317
TEA
EXOTIC TEAS
ONE PALACE RESTAURANT Bar & Grill
ONE PALACE RESTAURANT Bar & Grill
STORE FIXTURES
STORE 311 FIXTURES
PEN

1970'S

WHILE A WIDE VARIETY OF FAMOUS BANDS AND MUSICIANS GOT THEIR START AT THE CLUB, IT WAS MOST FAMOUS FOR BEING KNOWN AS THE BIRTHPLACE OF PUNK. CBGB'S LAST SHOW, IN 2006, WAS HEADLINED BY PATTI SMITH, A FREQUENT PERFORMER DURING THE CLUB'S EARLY DAYS. IT BEARS NOTING THAT IN 2013, THE MOVIE *CBGB* WAS RELEASED, AND IT WAS GARBAGE. IT WAS FREQUENTLY FACTUALLY INACCURATE, IRRITATING, AND RIDDLED WITH TIME-SENSITIVE ERRORS, LIKE PUTTING STICKERS OF BANDS THAT DIDN'T YET EXIST ON THE CLUB'S WALLS. IF YOU REALLY WANT TO KNOW THE HISTORY OF PUNK, DO WHAT EVERYONE DOES AND READ *PLEASE KILL ME: THE UNCENSORED ORAL HISTORY OF PUNK*, BY LEGS McNEIL AND GILLIAN McCAIN. AND READ A COUPLE OF SHITTY 80'S-90'S PUNK ZINES BECAUSE THEY'RE THE BEST.

1980'S

2000'S

UPTOWN FROM CBGB WAS MAX'S KANSAS CITY, WHICH FAMOUSLY CATERED TO THE GLAM ROCK SCENE. THE CLUB WAS OPENED IN 1965 BY MICKEY RUSKIN, A CORNELL LAW SCHOOL GRADUATE AND RESTAURANTEUR. THE SCENE WAS DECIDEDLY MORE ARTY DURING MAX'S EARLY YEARS, BEFORE GLAM AND PUNK TOOK OVER IN THE 70'S.

213 PARK AVE. SOUTH IN THE 1970'S

RUSKIN CLOSED THE FIRST INCARNATION OF MAX'S KANSAS CITY IN 1974, AS THE GLAM ROCK SCENE DIED OUT. A YEAR LATER, TOMMY DEAN MILLS REOPENED THE CLUB WITH THE INTENTION OF TURNING IT INTO A DISCO. BUT HE HIRED PETER CROWLEY, KNOWN FOR BOOKING THE SAME BANDS THAT PLAYED AT CBGB AND OTHER MUSIC CLUBS AROUND NYC. UNDER CROWLEY'S INFLUENCE, MAX'S BECAME ONE OF THE CITY'S MOST POPULAR PUNK VENUES. IT CLOSED IN 1981.

213 PARK AVE. SOUTH IN 2016

IN 1976, IRISH IMMIGRANT PAT KENNY MOVED HIS UPTOWN SUPPER CLUB KENNY'S CASTAWAYS INTO A SPACE AT 157 BLEECKER STREET. PREVIOUSLY, THE VENUE HAD BEEN HOME TO THE SLIDE, A NOTORIOUS GAY BAR AND BROTHEL IN THE LATE 1800'S THAT THE NEW YORK PRESS CALLED, "THE WICKEDEST PLACE IN THE CITY." KENNY'S IS OFTEN OVERSHADOWED BY THE CITY'S MORE ICONIC PUNK VENUES, BUT THROUGHOUT THE 70'S, ITS ROSTER RIVALED CBGB'S AND MAX'S. THE CLUB CLOSED IN 2012 AND BECAME CARROLL PLACE, A TITLE WHICH PAYS HOMAGE TO THE BLOCK'S ORIGINAL 1830'S NAME.

157 BLEECKER ST. IN THE 1970'S

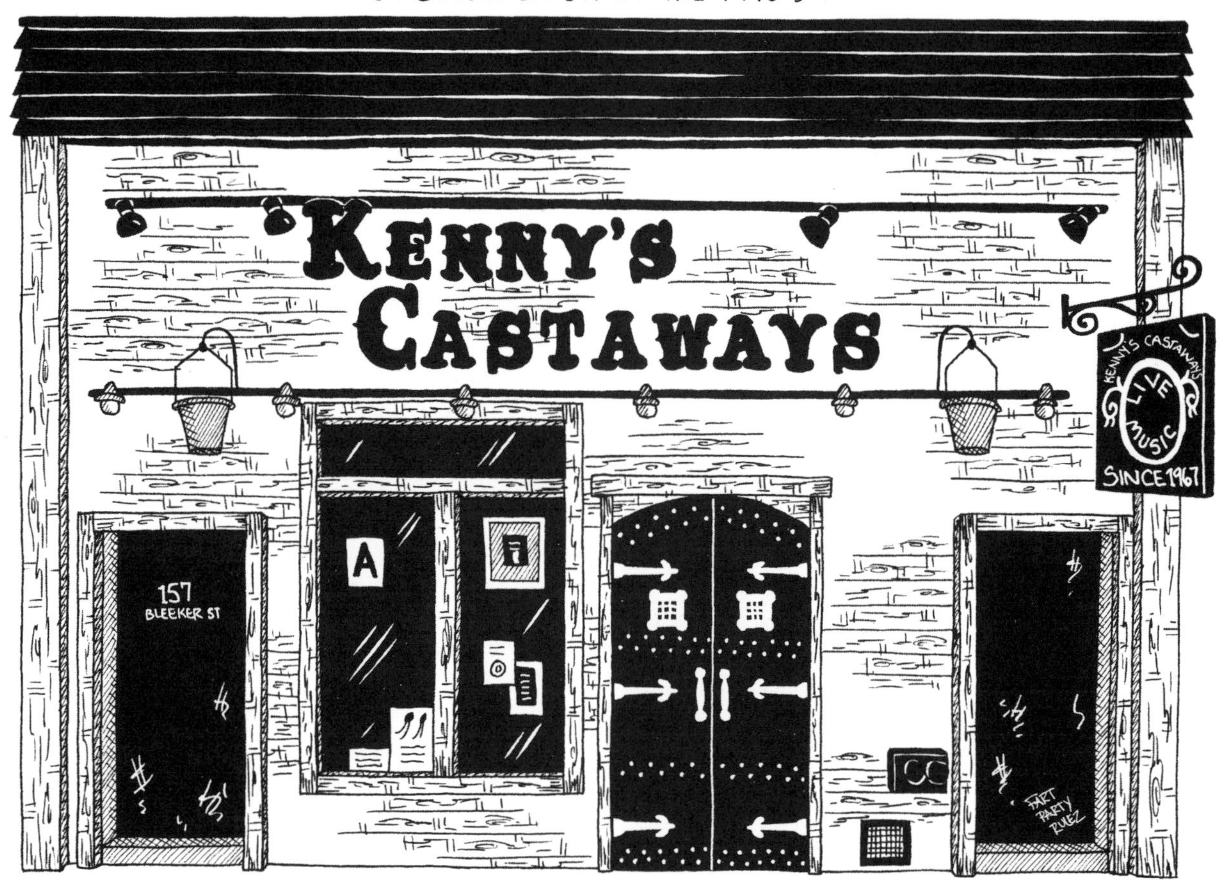

157 BLEECKER ST. IN 2016

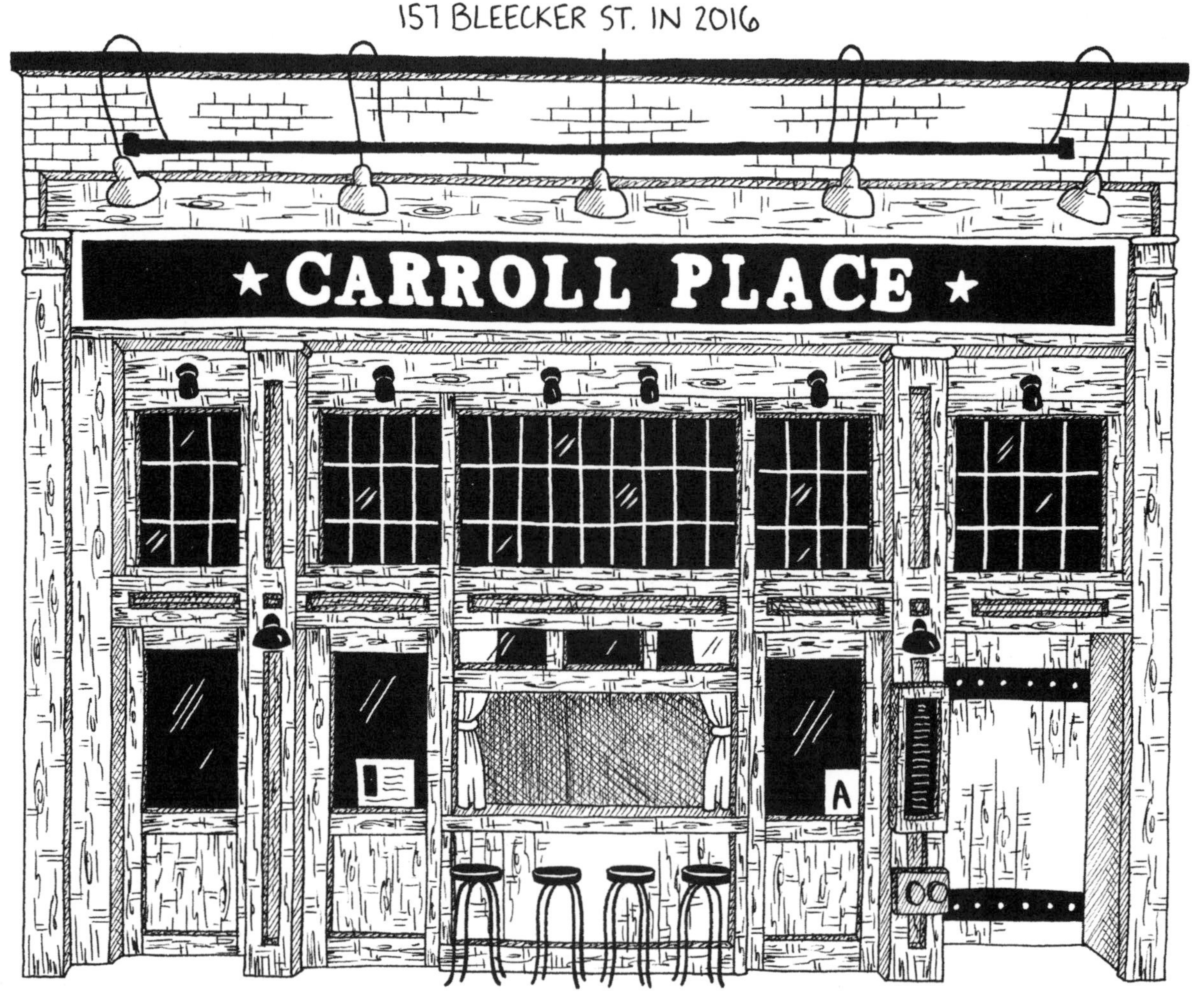

THE LOST HISTORY OF KIM'S VIDEO

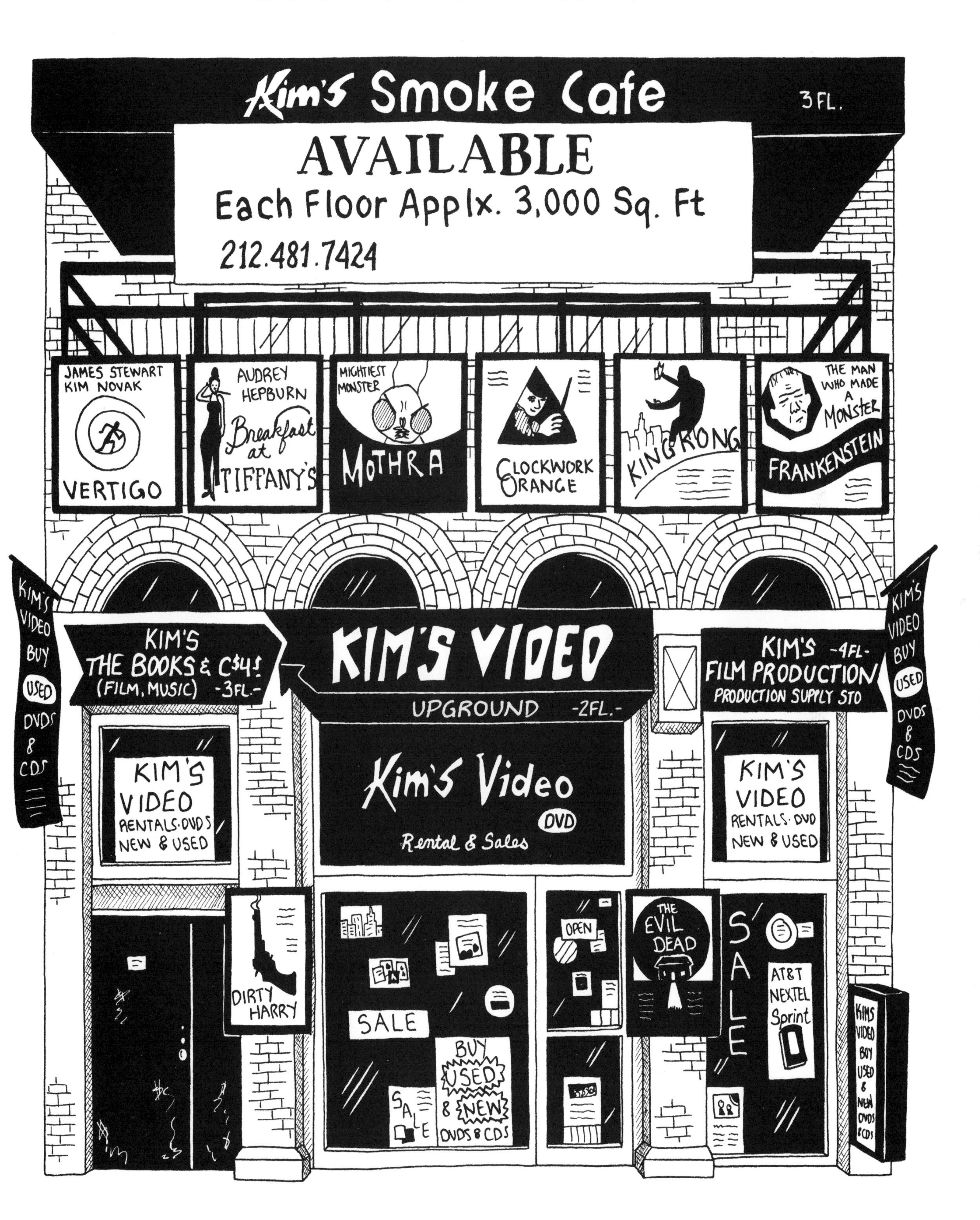

IN THE 1990'S, IF YOU WANTED AN OBSCURE MOVIE, A FOREIGN FILM, A B HORROR FLICK, OR A BOOTLEG RECORDING, KIM'S VIDEO WAS WHERE YOU WENT. (OR SO I'M TOLD. I WOULDN'T KNOW SINCE I WAS BUSY BEING A SHITTY, ANGSTY TEENAGER IN CALIFORNIA IN THE 90'S.) KIM'S WAS FAMOUS FOR HAVING A MASSIVE STOCK OF ECLECTIC VIDEOS SPREAD THROUGHOUT MULTIPLE STORES, MOSTLY CENTERED IN THE EAST VILLAGE. MANY FILMMAKERS CITE KIM'S FASTIDIOUS COLLECTION AS AN EARLY INFLUENCE ON THEIR WORK.

SOME CONSIDERED KIM'S A MECCA FOR FILM NERDS AND WEIRDOS, RUN BY A DAUNTINGLY COOL, VASTLY KNOWLEDGEABLE STAFF, WHILE OTHERS DISMISSED IT AS A JUNKY VIDEO SHOP POPULATED BY RUDE, CONDESCENDING ASSHOLES. I HAVE A FEELING THE REPUTATION OF KIM'S CLERKS PERSISTED DUE TO THE OLD IDIOM "YOU GET WHAT YOU EXPECT," BECAUSE I PERSONALLY KNOW A FEW EX-EMPLOYEES WHO ARE LOVELY, UNPRETENTIOUS PEOPLE. MANY OF KIM'S STAFF WENT ON TO BECOME SUCCESSFUL MUSICIANS, ARTISTS, ACTORS, AND FILMMAKERS.

THE MOST COMMONLY RECOUNTED HISTORY OF KIM'S VIDEO IS THIS: MR. KIM STARTED HIS RENTAL SHOP IN A CORNER OF HIS LAUNDROMAT ACROSS FROM TOMPKINS SQUARE PARK IN 1987. HIS SMALL BUT INTERESTING VIDEO COLLECTION GAINED A CULT FOLLOWING IN THE NEIGHBORHOOD, ALLOWING MR. KIM TO OPEN MULTIPLE VIDEO RENTAL STORES THROUGHOUT NYC. FOR ALMOST THREE DECADES, KIM'S VIDEO WAS FAMOUS FOR UNIQUE, DIVERSE, AND INCOMPARABLE INVENTORY. HOWEVER, LIKE THE MAJORITY OF VIDEO RENTAL SHOPS, KIM'S COULDN'T SURVIVE THE ADVENT OF THE INTERNET AND ONLINE STREAMING. THE LAST KIM'S VIDEO CLOSED IN 2014.

124 1ST AVE. EAST VILLAGE, MANHATTAN

HOWEVER, THAT STORY IS NOT QUITE TRUE. IT UNFORGIVABLY OMITS A MAN NAMED MATT MARELLO, WITHOUT WHOM KIM'S VIDEO MIGHT NOT EXIST. IN 1987, MARELLO WAS A YOUNG MUSICIAN FROM PHILADELPHIA WHO'D JUST MOVED TO NYC. HIS BAND, EXECUTIVE SLACKS, HAD BEEN OFFERED A RECORD DEAL THAT MARELLO TURNED DOWN IN ORDER TO PURSUE PAINTING. WITHOUT WORK EXPERIENCE, MARELLO'S FIRST JOB AT 7A CAFE WAS, IN HIS WORDS, "AN UNMITIGATED DISASTER," SO HIS BOSS SUGGESTED HE TRY THE LAUNDROMAT VIDEO STORE DOWN THE STREET. AT THAT TIME, MR. KIM'S OUTPOST HAD ABOUT 100 VIDEOS OF MOSTLY MAINSTREAM FARE. MARELLO, A FILM AND INDEPENDENT CINEMA BUFF, WAS GIVEN FULL CONTROL OF THE COLLECTION, WHICH HE STOCKED WITH OBSCURE AND FOREIGN FILMS. MARELLO ARRANGED THE VIDEOS BY COUNTRY OF ORIGIN AND DIRECTOR, AN UNUSUAL ORGANIZATION METHOD FOR WHICH KIM'S BECAME FAMOUS.

THE EAST VILLAGE IN THE 80'S WAS FULL OF ARTISTS, MUSICIANS, FILMMAKERS, AND NYU STUDENTS WHO BEGAN TO CONGREGATE AT KIM'S TINY VIDEO OUTPOST, WHERE MARELLO ORGANIZED A SECTION FEATURING LOCAL TALENT. USING HIS EXTENSIVE FILM KNOWLEDGE, AND THOSE OF KIM'S PATRONS, MARELLO WAS ABLE TO CREATE A FILM COLLECTION THAT WAS UNRIVALED IN ITS UNIQUENESS. HIS COLLECTION WAS SO POPULAR THAT MR. KIM OPENED A STORE FOR HIM TO RUN DOWN THE STREET. TWO YEARS LATER, MR. KIM OPENED MONDO KIM, HIS BIGGEST AND MOST FAMOUS LOCATION ON 2ND AVENUE AND ST. MARK'S PLACE. MR. KIM PUT MARELLO IN CHARGE OF CREATING MONDO KIM'S COLLECTION AS WELL.

MARELLO WORKED FOR MR. KIM FOR 13 YEARS BEFORE RESIGNING SO HE COULD FOCUS ON HIS FAMILY AND ARTISTIC EFFORTS. HE RECEIVED TWO NEW YORK FOUNDATION FOR THE ARTS GRANTS, AND WAS AWARDED THE GUGGENHEIM FOUNDATION FELLOWSHIP. HIS MOST RECENT SHOW WAS AT THE PIEROGI GALLERY IN THE LOWER EAST SIDE. ALTHOUGH MARELLO WAS THE LYNCHPIN OF KIM'S FAMOUS COLLECTION, HE HAS BEEN MOSTLY ERASED FROM THE STORE'S PUBLIC HISTORY, WHICH IS AN EGREGIOUS OMISSION, SINCE, AS EX-EMPLOYEE CHRISTOPHER PRAVDICA TOLD BEDFORD & BOWERY, "IT WAS ALL BECAUSE OF MATT MARELLO THAT THE WHOLE THING HAPPENED."

IT WAS PRAVDICA'S QUOTE THAT MADE ME RECONSIDER THE CONSPICUOUS HISTORY OF KIM'S VIDEO. I TRACKED MARELLO DOWN AND I PRESENTED HIM WITH MY THEORY OF HIS UNRECOGNIZED AND PIVOTAL ROLE IN KIM'S SUCCESS. MARELLO'S SIDE OF THE STORY CONFIRMED MY HYPOTHESIS, YET I WAS SURPRISED TO NOTE A LACK OF BITTERNESS OVER BEING CONSISTENTLY EXPUNGED FROM KIM'S ORIGIN STORY. NOR DID HE MENTION EMPLOYEE COMPENSATION, WHICH, ACCORDING TO MULTIPLE SOURCES, WAS ABYSMAL. WORKERS WERE REPORTEDLY PAID MINIMUM WAGE, SOMETIMES LESS, BUT MARELLO WAS QUICK TO NOTE THAT MR. KIM HAD BEEN VERY GENEROUS TO HIM OVER THE YEARS.

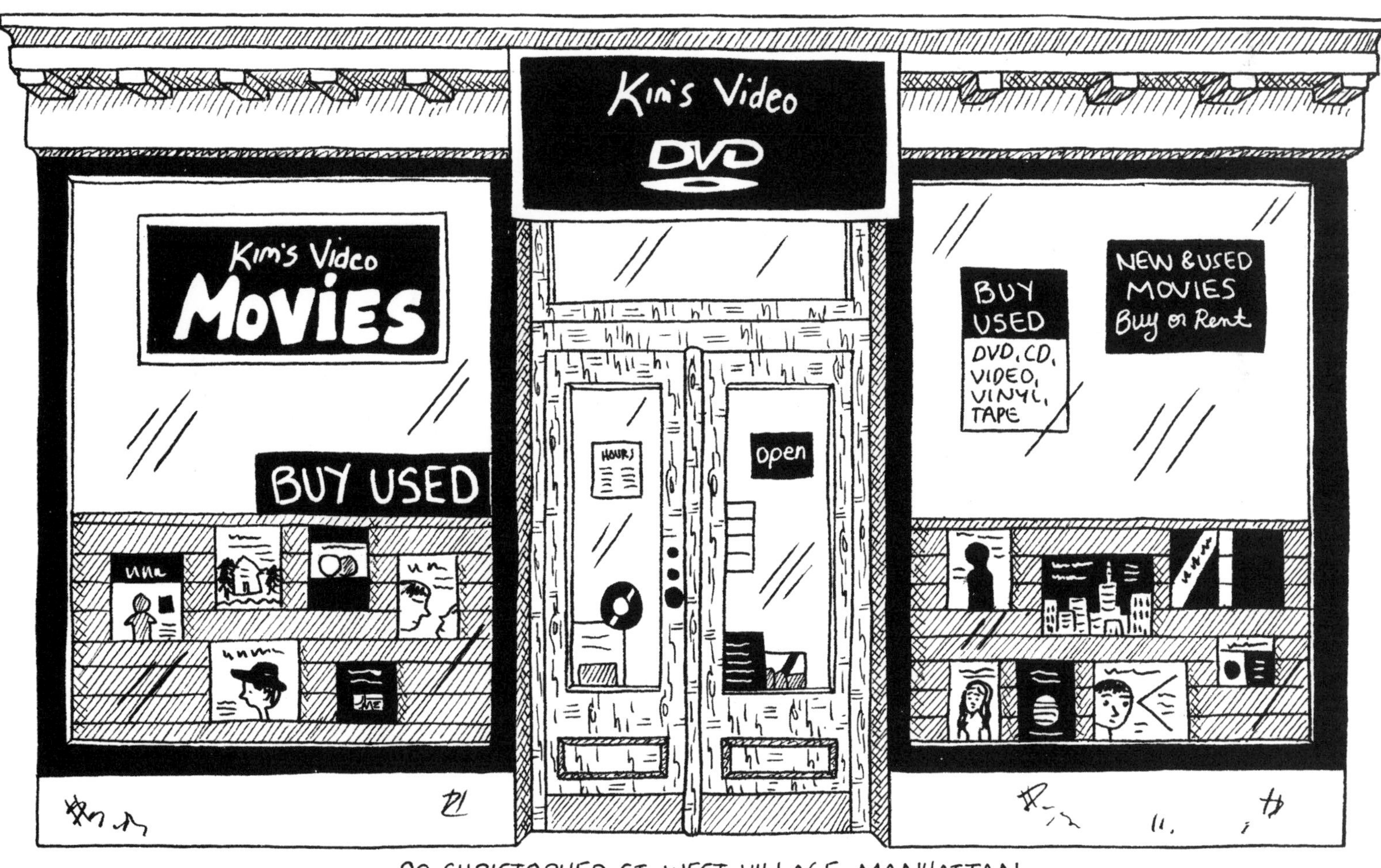

89 CHRISTOPHER ST. WEST VILLAGE, MANHATTAN

ACCOUNTS OF MR. KIM'S PERSONALITY VARY, PAINTING HIM AS A FASCINATING, SOMETIMES POLARIZING CHARACTER. SOME EX-EMPLOYEES ACCUSED HIM OF BEING A TYRANT WHO DIDN'T TAKE CARE OF HIS EMPLOYEES, BUT OTHERS SPOKE MORE FONDLY OF HIM, NOTING HIS LOVE OF FILM AND DESIRE TO BE A DIRECTOR. HE EVEN MADE A MOVIE BASED ON VARIOUS SCRIPT IDEAS TRANSCRIBED BY EMPLOYEE (LATER TURNED DIRECTOR) NICK ZEDD. THE SCRIPT, "A PERVERTED PSYCHODRAMA INVOLVING A BUDDHIST PRIEST AND SOME ASIAN SCHOOLGIRLS," MADE LITTLE SENSE. WHEN ZEDD ASKED FOR THE $500 HE WAS PROMISED UP FRONT—AFTER SIGNING A CONTRACT FOR $5,000 TOTAL—HE WAS FIRED. MR. KIM'S FILM SCREENED ONLY ONCE IN A THEATER ON AVENUE A.

THE OTHER HALF OF KIM'S UNKNOWN HISTORY IS WHAT BECAME OF MR. KIM AND MARELLO'S FAMOUS FILM COLLECTION AFTER THE STORES CLOSED. DESPITE ITS POPULARITY, KIM'S VIDEO SAW THE SAME DECLINE IN SALES THAT ALL VIDEO AND MUSIC STORES SAW IN THE LATE 90'S/EARLY 00'S WHEN PEOPLE STOPPED BUYING RECORDS AND RENTING VIDEOS. TECHNOLOGY MADE AN IRREPARABLE DENT IN SALES, AND VIDEO AND MUSIC STORES WORLDWIDE CLOSED DOWN. IN 2005, THE FBI RAIDED KIM'S AND CONFISCATED THEIR BOOTLEG STOCK. KIM'S CULT FOLLOWING WASN'T ENOUGH TO KEEP THE BUSINESS OPEN, AND THE STORES BEGAN CLOSING.

IN 2009, MR. KIM MADE A PUBLIC PLEA/OFFER FOR HIS VIDEO COLLECTION. HE PROMISED TO DONATE IT FOR FREE TO ANYONE WHO COULD MEET HIS THREE REQUIREMENTS: "KEEP THE COLLECTION INTACT, CONTINUE TO UPDATE IT, AND MAKE IT ACCESSIBLE TO KIM'S MEMBERS AND OTHERS." OFFERS ROLLED IN, BUT MR. KIM WAS NOT HAPPY WITH ANY OF THEM. THE ONLY OFFER HE FINALLY APPROVED WAS NOT ONE ANYONE EXPECTED. MR. KIM AGREED TO HAVE HIS COLLECTION OF NEARLY 55,000 DVDS AND VHS TAPES SENT TO THE TOWN OF SALEMI, ITALY, WHICH FOUGHT TO GET THE COLLECTION TO REVITALIZE THEIR TOWN'S ECONOMY. SALEMI'S PROPOSAL PROMISED TO KEEP THE VIDEOS PUBLICLY ACCESSIBLE, TO HOLD A 24-HOUR FILM FESTIVAL, AND TO NAME A COMMUNITY VIDEO CENTER AFTER MR. KIM.

NEW YORKERS WERE NOT HAPPY WITH MR. KIM'S DECISION TO ALLOW THE COLLECTION TO LEAVE NYC. THEY WERE UPSET THAT HE TURNED DOWN LOCAL INSTITUTIONS SUCH AS NYU AND COLUMBIA, WHOSE BIDS FOR THE COLLECTION STATED THEY COULD NOT TAKE ALL THE VIDEOS, ONLY SOME, DUE TO LACK OF SPACE. THAT STIPULATION DEFIED MR. KIM'S INSISTENCE THAT THE COLLECTION BE DONATED IN WHOLE. DESPITE PROTESTATION, THE COLLECTION WAS SHIPPED OVERSEAS TO ITALY, WHERE A SERIES OF TRUCKS TRANSPORTED IT TO SMALLER CARS WHICH TRANSPORTED IT TO PEOPLE WHO CARRIED THE BOXES OF VIDEOS BY HAND UP NARROW, WINDING ROADS TO THE CITY OF SALEMI. ONCE THERE, THE COLLECTION BASICALLY DISAPPEARED.

IN 2012, KARINA LONGWORTH, A WRITER FOR *THE VILLAGE VOICE*, WENT TO ITALY IN SEARCH OF THE FAMOUS COLLECTION, ONLY TO HAVE HER EFFORTS THWARTED. SALEMI OFFICIALS CLAIMED THE VIDEOS WERE BEING SAFELY STORED AND MAINTAINED UNTIL THEY CAN MAKE GOOD ON THE PROPOSAL, BUT OTHERS CLAIMED THEY HAD BEEN LEFT TO ROT IN BOXES BEING INFILTRATED BY MICE AND INSECTS. THE CONDITION OF THE COLLECTION IS UNKNOWN, BUT MANY SPECULATE THAT TIME, IMPROPER STORAGE, AND ANIMAL FECES HAVE DESTROYED SOME OF IT. LONGWORTH ALSO DISCOVERED THERE WAS NO ANNUAL FILM FESTIVAL AS PROMISED, AND THE PROPOSED COMMUNITY CENTER NAMED AFTER MR. KIM DID NOT EXIST.

AS OF 2016, THERE ARE NO UPDATES REGARDING THE COLLECTION. IT SEEMS THE FATE OF THE FILMS MIRRORED MR. KIM'S OWN WISHES FOR HIMSELF, WHICH HE MADE CLEAR TO THE NEW YORK *DAILY NEWS* UPON THE CLOSING OF HIS LAST STORE WHEN HE SAID, "I NOW DO NOT WANT TO FIGHT AGAINST THE NEW STREAM. I JUST WANT TO DISAPPEAR CALMLY." AND THAT HE DID.

THE ONLY PICTURE THAT EXISTS OF MATT MARELLO AT KIM'S VIDEO, 1991

PHOTO COURTESY OF MATT MARELLO. PHOTOGRAPHER UNKNOWN.

CIGAR STORES ON BROADWAY THEN & NOW

1691-1697 BROADWAY IN 1916
MIDTOWN, MANHATTAN

1691-1697 BROADWAY IN 2015

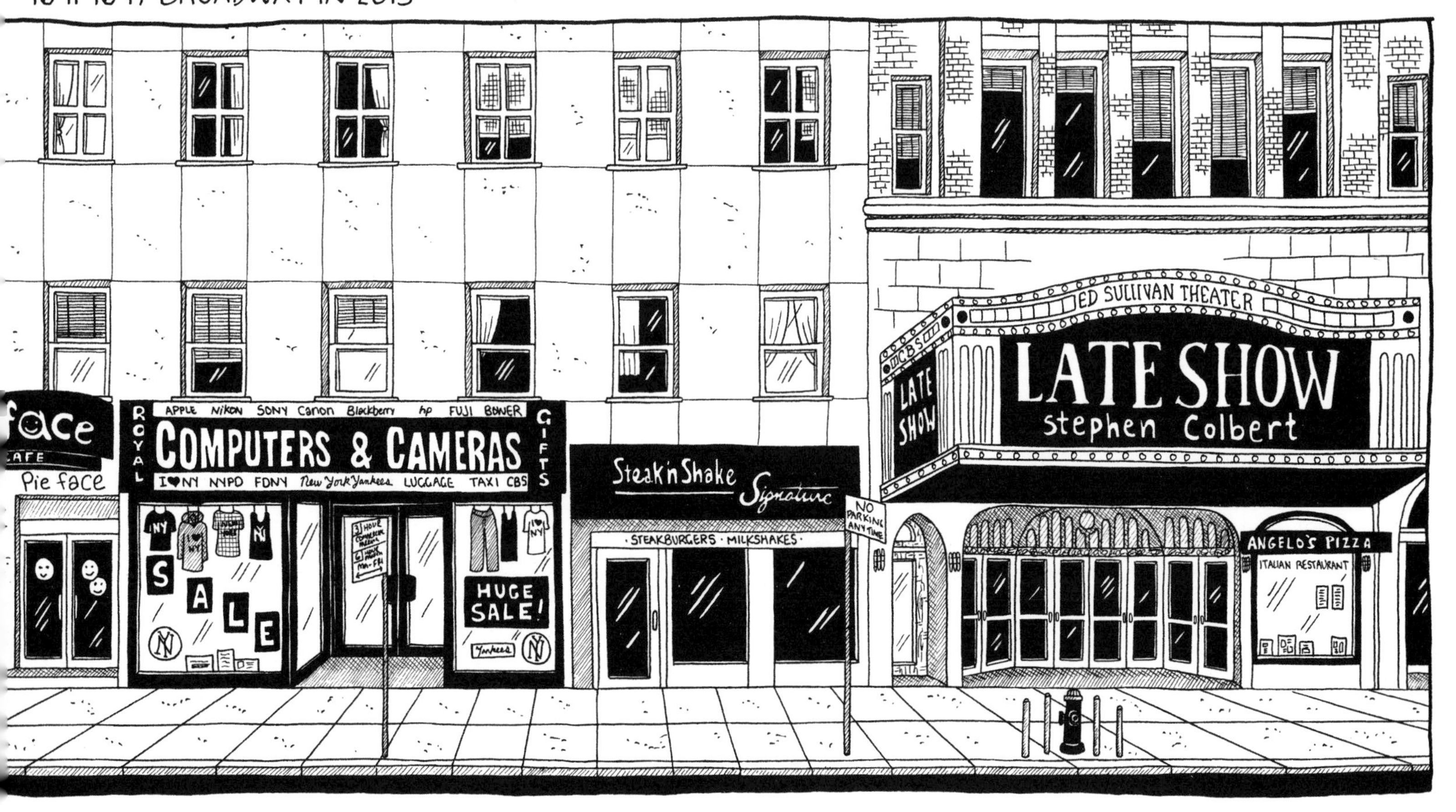

W.67TH ST. AND BROADWAY IN 1936
UPPER WEST SIDE, MANHATTAN

W.67TH ST. AND BROADWAY IN 2016

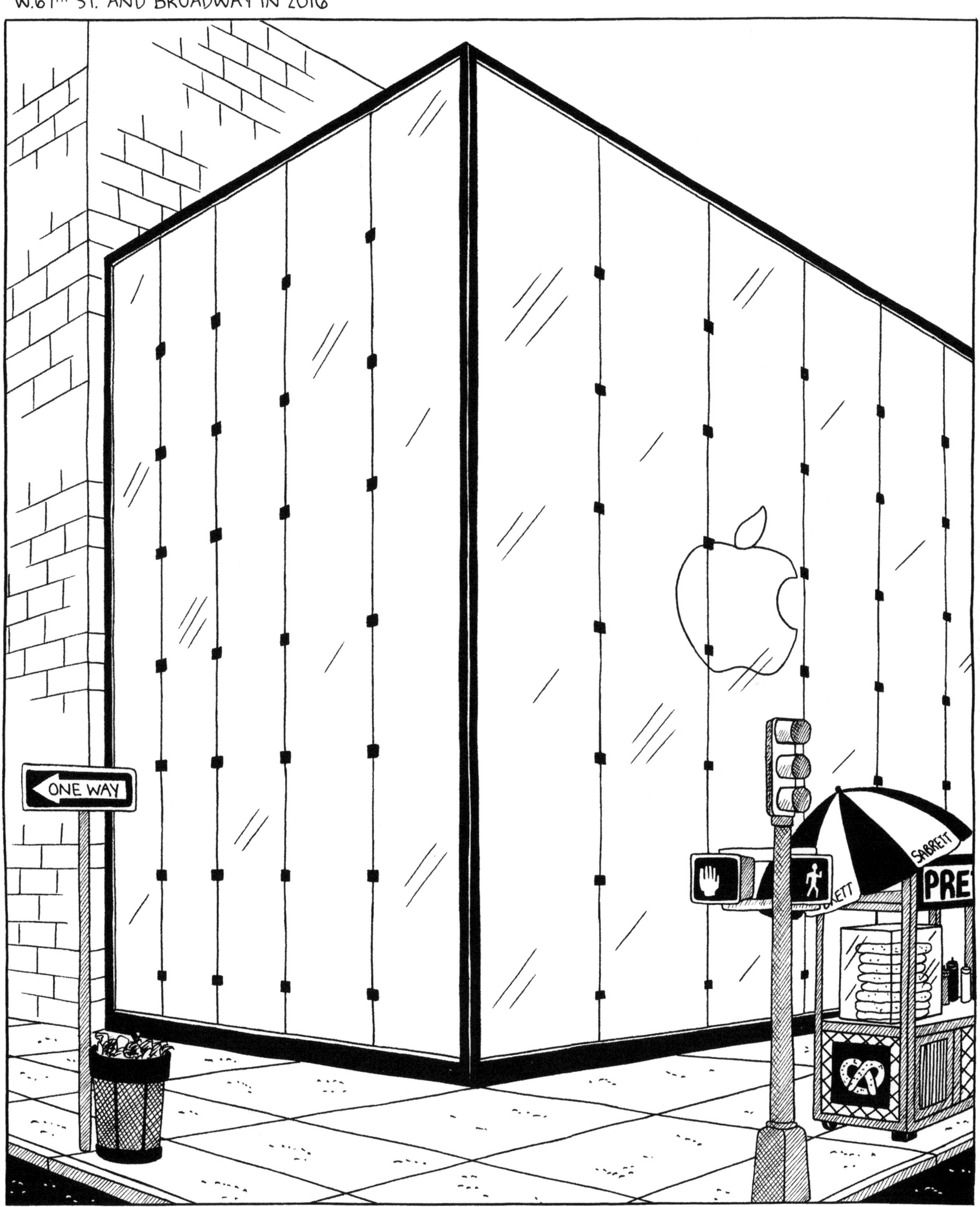

88 W.BROADWAY IN 1914

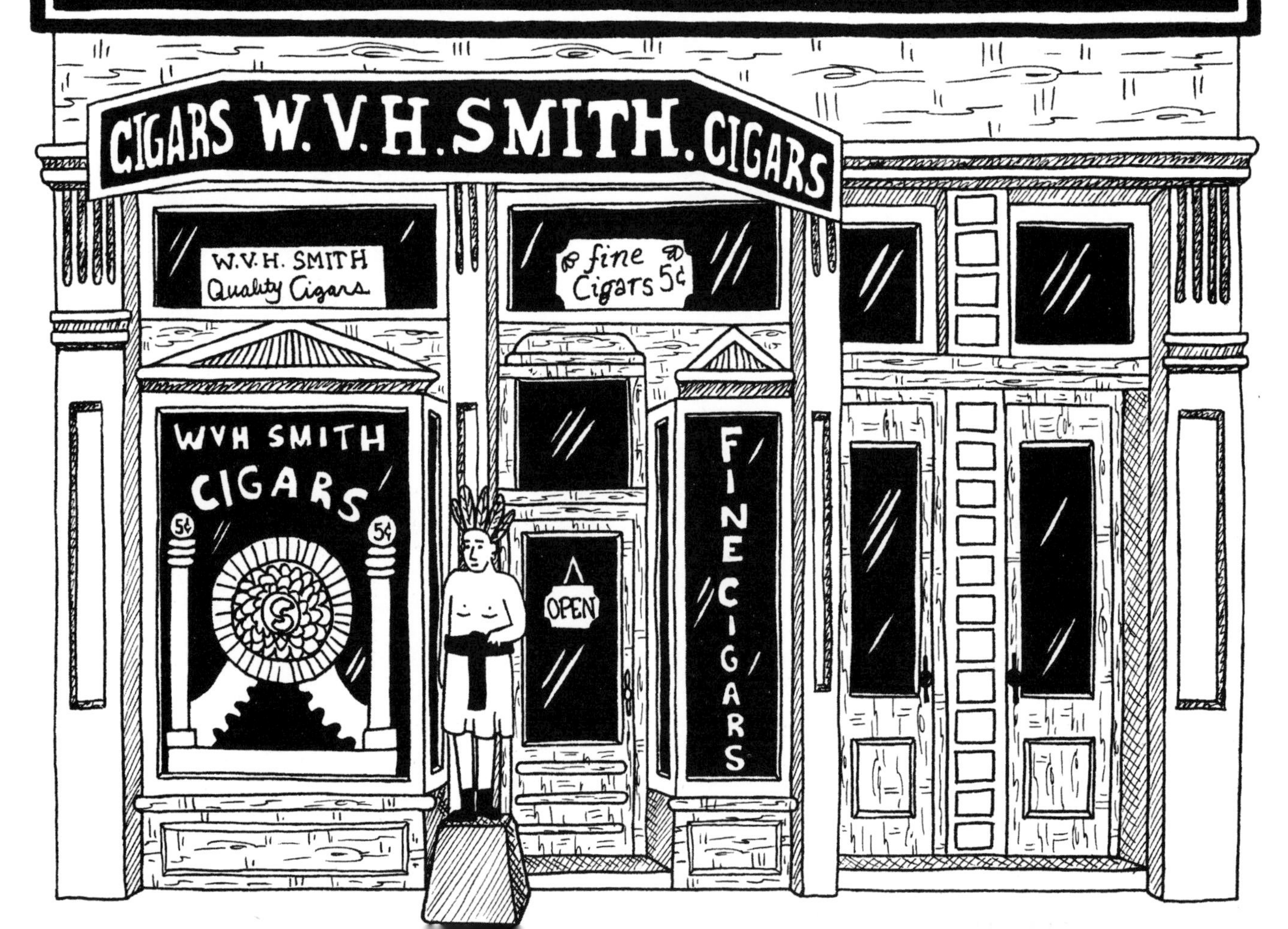

88 W.BROADWAY IN 2015. TRIBECA, MANHATTAN

VINTAGE TRASH & HORSE BONES: THE ORIGINS OF BOTTLE BEACH

RUBBER BOOTS, PLASTIC GLOVES, DIGGING TOOLS, AND TOTE BAGS ARE NOT TYPICAL BEACH SUPPLIES...
ALRIGHT, I'M READY, LET'S HIT THE ROAD!

...UNLESS YOU'RE GOING TO BOTTLE BEACH IN DEAD HORSE BAY IN BROOKLYN, NEW YORK.

AT THE TURN OF THE LAST CENTURY, BARREN ISLAND (A SMALL PATCH OF LAND OFF SOUTH BROOKLYN, NORTHEAST OF CONEY ISLAND) WAS HOME TO DOZENS OF RENDERING FACTORIES THAT USED ANIMAL CARCASSES TO MAKE VARIOUS INDUSTRIAL AND HOUSEHOLD PRODUCTS.
HORSE GLUE
COW DIRT
PIG SOAP
Lamb Candles

THE SIZE AND ABUNDANCE OF HORSES MADE THEM THE MOST COMMONLY, UH, "RECYCLED" ANIMALS.
GOOD OLD SEBASTIAN, HE SERVED US WELL. HE HELPED US BUILD OUR HOME AND BUSINESS, AND CARRIED US DAILY TO AND FRO, RAIN OR SHINE.
ALAS, HE'S OLD AS BALLS, AND IS OF NO USE TO US ANYMORE.
WHAT WILL WE DO WITH HIM, PAPA?

WELL, SON, WE'LL DO WHAT EVERYONE DOES WITH THEIR BELOVED BEASTS OF BURDEN WHO HAVE GOTTEN OLD OR MILDLY INJURED...
SHOOT 'EM IN THE HEAD AND TURN 'EM INTO GLUE.

UPON THEIR DEMISE, THE CITY'S HORSES AND OTHER DEAD ANIMALS WERE CARTED OUT TO BARREN ISLAND, WHERE THEIR CARCASSES WERE CLEANED, DISMEMBERED, PROCESSED AND TURNED INTO GOODS.
I KNOW WE ALL MISS SEBASTIAN, BUT HE IS HERE IN SPIRIT...
...AND IN THIS CANDLE MADE FROM HIS FATTY TISSUE.
HE'S IN THE SOUP TOO!

WHEN THE FACTORIES WERE DONE MINING THE CARCASSES, THEY CHOPPED THEM UP AND TOSSED THEM INTO THE WATER, WHICH IS HOW DEAD HORSE BAY GOT ITS NAME.
hi-ho hi-ho into the bay you go!

RENDERING FACILITIES WERE NOT THE ONLY FACTORIES IN THE AREA. THE BAY SHORES WERE ALSO HOME TO FISH OIL PLANTS, WASTE DISPOSAL, AND A RAPIDLY GROWING LANDFILL.
OH WOOF, IT SMELLS LIKE SOMEONE MURDERED A FART OUT THERE! THE DECAYING FISH IN THE BAY ARE BARELY MASKING THE SMELL OF THE ROTTING ANIMAL CARCASSES ON THE SHORE. WHAT'S FOR DINNER? UGH, SEBASTIAN STEW AGAIN, I SEE. WE NEED TO START RAISING PIGS, GET SOME BACON UP IN THIS MOTHER!

BY THE 1920'S, BARREN ISLAND WAS A WASTELAND. THE AUTOMOBILE HAD REPLACED HORSES AS MEANS OF TRANSPORTATION, RENDERING THE FACTORIES OBSOLETE. IN THEIR PLACE GREW A MASSIVE AND RAPIDLY EXPANDING LANDFILL. SOME OF THAT TRASH, ALONG WITH COAL AND SAND, WAS USED TO CONNECT BARREN ISLAND TO BROOKLYN, CREATING WHAT WAS LATER KNOWN AS FLOYD BENNETT FIELD. IN THE 1930'S, THE LANDFILL AT DEAD HORSE BAY WAS CAPPED AND FILLED IN WITH MARSHLANDS AND BAY WATER. BUT IN THE 1950'S, THE CAP BURST, FILLING THE BAY WITH GARBAGE AND HORSE BONES.

SINCE THEN, THE TRASH HAS BEEN CONTINUALLY WASHING UP, FILLING THE SHORELINE WITH MOSTLY BOTTLES AND THE OCCASIONAL SHOE, TOYS, APPLIANCES, AND OTHER BROKEN REMNANTS OF A BYGONE ERA.

ON QUIET DAYS AT BOTTLE BEACH, IF YOU STAND CLOSE TO THE WATER, YOU CAN HEAR THE MELODIC TINKLING OF BROKEN GLASS AS THE WATER LAPS THE SHORE.
IT'S JUST SO BEAUTIFUL!
THIS DISGUSTING HEAP OF GARBAGE IS MAKING ME HAVE ALL THE FEELINGS!

THE MAIN STRETCH OF BOTTLE BEACH, ACCESSIBLE FROM A PATH OFF FLATBUSH AVE. THE PATH DIVERGES INTO THREE PATHS, SO TO SEE ALL OF THE BEACH, TAKE THE SIDE ONES.

TRASH AND BOTTLES SPILLING OUT FROM THE LANDFILL THAT HELPED FORM FLOYD BENNETT FIELD.

BOTTLES ON THE BOTTLE TREE, WHICH LOST MOST OF ITS ORNAMENTS DURING HURRICANE SANDY.

URINE SPECIMEN BOTTLE CIRCA 1920'S.

HORRIFYING CHILDREN'S TOY.

BOTTLE TREE.

VINTAGE LEATHER SHOE.

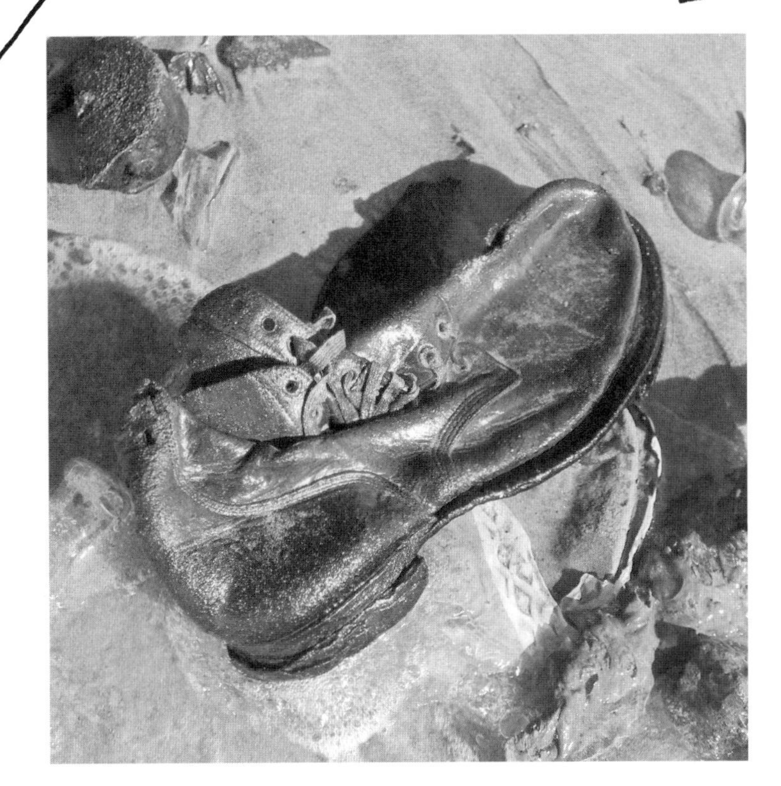

HORSE BONES AND A CAST IRON CIRCUS TOY.

RARE FIND: A PERFECTLY INTACT ROUND BOTTOM BOTTLE THAT WASHED UP ON SHORE AFTER A BIG STORM.

ABANDONED BOAT ON THE JAMAICA BAY SHORELINE.

HARLEM NIGHTCLUBS THEN & NOW

288 LENOX AVE. IN THE 1940'S

LENOX LOUNGE

288

RESTAURANT

288 LENOX AVE. IN 2016

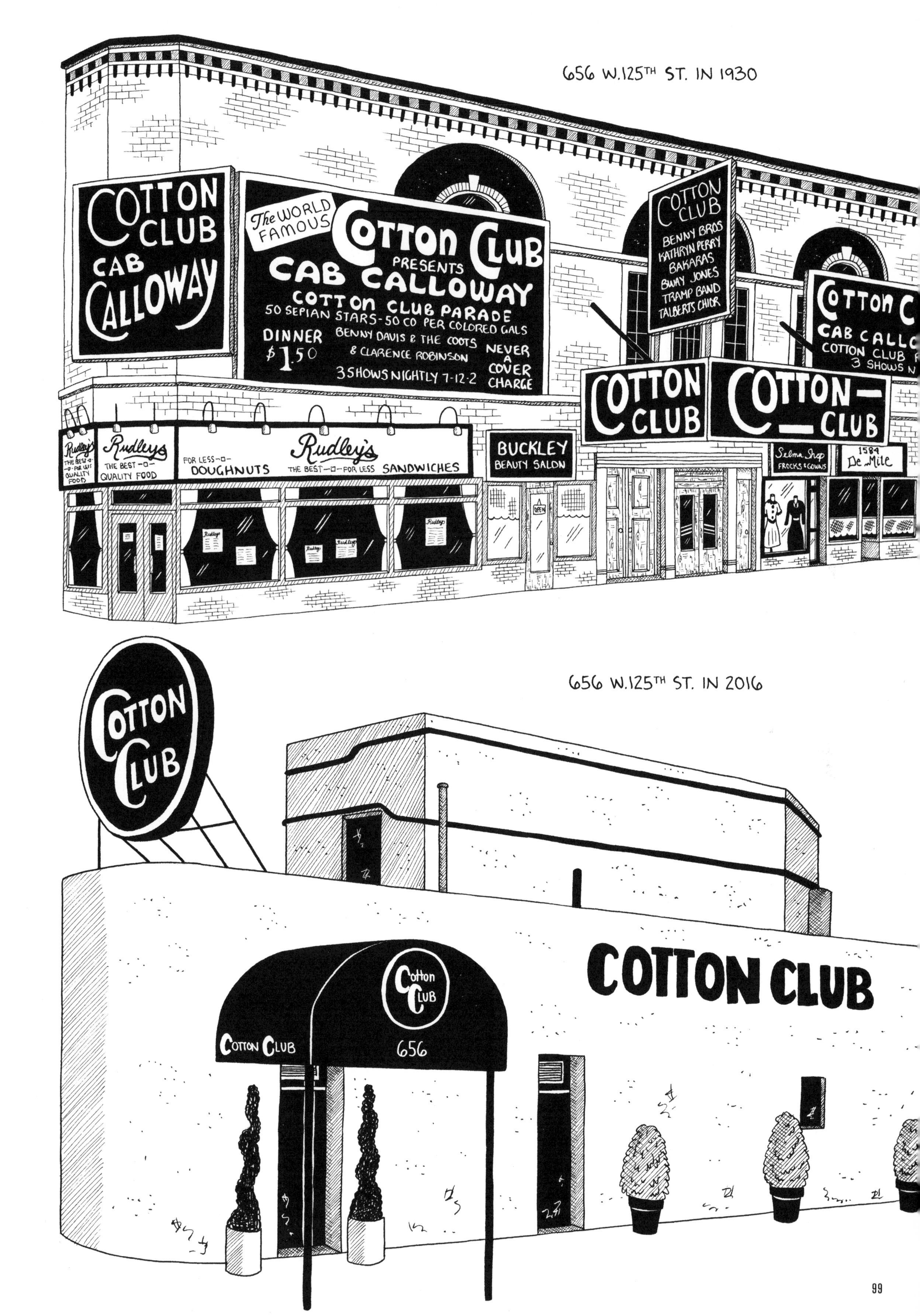
656 W.125TH ST. IN 1930
COTTON CLUB
CAB CALLOWAY
The WORLD FAMOUS
COTTON CLUB
PRESENTS
CAB CALLOWAY
COTTON CLUB PARADE
50 SEPIAN STARS-50 CO PER COLORED GALS
DINNER $1.50
BENNY DAVIS & THE COOTS
& CLARENCE ROBINSON
NEVER A COVER CHARGE
3 SHOWS NIGHTLY 7-12-2
COTTON CLUB
BENNY BROS
KATHRYN PERRY
BAKARAS
BWAY JONES
TRAMP BAND
TALBERTS CHIOR
COTTON CLUB
COTTON CLUB
Rudley's
THE BEST -□- QUALITY FOOD
FOR LESS -□- DOUGHNUTS
Rudley's
THE BEST -□- FOR LESS
SANDWICHES
BUCKLEY
BEAUTY SALON
OPEN
Selma Shop
FROCKS & GOWNS
1584
De Mile
656 W.125TH ST. IN 2016
COTTON CLUB
COTTON CLUB
Cotton Club
COTTON CLUB
656

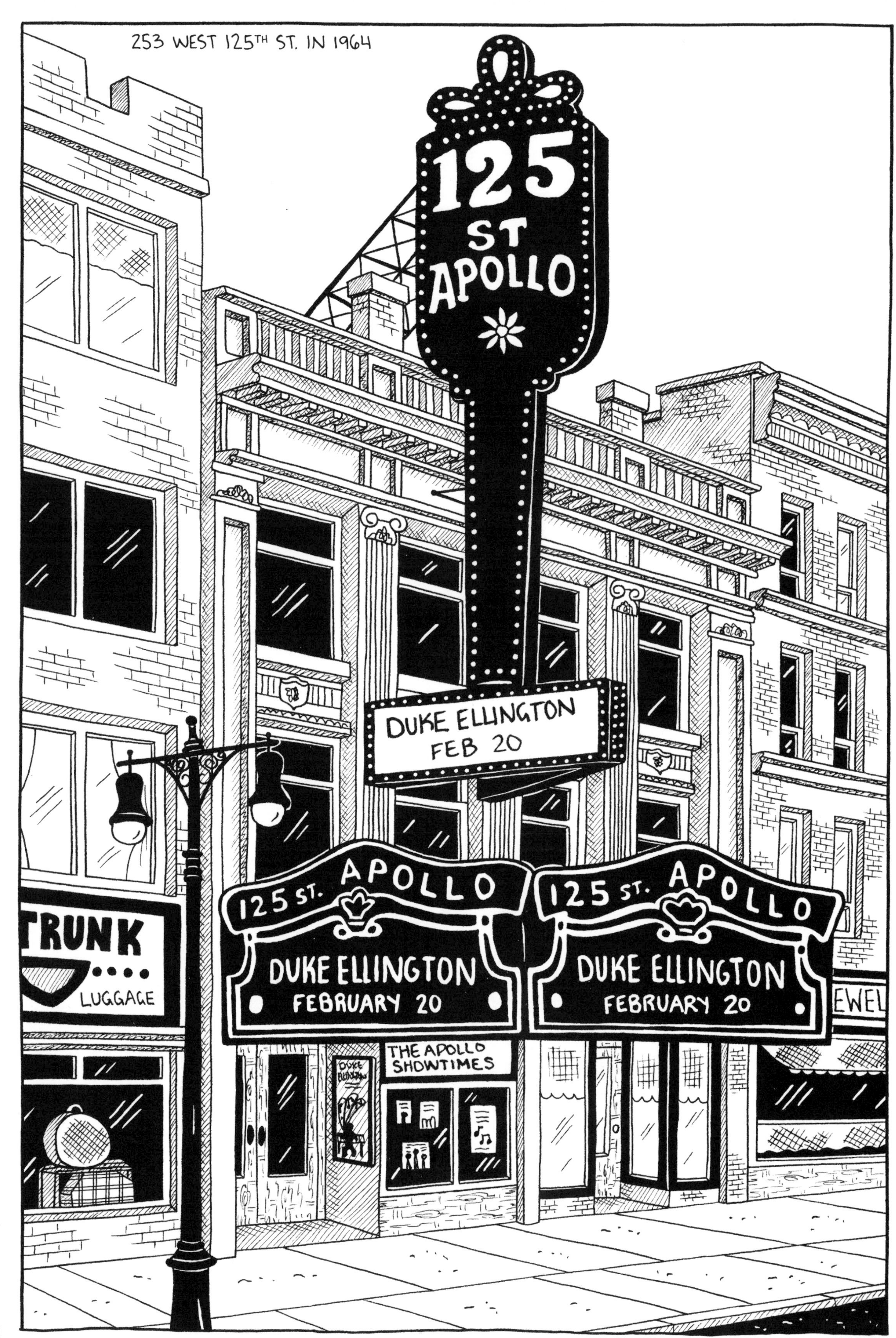
253 WEST 125TH ST. IN 1964
125 ST APOLLO
DUKE ELLINGTON FEB 20
125 ST. APOLLO
DUKE ELLINGTON FEBRUARY 20
125 ST. APOLLO
DUKE ELLINGTON FEBRUARY 20
TRUNK
LUGGAGE
THE APOLLO SHOWTIMES
EWEL

253 WEST 125TH ST. IN 2014
APOLLO
APOLLO
THE BOWERY PRESENTS
TV ON THE RADIO
TUES NOV 18 8PM
THE BOWERY PRESENTS
TV ON THE RADIO
TUES NOV 18 8PM
APOLLO MUSIC CAFE
CLEARANCE
2 FOR 1 VIDEO GAMES
GAME SALE
PIZZA ISLAND FER LIFE

NELLIE BLY: THE INTREPID JOURNALIST

BORN ELIZABETH COCHRAN IN 1864 IN PENNSYLVANIA, NELLIE BLY (HER PEN NAME) WAS A GROUNDBREAKING JOURNALIST, TRAVELER, INVENTOR, CHARITY WORKER, AND INDUSTRIALIST. BLY GOT HER START IN JOURNALISM AS A TEENAGER, WHEN SHE PENNED A RESPONSE TO A MISOGYNISTIC COLUMN TITLED "WHAT ARE GIRLS GOOD FOR?" IN HER HOMETOWN PAPER. BLY'S LETTER, WRITTEN UNDER THE PSEUDONYM LONELY ORPHAN GIRL AND TITLED "THE GIRL PUZZLE," IMPRESSED THE PAPER'S EDITOR SO MUCH THAT HE EVENTUALLY HIRED HER TO WRITE FULL TIME FOR THE *PITTSBURGH DISPATCH*.

DURING HER TIME AS A JOURNALIST FOR THE PAPER, BLY WROTE INVESTIGATIVE PIECES ABOUT WOMEN WHO WORKED IN FACTORIES AND HELD TRADITIONALLY MALE JOBS. HOWEVER, DUE TO HER GENDER, SHE WAS PRESSURED TO COVER MORE TYPICAL "WOMEN'S ISSUES" LIKE FASHION AND SOCIETY. BLY, THEN AGE 21, WAS LIKE 'FUCK THIS NOISE,' AND LEFT PITTSBURGH TO WORK AS A FOREIGN CORRESPONDENT IN MEXICO, WHERE SHE WROTE ABOUT CULTURE AND POLITICS. AFTER SIX MONTHS, BLY LEFT MEXICO UPON THREAT OF INCARCERATION OVER HER DISPARAGING PIECES ON THE MEXICAN DICTATOR PORFIRIO DIAZ.

WHEN BLY RETURNED TO PITTSBURGH, SHE WAS AGAIN ASSIGNED FASHION AND SOCIETY ARTICLES. DISMAYED, SHE QUIT AND WENT TO NEW YORK CITY. AFTER MONTHS OF STRUGGLING TO FIND WORK, SHE WAS HIRED AT THE *NEW YORK WORLD*, JOSEPH PULITZER'S FAMOUS NEWSPAPER, WHERE SHE WROTE HER MOST ENDURING AND INFLUENTIAL ARTICLES AT AGE 23.

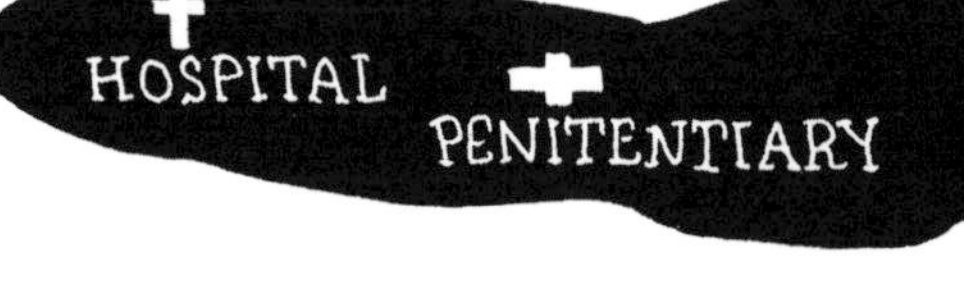

1840'S MAP OF BLACKWELL'S ISLAND, NOW ROOSEVELT ISLAND

BLACKWELL'S ISLAND

THE SERIES OF ARTICLES, TITLED "BEHIND ASYLUM BARS," WERE ABOUT HER TIME UNDERCOVER AT BLACKWELL'S ISLAND IN THE WOMEN'S LUNATIC ASYLUM. AFTER MUCH PRACTICE, BLY CONVINCINGLY FAKED INSANITY AND WAS COMMITTED TO THE ASYLUM BY A DOCTOR. BLY STAYED AS A PATIENT FOR TEN DAYS, WITNESSING AND TAKING NOTES ON, SQUALID CONDITIONS AND EGREGIOUS MISTREATMENT OF THE HELPLESS (AND OFTEN MISUNDERSTOOD AND/OR MISDIAGNOSED) PATIENTS.

BEHIND ASYLUM BARS.

The Mystery of the Unknown Insane Girl

Remarkable Story of the Successf

Impersonation of Insanity.

How Nellie Brown Deceived Judge

porters and Medical Expert

I succeeded in getting committed to the insane ward at Blackwell's Island, where I spent 10 days and nights and had an experience which I shall never forget. I took it upon myself to enact the part of a poor, unfortunate crazy girl, and felt it was my duty not to shirk any of the disagreeable results that should follow.

BLY'S NEWSPAPER ARTICLES IN THE NEW YORK WORLD IN 1887. IN THE ASYLUM, BLY WENT BY THE NAME NELLIE BROWN.

WHEN BLY'S ARTICLES WERE PUBLISHED, A GRAND JURY APPROVED AN INVESTIGATION INTO THE ASYLUM, WHICH ULTIMATELY LED TO BETTER TREATMENT OF PATIENTS, CLEANER FACILITIES, AND MORE FUNDING FROM THE DEPARTMENT OF PUBLIC CHARITIES AND CORRECTIONS. BLY'S WRITING WAS LATER COLLECTED AND PUBLISHED IN A BOOK TITLED *TEN DAYS IN A MAD-HOUSE.*

AFTER THE SUCCESS OF HER ARTICLES, BLY IMMEDIATELY BEGAN ANOTHER JOURNALISM VENTURE, INSPIRED BY JULES VERNE'S NOVEL *AROUND THE WORLD IN 80 DAYS.* BLY COMPLETED HER WORLD TRIP IN A RECORD-BREAKING 72 DAYS. HER AUDACIOUS JOURNEY EVEN LED TO THE CREATION OF A BOARD GAME. (THAT GAME HAS SINCE BEEN TURNED INTO A JIGSAW PUZZLE, WHICH I BOUGHT MYSELF AS A REWARD FOR FINISHING THIS BOOK, BECAUSE I PARTY HARD.)

The World.

NEW YORK, SUNDAY, JANUARY 26TH, 1890

NELLIE BLY'S BOOK

AROUND THE WORLD IN 72 DAYS

The famous reporter's own account of her astonishing record-breaking world-wide adventure.

ROUND THE WORLD
With
NELLIE BLY.
A NOVEL AND FASCINATING GAME WITH PLENTY OF EXCITEMENT ON LAND AND SEA.

AT AGE 31, BLY MARRIED A 73-YEAR-OLD MILLIONAIRE WHO OWNED THE IRON CLAD MANUFACTURING COMPANY. BLY RETIRED FROM JOURNALISM TO ASSIST HER HUSBAND AND BECOME AN INVENTOR, RECEIVING MULTIPLE PATENTS FOR HER INVENTIONS. WHEN BLY'S HUSBAND DIED, SHE BECAME PRESIDENT OF THE COMPANY, A GROUND-BREAKING POSITION FOR A WOMAN DURING THAT TIME.

THE IRON CLAD FACTORIES

ARE THE LARGEST

Of their kind and are owned exclusively

by

* NELLIE BLY *

The only woman in the world personally managing Industries of such a magnitude

PAN-AMERICAN EXPOSITION, 1901

NELLIE BLY

UNFORTUNATELY, THE BUSINESS WENT BANKRUPT SHORTLY AFTER BLY ASSUMED HER POSITION. SHE RETURNED TO JOURNALISM TO COVER WWII AND THE WOMAN'S SUFFRAGE MOVEMENT. BLY DIED OF PNEUMONIA AT AGE 57 AND WAS BURIED IN WOODLAWN CEMETERY IN THE BRONX.

DEDICATED JUNE 22, 1978
TO
NELLIE BLY
ELIZABETH COCHRANE SEAMAN
BY THE NEW YORK PRESS CLUB
IN HONOR OF
A FAMOUS NEWS REPORTER
MAY 5, 1864 - JAN 27, 1922

HOLDOUT BUILDINGS OF NEW YORK CITY

A "HOLDOUT" IS A REAL ESTATE TERM FOR BUILDINGS WHOSE OWNERS REFUSE TO VACATE OR BE BOUGHT OUT WHEN A DEVELOPER WANTS TO DEMOLISH THEIR PROPERTY FOR THE EXPANSION OF A NEIGHBORING PROJECT. MANY HOLDOUT BUIDLINGS AROUND THE WORLD HAVE BECOME FAMOUS, ESPECIALLY IN CHINA WHERE THEY'RE CALLED "NAIL HOUSES." (GOOGLE IT, THEY'RE AMAZING.)

FOR MANY DECADES, MACY'S IN HERALD SQUARE HAD ONE OF THE MOST NOTORIOUS HOLDOUT BUILDINGS IN NYC, ON WHAT WAS CALLED "MILLION DOLLAR CORNER" ON BROADWAY AND 34TH ST. THE NAME CAME FROM THE EVENTUAL LEASE BUYOUT FOR ONE MILLION DOLLARS, AN ASTONISHING AMOUNT AT THE TIME. THE BUILDING STILL EXISTS TODAY, BUT IT'S COVERED BY A GIANT MACY'S BAG BILLBOARD.

CURRENTLY, THERE ARE A NUMBER OF HOLDOUT BUILDINGS IN NYC, AS PROPERTY OWNERS EITHER WAIT FOR A HIGHER BUYOUT, OR SIMPLY WANT TO RESIST CHANGE. WHEN THAT HAPPENS, DEVELOPERS ARE OFTEN FORCED TO BUILD AROUND THE HOLDOUT STRUCTURE, WHICH CREATES AN INTERESTING AESTHETIC. THE FOLLOWING ARE SOME OF MY FAVORITE HOLDOUT BUILDINGS CURRENTLY* IN THE CITY.

**I LEFT THE CITY IN 2016, SO IT BEARS NOTING SOME OF THESE BUILDINGS MAY NO LONGER EXIST.*

3RD AVE. BETWEEN E.21ST ST.
AND E.22ND ST. IN 2015
GRAMERCY, MANHATTAN

SEPHORA
THE ANNEX
WRITING CLASSES
metro
THE VOICE
am
NEW YORK
134 E. 60TH ST.
MIDTOWN, MANHATTAN

1 2 3 4 5 6 7 8 9 10 11 12
00 01 02 03 04 05 06 07 08 09 10 11
12 13 14 15 16 17 18 19 20 21 22 23
24 25 26 27 28 29 30 31 32 33 34 35
36 37 38 39 40 41 42 43 44 45 46 47
48 49 50 51 52 53 54 55 56 51 58 59
STARBUCKS COFFEE
GAY CITY
metro
VOICE
VOICE
127 JOHN ST.
FINANCIAL DISTRICT, MANHATTAN

COFFEE
BAKERY
PANINI
SALAD
SOUP
PASTA
3
COMMERCIAL
VEHICLES ONLY
MON-FRI
6am-7pm
NO
HOTEL
pure fresh
A
58 W.36TH ST.
MIDTOWN, MANHATTAN

THE HISTORY OF NEW YORK CITY'S PNEUMATIC TUBES

IN THE LATE 1800'S, AS THE CITY'S POPULATION BOOMED, DELIVERING THE MAIL BECAME AN IMMENSE CHORE. THE MAIN POST OFFICES OF MANHATTAN WERE OVERLOADED, AND TRANSPORTING MAIL FROM ONE POST OFFICE TO THE OTHER WAS TRICKY IN AN ERA OF HORSE-DRAWN CARTS OR NEWLY INVENTED (AND OFTEN UNRELIABLE) ELECTRIC OR GAS VEHICLES.

IN A BID TO HASTEN MAIL DELIVERY, THE NEW YORK POSTAL SYSTEM BUILT AN EXTENSIVE UNDERGROUND TUBE SYSTEM. IT WAS BASED ON SCOTTISH INVENTOR WILLIAM MURDOCH'S EARLY-19TH-CENTURY INVENTION —THE PNEUMATIC TUBE— WHICH PUSHED MATERIAL THROUGH A SERIES OF UNDERGROUND TUBES USING PRESSURIZED AIR.

NYC'S PNEUMATIC MAILING SYSTEM OPERATED FROM 1897 TO 1953. STRETCHING THE WHOLE LENGTH OF MANHATTAN, THESE TUBES SENT MAIL SHOOTING UNDERGROUND THROUGH THE CITY FROM POST OFFICE TO POST OFFICE. DURING THE HEIGHT OF ITS USE, THE PNEUMATIC TUBE MAIL SYSTEM CARRIED AROUND 95,000 LETTERS A DAY, ABOUT ONE-THIRD OF THE MAIL BEING TRANSPORTED THROUGH THE CITY.

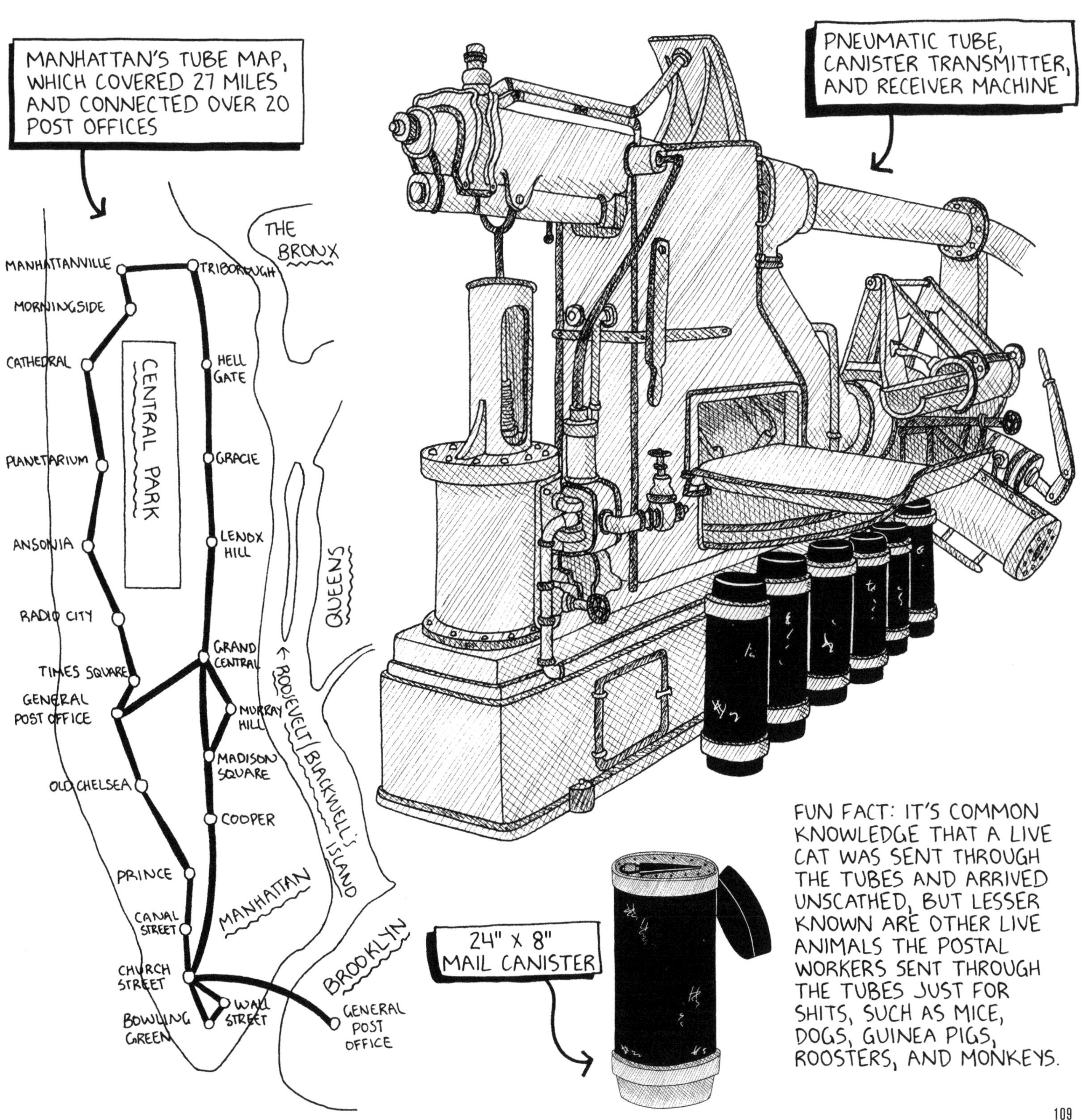

ALTHOUGH THE PNEUMATIC MAIL SYSTEM WAS THE MOST FAMOUS USE OF TUBES, IT WAS NOT THE MOST EXCITING. IN 1869, THE BEACH PNEUMATIC TRANSIT COMPANY ATTEMPTED TO CREATE A NEW METHOD OF TRANSPORTATION USING LARGER TUBES AND CYLINDRICAL CARS THAT COULD HOLD ALMOST TWO DOZEN PEOPLE.

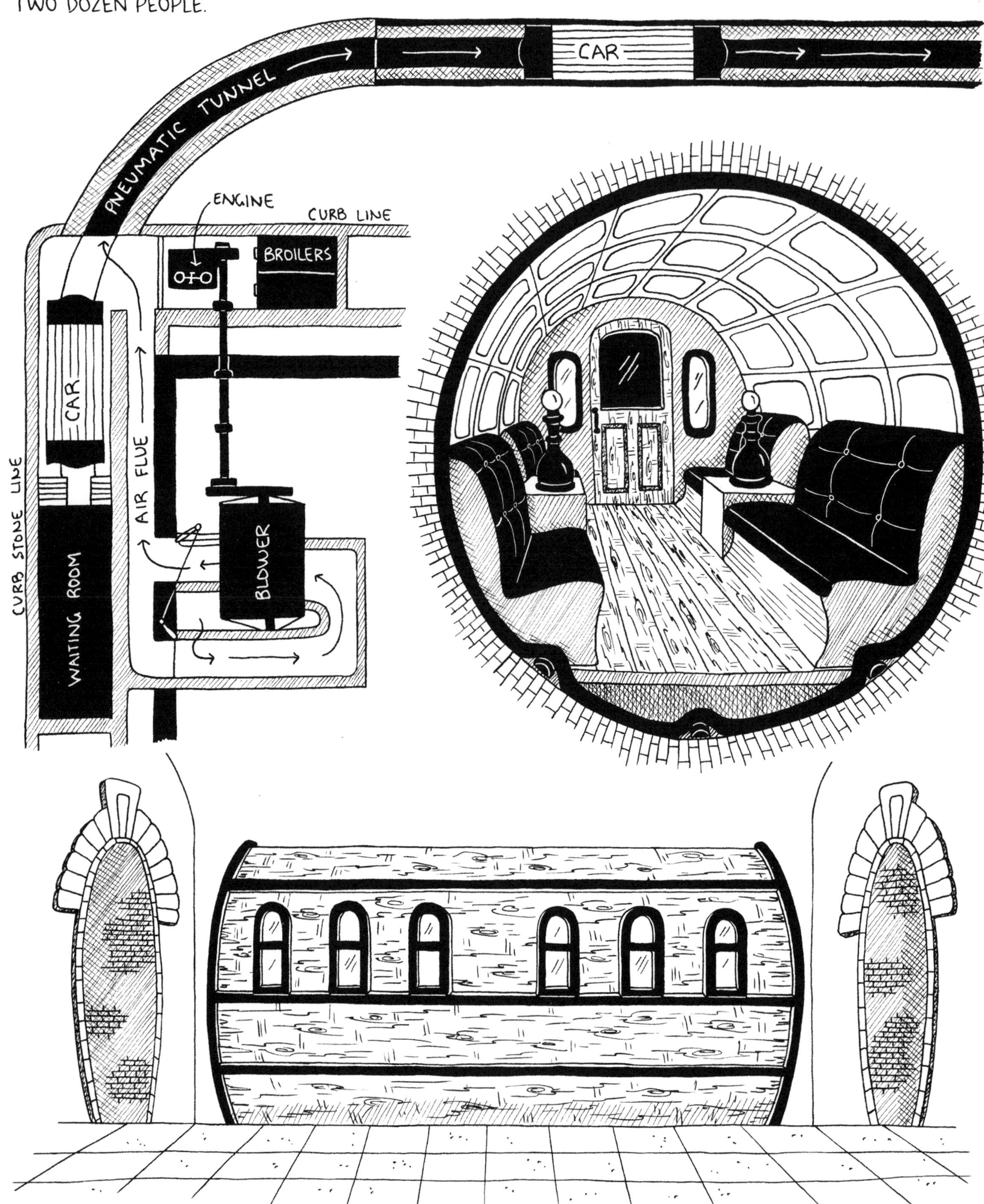

DURING ITS FIRST YEAR IN OPERATION, THE BEACH PNEUMATIC TRANSIT SOLD MORE THAN 400,000 RIDES AT 25 CENTS EACH, WITH PROCEEDS GOING TO THE UNION HOME AND SCHOOL FOR SOLDIERS' AND SAILORS' ORPHANS. THE TUBE RAN UNDER BROADWAY FROM WARREN STREET TO MURRAY STREET. UNFORTUNATELY, THE SYSTEM ULTIMATELY FAILED WHEN THE BPT COULDN'T GET PERMISSION TO EXPAND THE LINE. AFTER THREE YEARS, THE STATION AND TUBES WERE ABANDONED AND SEALED.

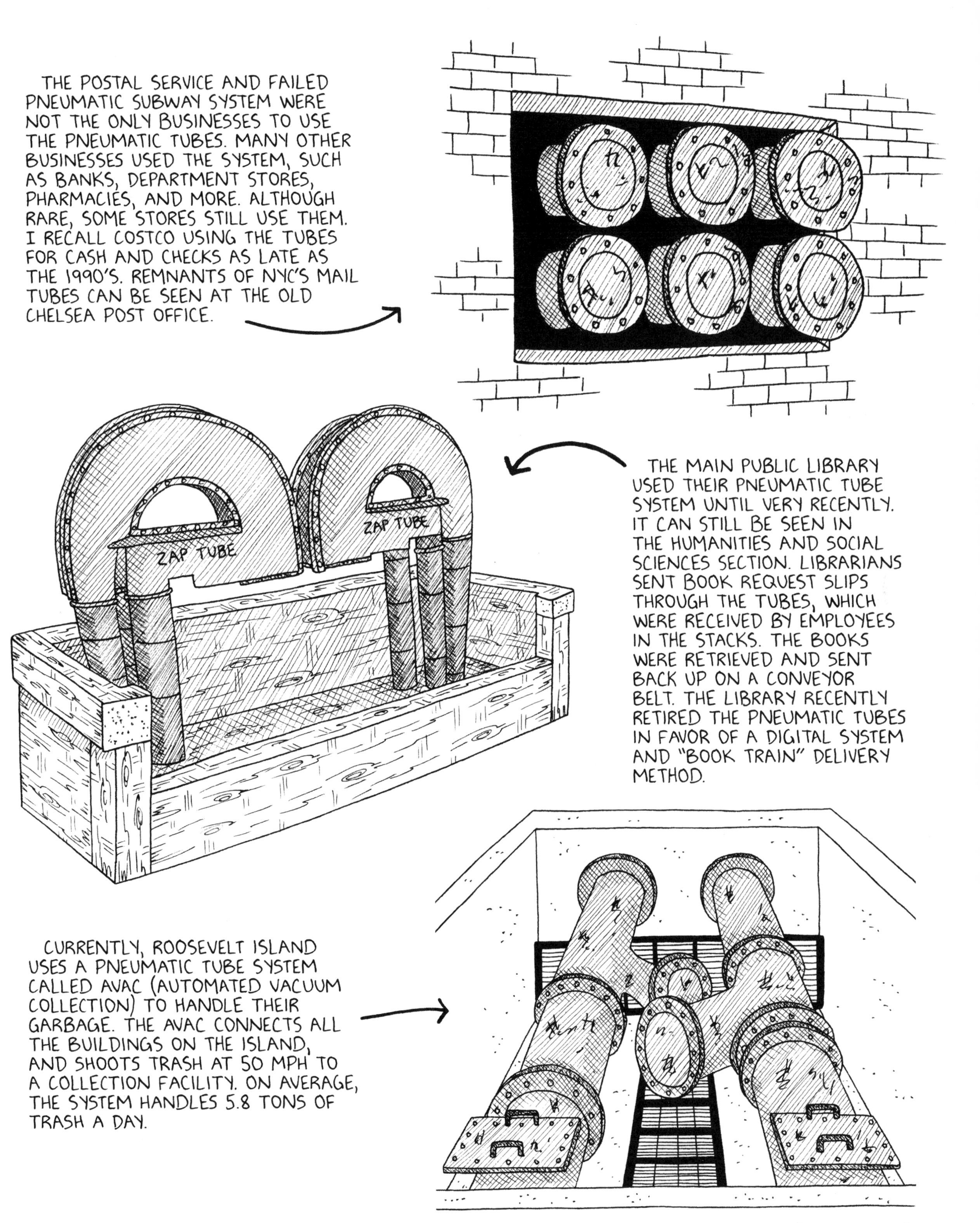

THE POSTAL SERVICE AND FAILED PNEUMATIC SUBWAY SYSTEM WERE NOT THE ONLY BUSINESSES TO USE THE PNEUMATIC TUBES. MANY OTHER BUSINESSES USED THE SYSTEM, SUCH AS BANKS, DEPARTMENT STORES, PHARMACIES, AND MORE. ALTHOUGH RARE, SOME STORES STILL USE THEM. I RECALL COSTCO USING THE TUBES FOR CASH AND CHECKS AS LATE AS THE 1990'S. REMNANTS OF NYC'S MAIL TUBES CAN BE SEEN AT THE OLD CHELSEA POST OFFICE.
ZAP TUBE
ZAP TUBE
THE MAIN PUBLIC LIBRARY USED THEIR PNEUMATIC TUBE SYSTEM UNTIL VERY RECENTLY. IT CAN STILL BE SEEN IN THE HUMANITIES AND SOCIAL SCIENCES SECTION. LIBRARIANS SENT BOOK REQUEST SLIPS THROUGH THE TUBES, WHICH WERE RECEIVED BY EMPLOYEES IN THE STACKS. THE BOOKS WERE RETRIEVED AND SENT BACK UP ON A CONVEYOR BELT. THE LIBRARY RECENTLY RETIRED THE PNEUMATIC TUBES IN FAVOR OF A DIGITAL SYSTEM AND "BOOK TRAIN" DELIVERY METHOD.
CURRENTLY, ROOSEVELT ISLAND USES A PNEUMATIC TUBE SYSTEM CALLED AVAC (AUTOMATED VACUUM COLLECTION) TO HANDLE THEIR GARBAGE. THE AVAC CONNECTS ALL THE BUILDINGS ON THE ISLAND, AND SHOOTS TRASH AT 50 MPH TO A COLLECTION FACILITY. ON AVERAGE, THE SYSTEM HANDLES 5.8 TONS OF TRASH A DAY.

ALTHOUGH PNEUMATIC TUBES ALMOST DISAPPEARED COMPLETELY, THE SYSTEM IS NOW BEING REVIVED BY ENVIRONMENTALLY CONCERNED ENTREPRENEURS WHO SEE IT AS A WAY TO TRANSPORT GARBAGE WITHOUT USING VEHICLES, TO PREVENT OVERFLOWING TRASH CANS, AND TO ABOLISH THE UBIQUITOUS PILES OF TRASH BAGS ON THE CITY'S SIDEWALKS. THE PNEUMATIC TRASH SYSTEM PROPOSAL IS BASED ON SWEDEN'S SYSTEM, WHICH IS VERY SUCCESSFUL. IF THE PROPOSAL IS ACCEPTED, PNEUMATIC TUBES WILL SOON RETURN TO NEW YORK CITY.

ART DECO DOORS OF MANHATTAN

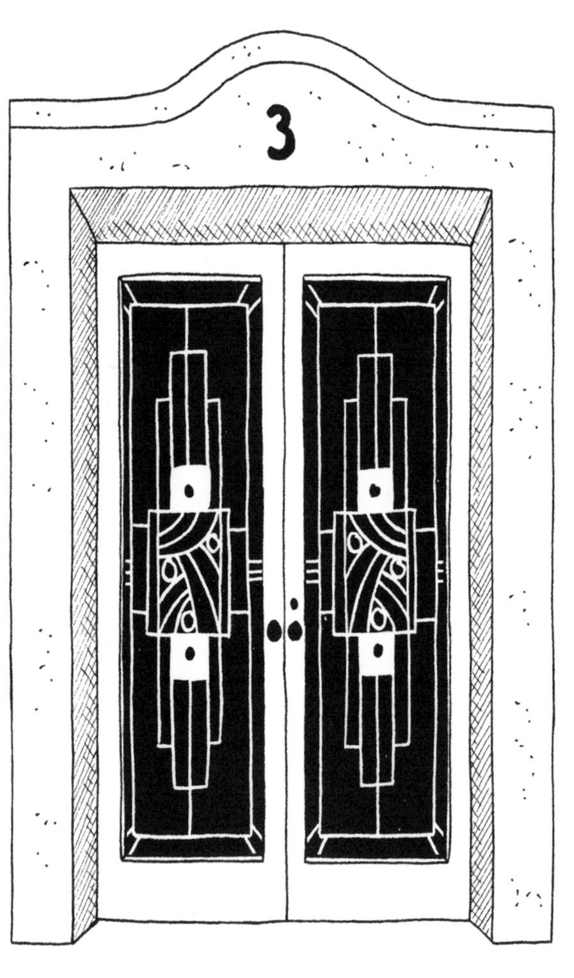

GOTHIC DOORS OF MANHATTAN

MADE IN NEW YORK

TOILET PAPER

ORIGINALLY ADVERTISED AS "MEDICATED PAPER FOR THE WATER CLOSET," TOILET PAPER WAS INVENTED IN 1857 BY JOSEPH GAYETTY. HE SOLD 1,000 SHEETS FOR ONE DOLLAR.

INITIALLY, THE PAPER WAS MARKETED AS AN ANTI-HEMORRHOID MEDICINAL PRODUCT, BUT GAYETTY QUICKLY SAW ITS BROADER POTENTIAL.

THIS IS GOING TO CHANGE EVERYTHING FOR FOREVER FOR ALL THE BUTTS EVERYWHERE!

GAYETTY MARKETED HIS PRODUCT TO THE GENERAL PUBLIC, WARNING THEM OF THE DANGERS OF THEIR CURRENT SANITARY METHODS, SUCH AS WIPING WITH NEWSPAPERS AND MAGAZINES.

THE PAPER WAS MADE OF ROUGH MANILA HEMP, TREATED WITH ALOE TO SOFTEN IT.

*A POPULAR JOKE ABOUT USING THE SEARS & ROEBUCK CATALOGUE AS TOILET PAPER.

THE TOM COLLINS

WHAT BEGAN AS A PRANK, THE TOM COLLINS WAS SUPPOSEDLY INVENTED IN 1874 BY BARTENDER JERRY THOMAS. EVEN THOUGH CREDIT FOR THE DRINK'S INVENTION IS DISPUTED, IT WAS NOTED THAT THE FIRST OFFICIAL TOM COLLINS RECIPE (IN AMERICA) APPEARED IN THOMAS'S BARTENDING GUIDE.

SPECIFICS OF THE PRANK VARY, BUT A POPULAR VERSION INVOLVED A FABRICATED SHIT-TALKING BAR PATRON.

HAVE YOU SEEN TOM COLLINS?
I DON'T KNOW A TOM COLLINS.
WELL, HE'S AT THE BAR AROUND THE CORNER TALKING MAD SHIT ABOUT YOU!

POTATO CHIPS

THE FIRST POTATO CHIPS WERE INVENTED BY ACCIDENT, IN 1853, BY CHEF GEORGE CRUM, AS REVENGE ON COMPLAINING CUSTOMERS.
WHINE ABOUT MY FRENCH FRIES, EH? WELL I'LL GIVE THEM SOMETHING TO WHINE ABOUT!
FLOUR

OUT OF SPITE, CRUM ANGRILY SLICED A BATCH OF FRIES TOO THIN, THEN OVER-FRIED AND OVER-SALTED THEM.
I'LL SHOW THEM! THEY'LL HATE THESE! WHATEVER THE FUCK THEY ARE.

ALTHOUGH CRUM'S INTENTION WAS TO ANGER HIS PATRONS, HIS SCHEME BACKFIRED. THEY LOVED HIS CREATION.
WHAT ARE THESE? THEY'RE DELICIOUS!
YOU, UH, YOU ACTUALLY LIKE THEM?
WE LOVE THEM! WHAT ARE THEY?
UM...POTATO FLATS? NO. POTATO CHIPS? YEAH, POTATO CHIPS!

CRUM CONTINUED TO SERVE HIS POPULAR CHIPS TO MUCH ACCLAIM. EVENTUALLY HIS CREATION WENT COMMERCIAL, UNDER THE NAME "SARATOGA CHIPS," WHICH ARE STILL AVAILABLE TODAY.
MOON
TRADE MARK
BRAND
Saratoga Chips
Saratoga Springs

JELL-O

INDUSTRIALIST PETER COOPER INVENTED POWDERED GELATIN, THE BASE OF JELL-O, IN 1845. (GELATIN HAS BEEN AROUND SINCE THE 15TH CENTURY.) IN 1897, HE SOLD HIS PATENT TO PEARLE B. WAIT, WHO, ALONG WITH HIS WIFE, MAY, PATENTED "JELL-O."
THE DELICIOUS DESSERT
JELL-O
DELICATE DELIGHTFUL DAINTY
PRICE
LEMON
10¢
PURE FRUIT FLAVOR
THE GENESEE PURE FOOD CO.
LEROY, N.Y

UNABLE TO FIND COMMERCIAL SUCCESS, THE RECIPE EXCHANGED HANDS NUMEROUS TIMES. EVENTUALLY IT LANDED AT THE GENESEE FOOD COMPANY IN 1899, WHICH SOON MADE JELL-O A HOUSEHOLD NAME.
THANKS TO THE NEW JELL-O COOKBOOK™, I CAN NOW MAKE ALL KINDS OF REVOLTING MEALS OUT OF GELATINOUS, ARTIFICIALLY FLAVORED, UH, WHATEVER THE FUCK THIS SHIT IS.

CRONUTS

IN 2013, PASTRY CHEF DOMINIQUE ANSEL MARRIED A DONUT WITH A CROISSANT AND CREATED AN EPIC CONFECTIONARY SCAM. PEOPLE LINED UP AROUND THE BLOCK FOR THIS BULLSHIT, EAGER TO WASTE THEIR MONEY ON NYC'S NEXT "IT" FOOD.

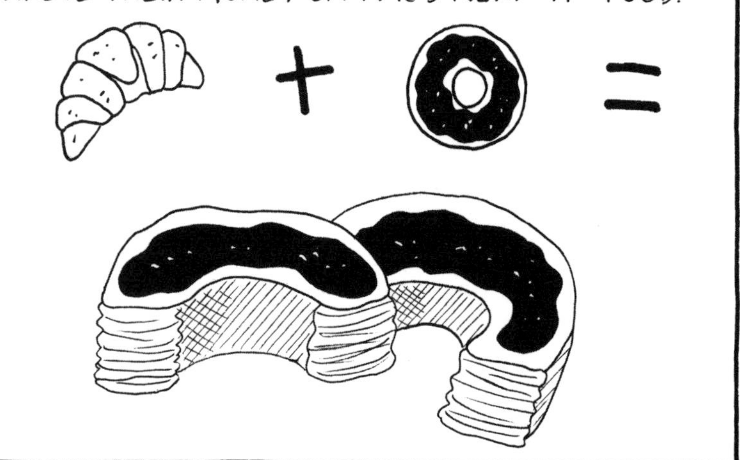

TO HIS CREDIT, ANSEL WAS A SAVVY BUSINESSMAN. HE TRADEMARKED HIS CRONUTS AND ARTIFICIALLY LIMITED THE SUPPLY, CREATING A HUGE DEMAND THAT ALLOWED HIM TO CHARGE $5 PER PASTRY. A CRONUT BLACK MARKET SPRUNG UP, WHERE IT WAS REPORTED SOME IDIOT ACTUALLY PAID $5,000 FOR A BOX OF 20 CRONUTS.

YEAH, *FIVE THOUSAND* DOLLARS. EVEN IF THAT'S NOT ACTUALLY TRUE, I'M STILL FOREVER UPSET ABOUT CRONUTS.

MR. POTATO HEAD

INVENTED BY TOY DESIGNER GEORGE LERNER, THE ORIGINAL MR. POTATO HEAD WAS A REAL POTATO (AND OTHER FRUITS & VEGETABLES) WITH PLASTIC BODY PARTS JABBED INTO HIM. THE KIT CAME WITH ONLY PLASTIC EXTREMITIES, THE ORGANIC MATTER WAS SUPPLIED BY THE BUYER.

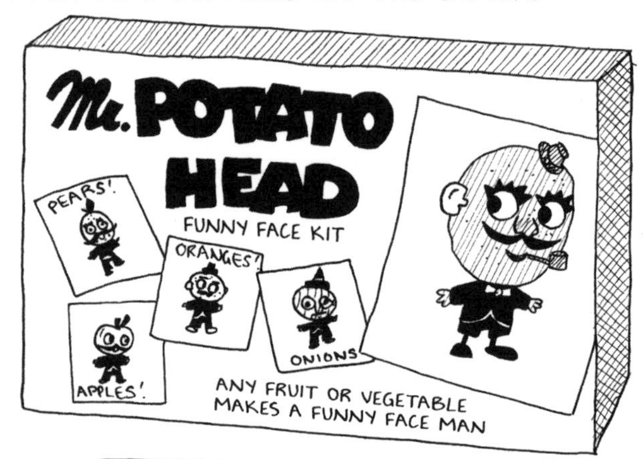

LERNER SOLD HIS INVENTION TO HASBRO TOY COMPANY IN 1952. ALTHOUGH IT WAS AN INSTANT HIT, IN A POST WWII ECONOMY, CONSUMERS WERE RELUCTANT TO WASTE FOOD, SO MR. POTATO HEAD WAS REDESIGNED AND GIVEN A FULLY PLASTIC MAKEOVER IN 1964.

CREDIT CARDS

IN 1946, BANKER JOHN BIGGINS CREATED THE FIRST BANK CARD, THE "CHARG-IT." CREDIT PROGRAMS ALREADY EXISTED (AS ILLUSTRATED BELOW), BUT WERE LIMITED TO SPECIFIC LOCATIONS. BIGGINS WAS THE FIRST TO ALLOW HIS CUSTOMERS TO USE THEIR CARDS AT MULTIPLE STORES. HOWEVER, THEY HAD TO HAVE AN ACCOUNT AT BIGGINS'S BANK.

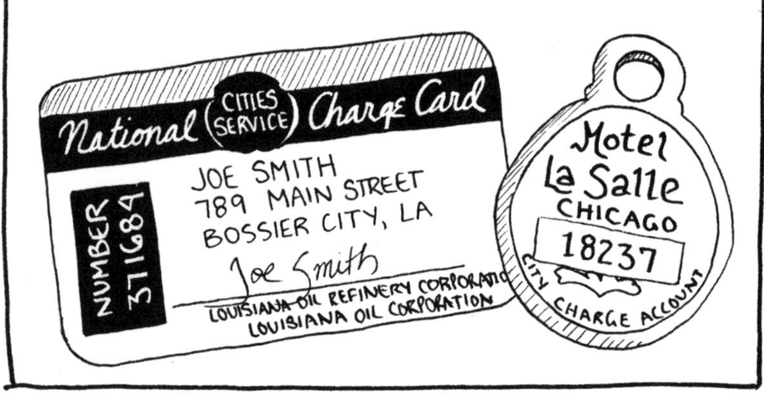

IN 1950, DINERS CLUB INTRODUCED A UNIVERSAL PAPER CHARGE CARD THAT COULD BE USED IN MULTIPLE LOCATIONS NO MATTER WHERE YOU BANKED. EVENTUALLY THOSE CARDS BECAME THE SAME PLASTIC CARDS WE USE TODAY.

THE BLOODY MARY

ALTHOUGH A TOMATO JUICE AND VODKA DRINK ALREADY EXISTED IN FRANCE, FERNAND PETIOT IS CREDITED WITH CREATING THE FIRST BLOODY MARY AT THE ST. REGIS HOTEL'S KING COLE BAR WHEN HE ADDED WORCESTERSHIRE SAUCE, BLACK PEPPER, CAYENNE, AND LEMON TO THE DRINK, CREATING ITS SIGNATURE RECIPE.

THE WALDORF SALAD

THIS GARBAGE SALAD OF MAYONNAISE, APPLES, CELERY, AND OTHER STUFF THAT OUGHT NOT BE IN A SALAD WAS CREATED IN THE 1890'S AT THE FAMOUS WALDORF ASTORIA HOTEL.

I WAS GOING TO DRAW THE SALAD BUT WAS LIKE, EH, WHO CARES? DOES ANYONE EVEN LIKE WALDORF SALAD? HAVE YOU EVEN SEEN IT? IT LOOKS LIKE A PILE OF PUKE! I'M SO MAD ABOUT THAT STUPID SALAD.

TEDDY BEARS

IN 1902, AMERICA WAS ERRONEOUSLY CHARMED WHEN PRESIDENT TEDDY ROOSEVELT DECLINED TO SHOOT AN INJURED BLACK BEAR WHILE OUT HUNTING. BROOKLYN CANDY STORE OWNERS MORRIS AND ROSE MICHTOM WERE INSPIRED TO SEW A STUFFED BEAR CALLED "TEDDY'S BEAR" IN HONOR OF ROOSEVELT.

THE FACT THAT ROOSEVELT WAS STILL AN AVID HUNTER WAS SWEPT UNDER THE RUG AS TEDDY BEARS SURGED IN POPULARITY.

SURE, I SAVED THAT ONE BEAR, BUT I'M STILL GONNA SHOOT THE SHIT OUT OF EVERYTHING ELSE!

THE KODAK CAMERA

GEORGE EASTMAN INTRODUCED THE KODAK CAMERA IN 1885, AND IT REVOLUTIONIZED PHOTOGRAPHY.

THIS IS GOING TO CHANGE EVERYTHING FOR FOREVER FOR EVERYONE EVERYWHERE!
AND NO, CAMERAS DON'T STEAL YOUR ESSENCE WHEN YOU GET YOUR PICTURE TAKEN, YOU IDIOTS.

THE ROLL OF TRANSPARENT PHOTOGRAPHIC FILM REPLACED THE MESSY, TIME-CONSUMING LIQUID EMULSION PROCESS. THE KODAK CAMERA WAS MADE AVAILABLE TO THE PUBLIC IN 1888.

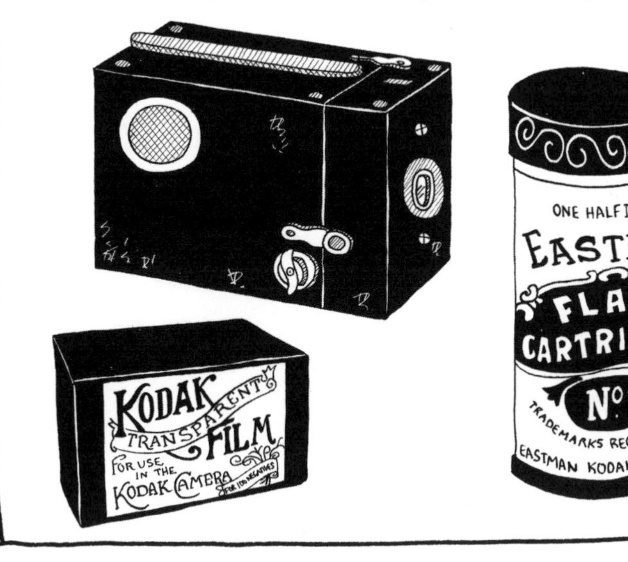

THE AIR CONDITIONER

THE FIRST ELECTRIC AIR CONDITIONER WAS INVENTED IN 1902 BY ENGINEER WILLIS CARRIER. ORIGINALLY, IT WAS CREATED TO PROTECT PAPER FROM HUMIDITY DAMAGE, NOT TO PAMPER PEOPLE, BUT WAS EVENTUALLY ADOPTED BY BUSINESSES LOOKING TO LURE CUSTOMERS INTO THEIR STORES.

THE AIR CONDITIONER BECAME A HUGE COMMERCIAL SUCCESS IN THE 1950'S WITH THE SUBURBAN BOOM.

IT'S AMAZING! MY HAPPY HOME IS COMPLETE! WELL, ALMOST, IT'LL BE COMPLETE WHEN THE SEARS & ROEBUCK'S CATALOGUE TELLS ME IT'S COMPLETE.
AIR CONDITIONER
THIS IS JUST AN EMPTY BOX, I CAN'T BRING MYSELF TO THROW IT AWAY.

SCRABBLE

SCRABBLE WAS INVENTED BY ALFRED MOSHER BUTTS IN 1949. BUTTS, AN UNEMPLOYED ARCHITECT, COMBINED HIS LOVE OF ANAGRAMS AND CROSSWORD PUZZLES, CREATING "CRISS CROSS WORDS." THE GAME SOLD SLOWLY AT FIRST, BUT RUMOR HAS IT THAT ONCE IT WAS DISCOVERED BY THE PRESIDENT OF MACY'S, IT BECAME HUGELY SUCCESSFUL.

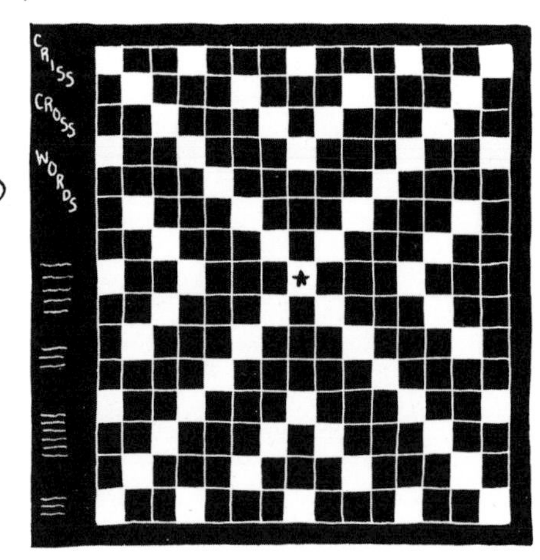

HOT DOGS

THE INVENTION OF THE HOT DOG IS CREDITED TO CONEY ISLAND BAKER AND PUSHCART OPERATOR CHARLES FELTMAN IN THE 1860'S.

ALTHOUGH FELTMAN INVENTED HOT DOGS, HIS EMPLOYEE NATHAN HANDWERKER TOOK THE INVENTION ONE STEP FURTHER AND OPENED THE FIRST NATHAN'S FAMOUS HOT DOGS.

HONORABLE MENTIONS:

THE REMOTE CONTROL
SYNTHETIC PENICILLIN
SCENTED CARDBOARD TREES
EGGS BENEDICT
GENERAL TSO'S CHICKEN
CHICKEN & WAFFLES
ATM MACHINES
THE PACEMAKER
THE PNEUMATIC RAILWAY
THE TYPEWRITER
PEPTO-BISMOL
THE REUBEN SANDWICH
HIP HOP

BED-STUY THEN & NOW

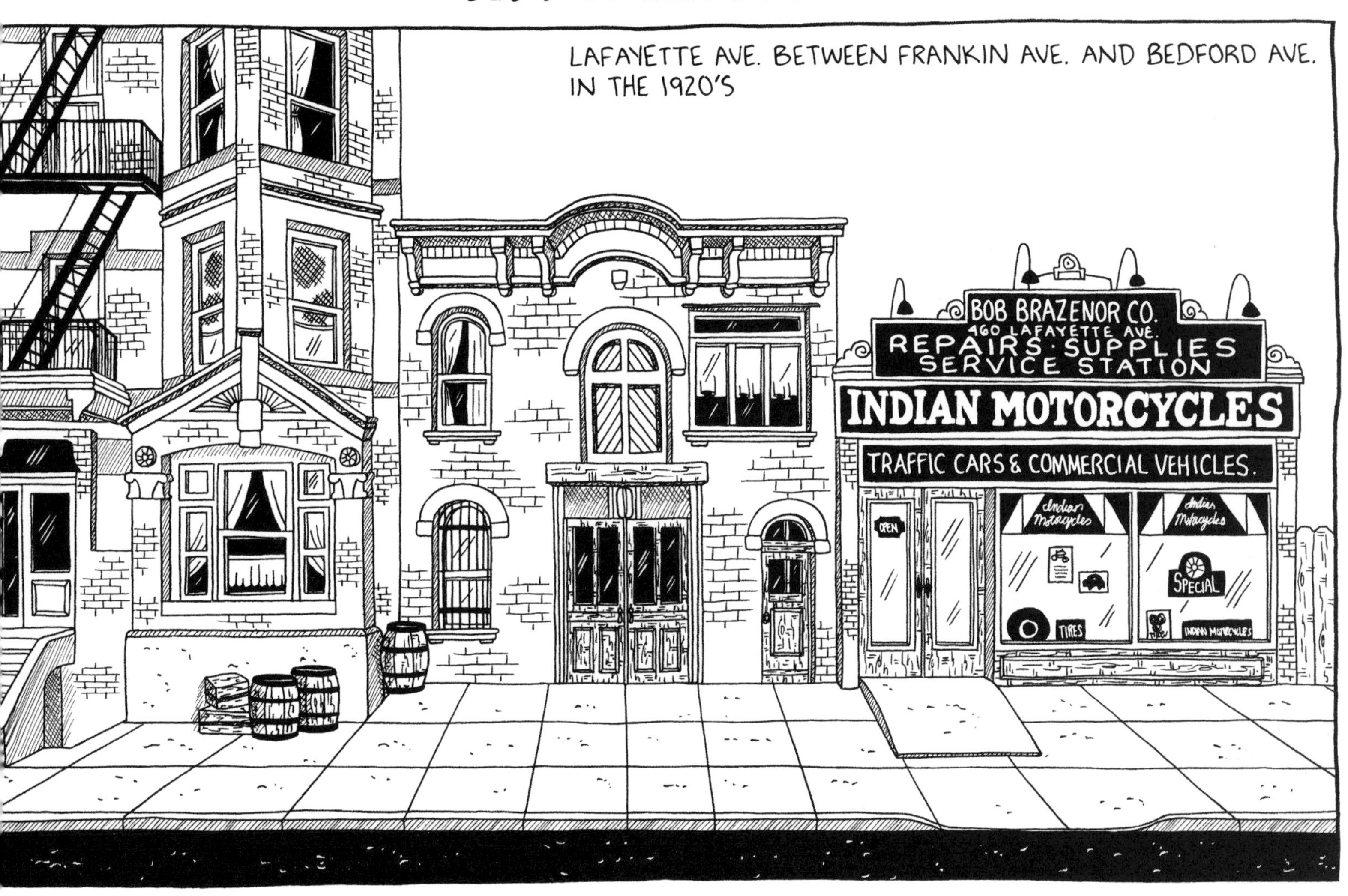

FULTON ST. BETWEEN NEW YORK AVE. AND MARCY AVE. IN THE 1940'S

FULTON ST. BETWEEN NEW YORK AVE. AND MARCY AVE. IN 2016

811 MYRTLE AVE. IN 1942
JEFFERSON
CASABLANCA
SINTOWN
FLYING TIGERS
SINTOWN
the Black Swan
Casablanca
FRESH BREAD & PASTRIES
BAKERY
FRESH BREAD & PASTRIES
SINTOWN
THE CITY WITHOUT A SOUL
JOHN WAYNE
James Cagney
YANKEE DOODLE DANDY
The Black Swan
CIGARS & CIGARETTES
Murad Cigarettes
Coca-Cola
Cigar SALE

811 MYRTLE AVE. IN 2016
WE BUY GOLD & DIAMONDS
JEWELRY
& BUY GOLD & DIAMONDS
BIOTECH
BUILDING SOLUTIONS CORP
GENERAL CONTRACTOR CONSTRUCTION
718-455-2813
Miguel SIGNS Painter
467-0222
MoMo
LOVE TRUMPS HATE
TO ANONYMOUSLY REPORT UNSAFE CONDITIONS AT THIS SITE, CALL 311
NO PARKING
NO PARKING ANY TIME

THE COMPLICATED AND UNFINISHED HISTORY OF RAY'S PIZZA

THE PLETHORA OF RAY'S PIZZA PARLORS, AND VARIATIONS THEREOF, IS ONE OF NYC'S MOST POPULAR AND ENDURING JOKES. IN A 1998 EPISODE OF *SEINFELD*, JERRY SUCCINCTLY SUMS UP THE SITUATION WHEN HE ASKS KRAMER IF HE IS AT "RAY'S PIZZA, FAMOUS RAY'S, OR FAMOUS ORIGINAL RAY'S." MOST NEW YORKERS ARE AWARE THAT NOT ALL THE RAY'S ARE CONNECTED, AND HAVE HEARD RUMBLINGS OF VARIOUS LAWSUITS AND LEGAL DEBACLES. THE INTRICACY OF THE PIZZA PARLORS' HISTORY IS EXTENSIVE, AND COMPLICATED BY A WEALTH OF MISINFORMATION, BOTH VERBALLY AND ONLINE. BUT THE BEST PART OF THE STORY IS OFTEN OMITTED IN LIEU OF BORING LEGAL STUFF, WHICH IS THAT THE FIRST RAY'S PIZZA WAS A FRONT FOR A MAFIA-RUN DRUG OPERATION.

RAY'S PIZZA
27 PRINCE ST.
SOHO, MANHATTAN

THE FIRST RAY'S PIZZA WAS OPENED BY RALPH CUOMO AT 27 PRINCE ST. IN LITTLE ITALY IN 1959. THE RESTAURANT WAS A HANGOUT FOR THE "PRINCE STREET CREW," AN INFAMOUS GROUP OF DRUG TRAFFICKERS FROM THE LUCCHESE CRIME FAMILY. UNLIKE MOST FRONTS, RAY'S WAS A FULLY FUNCTIONAL AND VERY POPULAR EATERY, DRIVEN BY CUOMO'S LOVE OF MAKING PIZZAS, SPECIFICALLY HIS FAMOUS TOMATO-FREE WHITE PIZZA. FLUSH WITH SUCCESS, CUOMO OPENED A SECOND PIZZERIA IN THE 1960'S, BUT SOLD IT TO FRANCES GIAIMO, WHO SOLD IT TO ROSOLINO MANGANO SHORTLY AFTER.

FAMOUS RAY'S PIZZA
465 6TH AVE.
GREENWICH VILLAGE, MANHATTAN

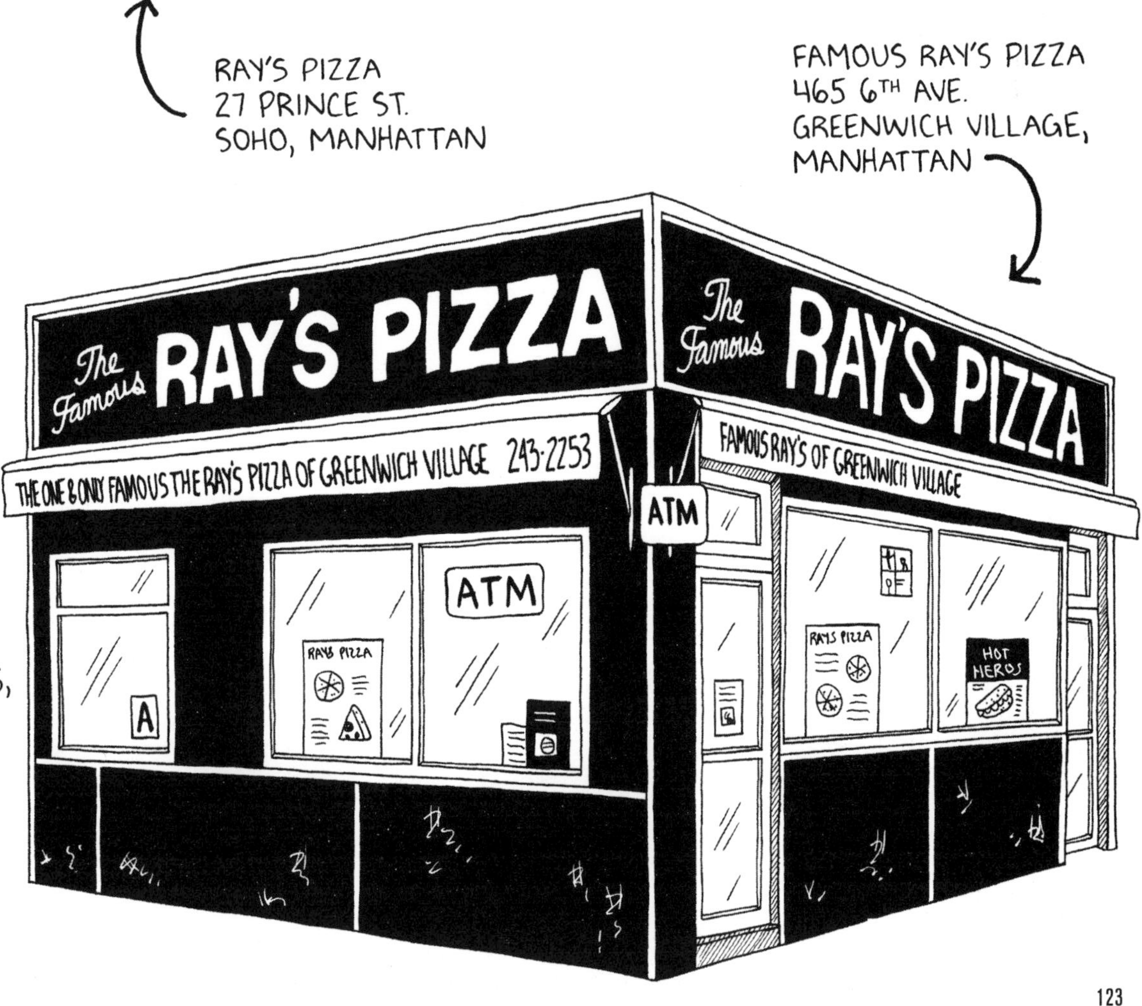

THIS IS WHERE THE STORY GETS COMPLICATED. NO SOURCES SEEM TO AGREE ABOUT WHO OWNED WHAT AND WHEN OR HOW THE PIZZA PARLORS WERE RUN. SOME SOURCES SAY THAT MANGANO WAS KNOWN FOR HIRING IMMIGRANTS, SOME OF WHOM QUIT TO OPEN THEIR OWN RAY'S AND CAPITALIZE ON THE NAME. OTHERS CLAIM IT WAS THE WORK OF A FEW SAVVY BUSINESSMEN. AS OWNERSHIP PASSED FROM PERSON TO PERSON AND MORE RAY'S PIZZAS SPRANG UP, THE STORY BECAME MUDDLED BY MERGERS, LEGAL BATTLES, AND LAWSUITS. IT'S ALSO PRETTY FUCKING BORING, SO LET'S GET BACK TO THE EARLY, FAR MORE FASCINATING DAYS OF THE FIRST RAY'S ON SPRING STREET.

FAMOUS ORIGINAL RAYS
204 9TH AVE. # 1
CHELSEA, MANHATTAN

FAMOUS ORIGINAL RAY'S
831 7TH AVE.
MIDTOWN, MANHATTAN

FAMOUS ORIGINAL RAY'S
811 LEXINGTON AVE.
UPPER EAST SIDE,
MANHATTAN

ACCORDING TO THE BOOK **MOB BOSS**, WRITTEN BY FORMER MAFIOSO ALFONSO D'ARCO, RALPH CUOMO AND HIS CREW WERE RUTHLESS ABOUT THEIR LUCRATIVE HEROIN OPERATION, WHICH THEY RAN OUT OF THE BASEMENT OF RAY'S. THE CREW MADE LESS THAN DISCREET DRUG DEALS, WHICH DREW UNWANTED ATTENTION. D'ARCO RECALLED ONCE SEEING CUOMO RUN DOWN THE STREET WITH TWO BRICKS OF HEROIN UNDER HIS ARM. THEY OPENLY SOLD TO KIDS, WHICH IRKED MANY OLDER MAFIA MEMBERS WHO HAD CHILDREN IN THE COMMUNITY. IN 1969, CUOMO WAS ARRESTED FOR HAVING AROUND $25 MILLION WORTH OF HEROIN IN HIS CAR TRUNK. UPON HIS RELEASE, HE WENT RIGHT BACK TO WORK SELLING PIZZA AND DRUGS.

THE MANHATTAN DISTRICT ATTORNEY'S OFFICE TRACKED CUOMO FOR YEARS, MOSTLY UNSUCCESSFULLY. CUOMO DID A FEW SHORT STINTS IN PRISON, BUT ALWAYS RETURNED TO HIS PIZZA PARLOR. MY FAVORITE ANECDOTE IS WHEN DETECTIVES WATCHED CUOMO PUT A WHITE SHOPPING BAG IN HIS TRUNK, AND INVITED HIS CREW TO TAKE A LOOK. INVESTIGATORS NOTED THAT D'ARCO APPEARED TO PUT HIS FINGER IN THE BAG, REMOVE IT, AND LICK IT, A CLASSIC DRUG-TESTING MOTION. HOWEVER, IN HIS MEMOIR, D'ARC CLAIMS THE BAG WAS FILLED WITH FRESHLY MADE SAUSAGES AND PEPPERS. WHY THE MEN NEEDED TO TRY TRUNK FOOD ON A LATE, COLD FEBRUARY NIGHT CAN ONLY BE LEFT TO SPECULATION.

FAMOUS ORIGINAL RAY'S PIZZA
736 7TH AVE.
MIDTOWN, MANHATTAN

RAY'S PIZZA & BAGEL CAFE
2 ST. MARK'S PL.
EAST VILLAGE, MANHATTAN

THE ORIGINAL RAY'S PIZZA
462 COLUMBUS AVE.
UPPER WEST SIDE, MANHATTAN

RALPH CUOMO DIED IN 2008, AND RAY'S PIZZA CLOSED IN 2011, DUE TO LEASE ISSUES. TODAY IT'S PRINCE STREET PIZZA, WHICH I HATE TO SAY HAS GREAT PIZZA BECAUSE IT FEELS LIKE A BETRAYAL, BUT IT'S TRUE. I'VE EATEN AT A NUMBER OF DIFFERENT RAY'S OVER THE YEARS, MORE OUT OF NECESSITY THAN CHOICE, AND I'VE NEVER BEEN THRILLED NOR DISAPPOINTED. THEY ALL HAVE THE KIND OF BASIC SLICE THAT FOR SOME REASON TASTES AMAZING AFTER SPENDING A DAY IN THE BUTTHOLE OF MIDTOWN.

CURRENTLY, NO ONE KNOWS EXACTLY HOW MANY RAY'S ARE IN THE CITY, SINCE THEY OPEN AND CLOSE CONSTANTLY, BUT IT'S ESTIMATED AROUND 20–40. TWO OF THE RAY'S I DREW FOR THIS PIECE —THE FIRST AND SECOND LOCATIONS— CLOSED DURING THE TWO YEARS I WORKED ON THIS BOOK.

SNACK CARTS, DELIVERY BIKES, AND FOOD TRUCKS OF NEW YORK CITY, 1800'S TO TODAY

Junior Lunch Car
No1
PIES & COFFEE Sandwiches
CIGARS AND CANDIES
PIE & COFFEE CIGARS
LUNCH SOFT DRINK

HOT SANDWICH
HOT SANDWICHES COLD CUTS & HEROES

Vegetarian Kitchen
HEALTHY VEGETARIAN HOME COOKIN
MENU
SMOOTHIES
MIXED BERRY
BANANA
CARROT
COCONUT
SANDWICH
VEGGIES
GRILLED TOFU
HUMMUS
GRILLED CHEESE
COOKIES
OATMEAL
CHOC CHIP

FROSTEE
SUNDAES · SHAKES
CONES

SABRETT
PRETZEL
DAYTONA DOG

SWEETERYNYC.COM
CHOPPER
HELLO!
DELICACY
WANT
MENU
SWEETERY NYC
Fabulous
enjoy
sensational
THE LINE BEGINS HERE
COOL
CHOCOLATES
DIVINE
YUM
DELIGHTFUL
WARM

BIG GAY ICE CREAM
LA or BUST!

SABRETT
HALAL FOOD
HALAL FOOD

IN THE DRINK: WHAT'S REALLY IN NEW YORK CITY'S TAP WATER

NEW YORK IS RENOWNED FOR HAVING SOME OF THE CLEANEST TAP WATER IN THE WORLD. YOU CAN DRINK IT RIGHT OUT OF THE FAUCET!

OUT OF THE FAUCET? SURE, IF YOU'RE A SAVAGE!

I KNOW IT'S SAFE, BUT I STILL RUN IT THROUGH A BRITA FILTER, AND STORE IT IN A BPA-FREE PLASTIC CONTAINER IN THE ECO-FRIENDLY THERMADOR™.

I ONLY DRINK SELTZER.
FLAT WATER IS A PEASANT'S BROTH.

UNBEKNOWNST TO MOST NEW YORKERS, THE CITY'S DRINKING WATER CONTAINS MICROSCOPIC SHRIMP, KNOWN AS COPEPODS. THEY ARE MOSTLY INVISIBLE TO THE NAKED EYE, BUT A FEW SPECIES ARE LARGE ENOUGH TO SPOT, ALTHOUGH THE FACT THAT THEY'RE TRANSLUCENT MAKES IT DIFFICULT.

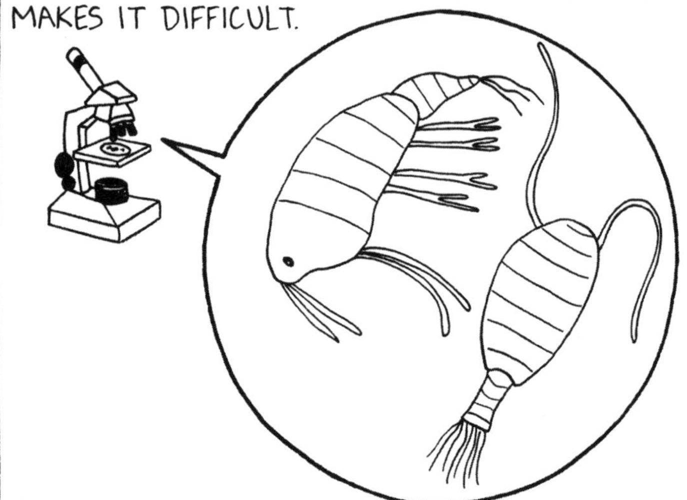

COPEPODS CAN BE FOUND IN ALMOST EVERY BODY OF WATER. THEY ASSIST IN THE CLEANSING PROCESS, AND EVEN EAT MOSQUITO LARVA. THEY ARE A DISTANT RELATIVE OF THE LOBSTER.

VERY DISTANT, IF YOU ASK ME.
AW!

THEY ARE NOT HARMFUL TO THE HUMAN BODY, NOR DO THEY TRIGGER SHELLFISH ALLERGIES, BUT THEY DID CAUSE A STIR AMONG THE JEWISH RESIDENTS OF NEW YORK CITY IN 2004, WHEN THEIR EXISTENCE WAS FIRST WIDELY REPORTED, BECAUSE SHELLFISH ARE NOT KOSHER. SALES OF FILTERED WATER SKYROCKETED, UNTIL THE CITY'S RABBIS DECLARED THEM EXEMPT FROM KOSHER LAW.

PURE H^2O
COPEPOD FREE, SUGAR FREE GLUTEN FREE, SOY FREE, BPA FREE, HYPOALLERGENIC, NON-COMEDOGENIC, NON-CARCINOGENIC, ORGANIC, HAND CRAFTED, PURE ARTISANAL BULLSHIT. NOT TESTED ON ANIMALS.

THE PRESENCE OF THE COPEPODS SIGNIFIES HEALTHY, CLEAN WATER, SO YOU CAN DRINK WITHOUT CONCERN! BESIDES, IT'S NOT LIKE YOU EVER NOTICED THEM BEFORE, ANYWAY.

WELL IT'S NOT LIKE I WANT TO BE HERE, EITHER!!

BROOKLYN THEATERS THEN & NOW

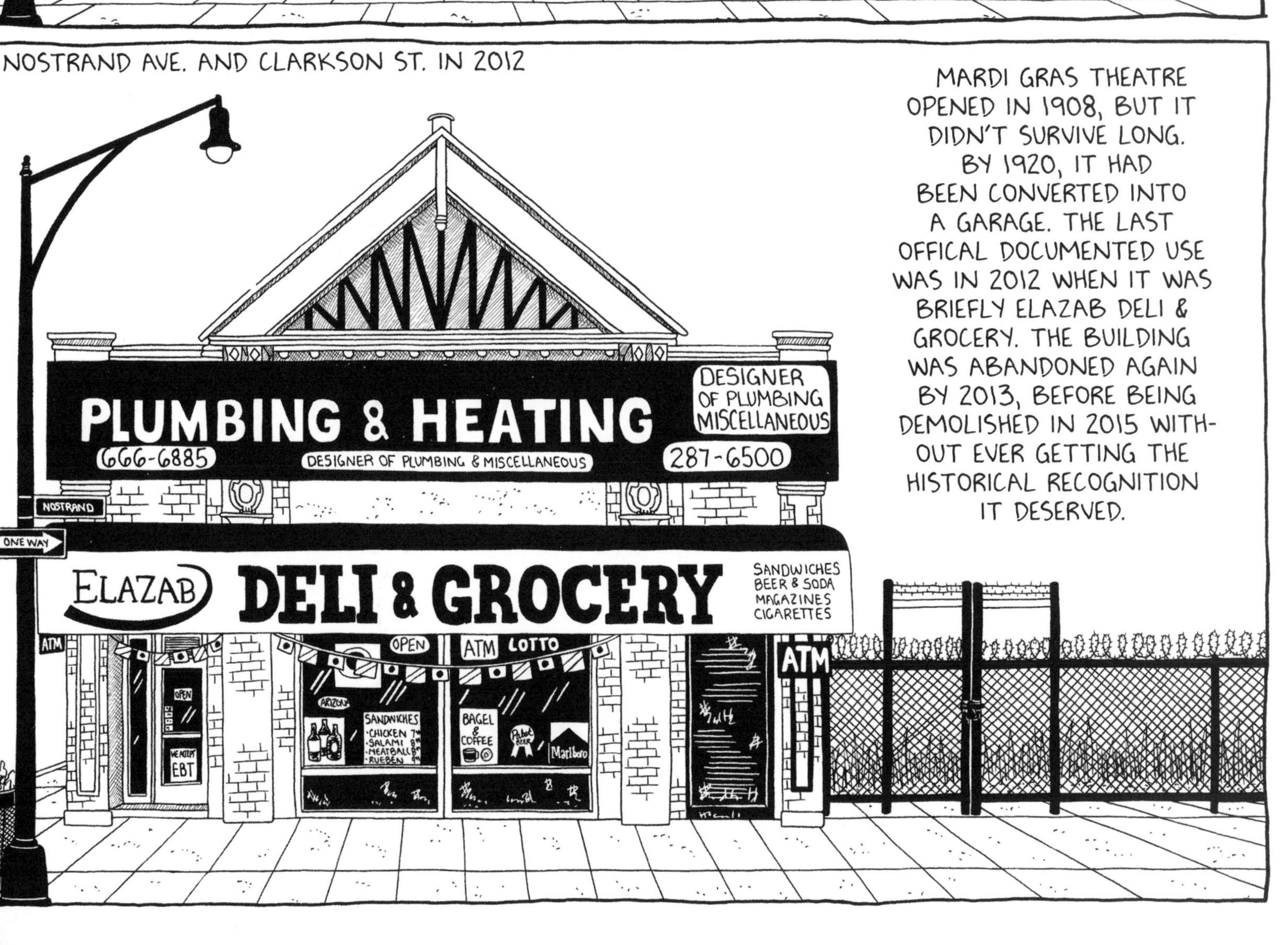

THE MAJESTIC OPENED IN 1904 AS A PLAYHOUSE THAT SHOWCASED VAUDEVILLE, MUSICALS, FILMS AND PLAYS. SHOWS HOPING TO MAKE IT TO BROADWAY OFTEN USED THE MAJESTIC FOR THEIR TRYOUTS. IN 1942 THE PLAYHOUSE WAS PURCHASED BY A PARISIAN AND HIS SONS AFTER THEY FLED NAZI GERMANY. THE FAMILY TRANSFORMED THE MAJESTIC INTO A LUXURIOUS EUROPEAN STYLE FIRST-RUN MOVIE THEATER. THE MAJESTIC CLOSED IN THE 1960'S.

651 FULTON ST. IN 1939. FORT GREENE, BROOKLYN

AFTER BEING EMPTY AND NEGLECTED FOR ALMOST TWO DECADES, BROOKYN ACADAMY OF MUSIC PRESIDENT HARVEY LICHTENSTEIN SNAPPED UP THE DERELICT BUILDING, WHICH HE'D WALKED PAST DAILY ON HIS WAY TO BAM. LICHTENSTEIN CAREFULLY RENOVATED THE THEATER, PRESERVING ORIGINAL ARCHITECTURAL DETAILS ON THE INTERIOR AND EXTERIOR, AND REOPENED IT IN 1987. TODAY BAM HARVEY THEATER (RENAMED IN 1999 TO HONOR LICHTENSTEIN WHEN HE RETIRED) STAGES A VARIETY OF SHOWS INCLUDING DANCE, OPERA, MUSIC, PLAYS, FILM, AND MORE.

651 FULTON ST. IN 2016

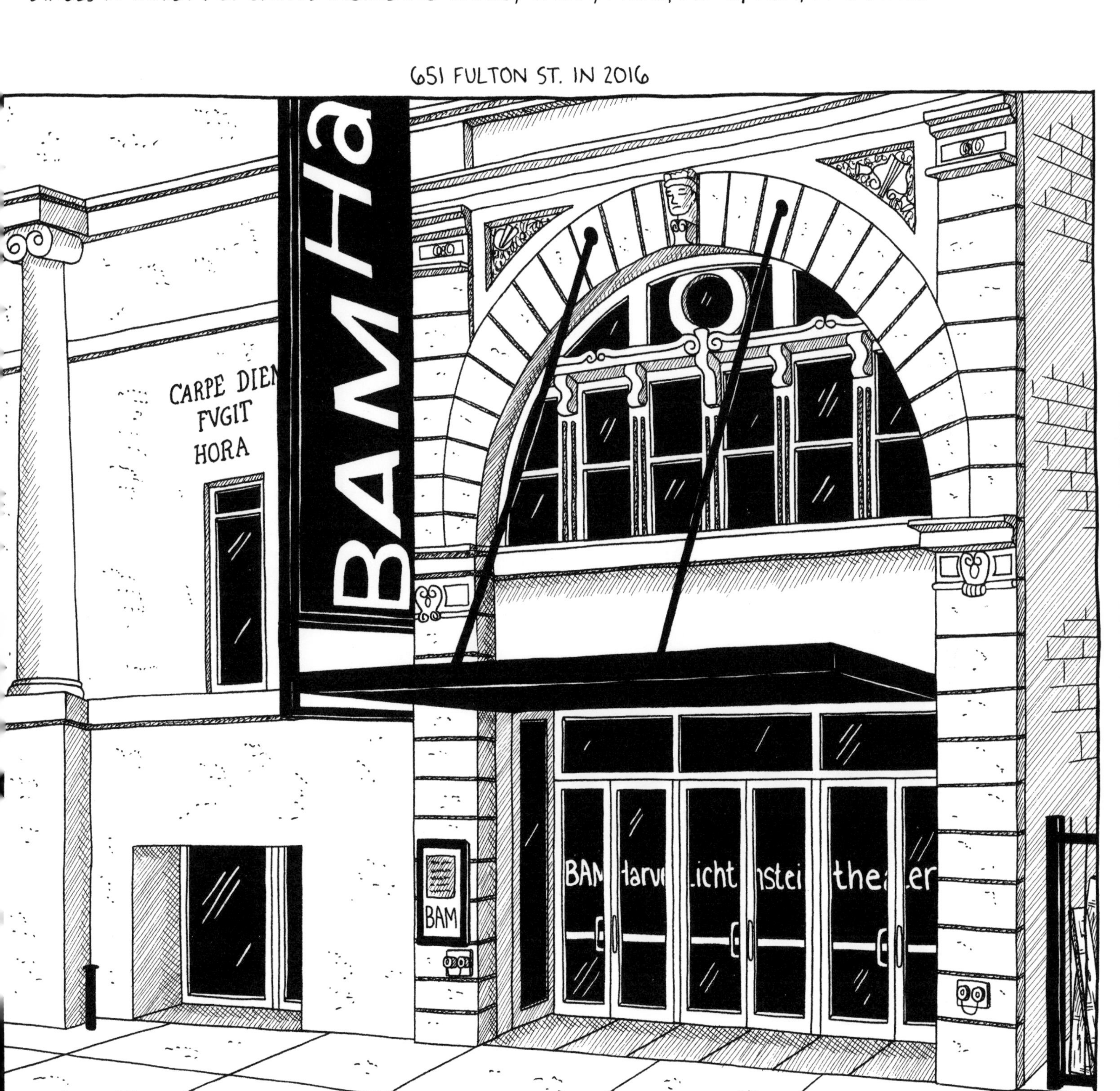

THE RKO KEITH OPENED IN 1928 AS A VAUDEVILLE THEATER. AT THAT TIME, THE THEATER WAS CALLED THE KEITH-ALBEE KENMORE THEATRE, AND BELONGED TO THE TILYOU FAMILY, WHO ALSO OWNED STEEPLECHASE PARK IN CONEY ISLAND. IT WAS AN ELEGANT THEATER, DESIGNED BY EUGENE DEROSA, AND HAD MURALS BY WILLY POGANY PAINTED ON THE WALLS. IN 1932 THE THEATER WAS SOLD TO THE B.F. KEITH'S CIRCUIT AND WAS CONVERTED TO A SINGLE-SCREEN THEATER.

2101 CHURCH AVE. IN 1946. PROSPECT PARK SOUTH, BROOKLYN

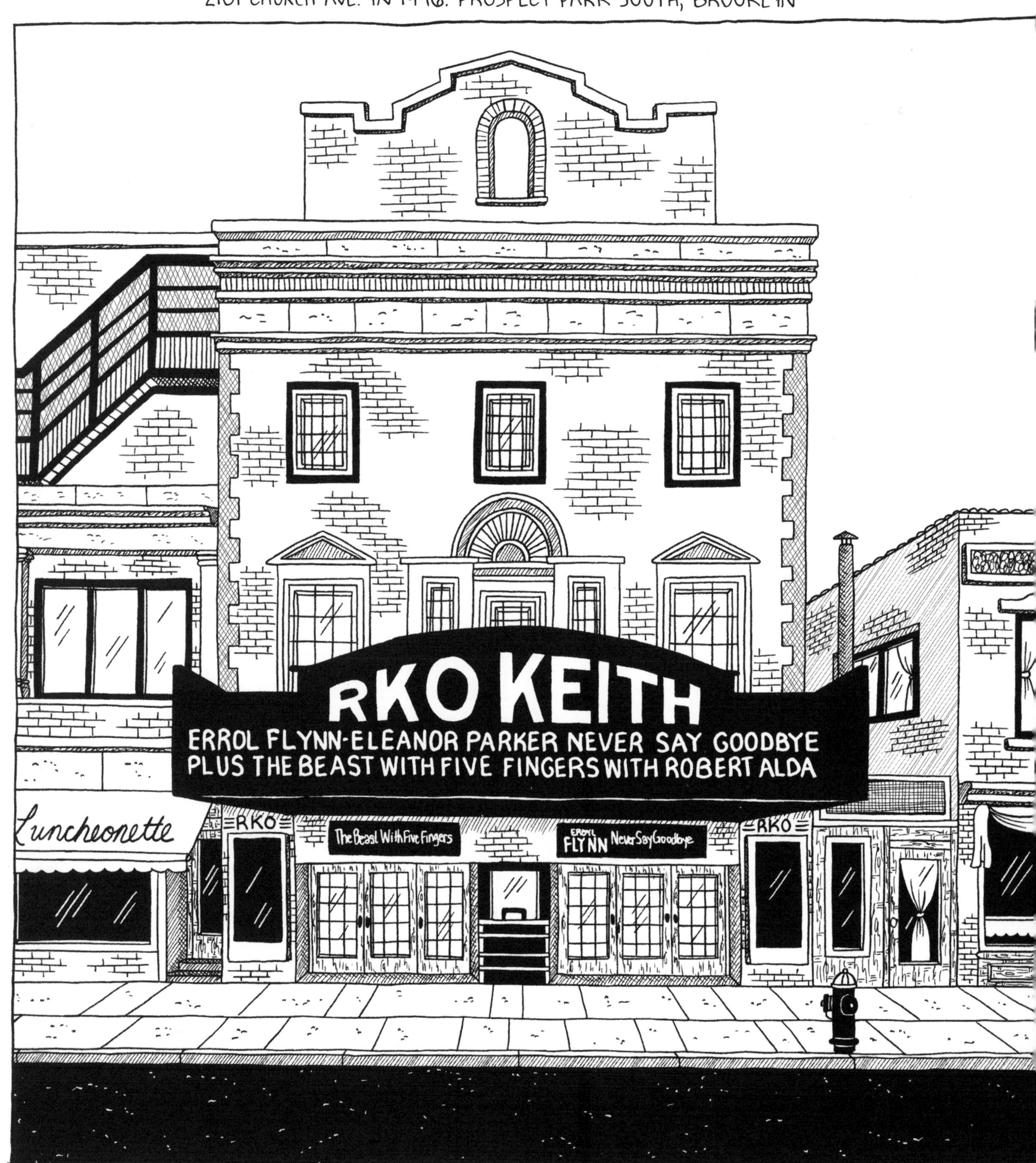

IN THE 1980'S, IT WAS SOLD TO THE CINEPLEX ODEON THEATER CHAIN. THE THEATER FELL ON HARD TIMES AS THE NEIGHBORHOOD GREW INCREASINGLY VIOLENT. AFTER A GANG-RELATED SHOOTING INSIDE THE THEATER IN 1999, IT FINALLY WENT UNDER. THE BUILDING WAS GUTTED AND TURNED INTO A MODELL'S SPORTING GOODS STORE. NO ONE KNOWS FOR SURE WHAT BECAME OF THE POGANY MURALS, BUT THEY'D BE VERY VALUABLE IF THEY SURVIVED.

2101 CHURCH AVE. IN 2016

1507 40TH ST. IN 1933
BOROUGH PARK,
BROOKLYN
THE WINDSOR THEATRE OPENED IN 1928
AND CLOSED IN 1959.
WINDSOR
THE INVISIBLE MAN
LITTLE WOMEN
DIES SHOES
SODA · CIGARS · CIGARETTES
CANDY · SODA · CIGARS
Formal Hats
KING KONG
LITTLE WOMEN
KING KONG
1507 40TH ST. IN 2016
THE THEATER WAS CONVERTED INTO
A SHORT-LIVED BOWLING ALLEY THAT
BURNED DOWN IN 1964. THE BUILDING
WAS DEMOLISHED AFTER THE FIRE.
40TH ST.
ONE WAY
Kol Tuv
כל טוב
SUPERMARKET
FREE DELIVERY
Kol Tuv

AN INCOMPLETE* GUIDE TO NEW YORK CITY REAL ESTATE

WHEN I FIRST MOVED TO NYC, MY INTRODUCTION TO THE CITY'S REAL ESTATE MARKET WAS BY FULL IMMERSION. I SPENT EVERY DAY FOR WEEKS VIEWING APARTMENTS, TALKING TO LANDLORDS, EMAILING AGENTS, CALLING BROKERS, AND COMBING THROUGH CRAIGSLIST. I WAS LOOKING FOR A TWO-BEDROOM UNDER $1500 TO SHARE WITH A FRIEND OF MINE WHO WAS ALSO NEW TO THE CITY. FINDING A TWO-BEDROOM FOR THAT PRICE ANYWHERE IN NYC IS NEARLY IMPOSSIBLE NOW, BUT IT WASN'T TEN YEARS AGO.

NAVIGATING THE MARKET WAS A DAUNTING TASK FOR ME, HAVING COME FROM SAN FRANCISCO WHERE THE USE OF BROKERS WASN'T AS COMMON AND RENT HADN'T SKYROCKETED YET. IN SF, I GOT ALL MY APARTMENTS SIMPLY BY RESPONDING TO A CRAIGSLIST AD, SHOWING UP, AND WRITING A CHECK. MANY LISTINGS WERE FIRST COME, FIRST SERVE, SO I DIDN'T HAVE TO COMPETE WITH HUNDREDS OF OTHER, MORE QUALIFIED APPLICANTS. I WAS TOTALLY UNPREPARED FOR WHAT AWAITED ME IN NYC, WHERE ALMOST ALL LISTINGS HAVE BROKERS, AND APPLICANTS ARE JUDGED BY THEIR INCOME, NOT THEIR PUNCTUALITY.

I ENCOUNTERED A FEW SCAM ARTISTS DURING MY APARTMENT HUNTING WEEKS. ONE WOMAN, POSING AS A BROKER, SPENT AN AFTERNOON SHOWING ME APARTMENTS AROUND BROOKLYN. WHEN WE LOOKED AT A TWO-BEDROOM IN CLINTON HILL, I WAS SURPRISED TO HEAR HER TELL THE LANDLORD WE WERE ROOMMATES. WHEN I OBJECTED, THE LANDLORD IMMEDIATELY FIGURED OUT WHAT WAS HAPPENING AND TOLD ME THERE WAS NO BROKER ON THE LISTING. TURNED OUT THE WOMAN WAS A CON ARTIST LOOKING TO STEAL ILLEGITIMATE BROKER'S FEES ON RANDOM APARTMENTS SHE FOUND ON CRAIGSLIST. ANOTHER BROKER REQUESTED A "SEARCHER'S FEE" PRIOR TO EVEN LOOKING AT HIS LISTINGS, WHICH IS NOT A THING. THANKFULLY, I DIDN'T FALL FOR IT.

AFTER MANY LONG, HOT, FRUSTRATING DAYS, I FINALLY SETTLED FOR A CRAPPY TWO-BEDROOM ON ELLERY STREET OFF BROADWAY, ON THE BORDER OF BUSHWICK AND BED-STUY. I KNEW I WOULDN'T BE THERE LONG, SO THE BROKEN LOCKS, SLANTED FLOOR, AND WINDOWLESS HALLWAY THAT SERVED AS THE KITCHEN AND LIVING ROOM DIDN'T BOTHER ME. YEARS LATER, A READER RECOGNIZED THE BUILDING FROM A DRAWING AND EMAILED TO INFORM ME THAT SHE HAD LIVED IN THE APARTMENT BELOW MINE. SHE SAID THAT A FEW YEARS AFTER I LEFT, THE BATHTUB IN MY OLD APARTMENT FELL THROUGH THE FLOOR AND INTO HER BATHROOM. NO ONE WAS HURT, BUT WHAT THE FUCK.

I APARTMENT-HOPPED FOR A LITTLE OVER A YEAR BEFORE I FOUND MY BELOVED GREENPOINT STUDIO. I WAS SO RELIEVED TO HAVE FOUND A PLACE I LIKED THAT I STAYED THERE FOR THE NEXT DECADE. ALTHOUGH I WAS GLAD TO HAVE THE TRAUMA OF APARTMENT HUNTING BEHIND ME, IT PIQUED MY CURIOSITY ABOUT OTHER TYPES OF BUILDINGS AND HOUSING I WOULD NOT EXPERIENCE IN THE CITY. I'D BEEN INTRODUCED TO TERMS LIKE CO-OP, PREWAR, CARRIAGE HOUSE, RAILROAD APARTMENT, AND SO MUCH MORE, AND I WAS FASCINATED BY IT ALL. I DECIDED TO INCLUDE A SECTION IN THIS BOOK DEVOTED TO NEW YORK REAL ESTATE, JUST SO I COULD DRAW ALL THE DIFFERENT TYPES OF BUILDINGS AND APARTMENTS I WOULD NEVER LIVE IN, WITH THE EXCEPTION OF MY STUDIO, WHICH IS INCLUDED IN THIS PIECE.

*THIS GUIDE IS INCOMPLETE SIMPLY BECAUSE I COULD NOT COVER ALL TYPES OF BUILDINGS AND APARTMENTS, SO I CHOSE A FEW OF MY FAVORITE PLACES THAT HAD MULTIPLE ARCHITECTURAL AND FLOOR-PLAN STYLES.

VICTORIAN TWO-BEDROOM
IN A QUEEN ANNE BROWNSTONE
196 HANCOCK ST. BED-STUY, BROOKLYN

QUEEN ANNE ARCHITECTURE EMERGED FROM THE VICTORIAN ERA AND WAS POPULAR IN THE UNITED STATES IN THE LATE 1800'S TO THE EARLY 1900'S. QUEEN ANNE BUILDINGS ARE CHARACTERIZED BY STEEPLY PITCHED ROOFS THAT OFTEN HAVE IRREGULAR SHAPES, TURRETS, TOWERS, AND FORWARD-FACING GABLES. THIS BED-STUY QUEEN ANNE BROWNSTONE WAS BUILT IN 1899 AND IS CURRENTLY SPLIT INTO THREE APARTMENTS. HERE'S THE LAYOUT FOR THE FIRST OF FOUR FLOORS. THIS APARTMENT INCLUDES TWO FLOORS (BEDROOMS ON THE SECOND FLOOR) AND THE TOP TWO LEVELS ARE SINGLE-FLOOR, TWO-BEDROOM APARTMENTS.

QUEEN ANNE INTERIOR SCENES

THREE-STORY PENTHOUSE IN A CLOCK TOWER
1 MAIN ST. DUMBO, BROOKLYN

DUMBO'S CLOCKTOWER BUILDING WAS DESIGNED IN 1914 BY WILLIAM HIGGINSON. INITIALLY THE BUILDING WAS INTENDED FOR INDUSTRIAL PURPOSES, AND HOUSED A SERIES OF FACTORIES KNOWN AS "GAIRVILLE," NAMED AFTER OWNER ROBERT GAIR. BY THE 1920'S, IT WAS HOME TO THE CHARLES WILLIAMS STORES, A LARGE FASHION AND HOUSEHOLD MAIL-ORDER BUSINESS. IN 1998, IT WAS CONVERTED INTO A 16-FLOOR, 124-UNIT RESIDENTIAL BUILDING. THE PENTHOUSE WAS LISTED FOR $25 MILLION IN 2010, BUT SOLD FOR $15 MILLION IN 2017. IT WAS THE MOST EXPENSIVE CONDO EVER SOLD IN BROOKLYN.

THE THREE-STORY, 11.5-ROOM PENTHOUSE IS NEARLY 7,000 SF WITH 3 BEDROOMS AND 3.5 BATHROOMS. IT HAS A PRIVATE GLASS ELEVATOR, AND CEILING HEIGHTS RANGING FROM 16 TO 50 FEET. THE FOUR 14-FOOT CLOCKS PROVIDE A 360-DEGREE VIEW OF THE CITY.

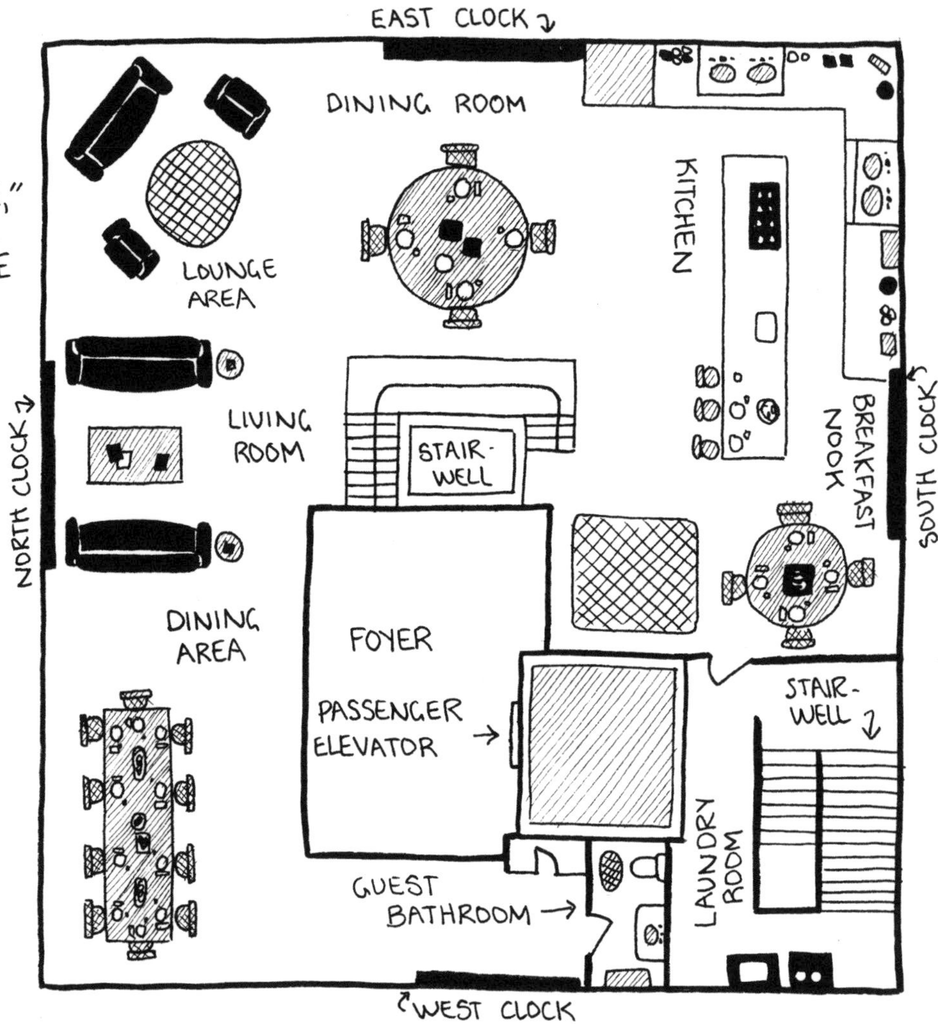

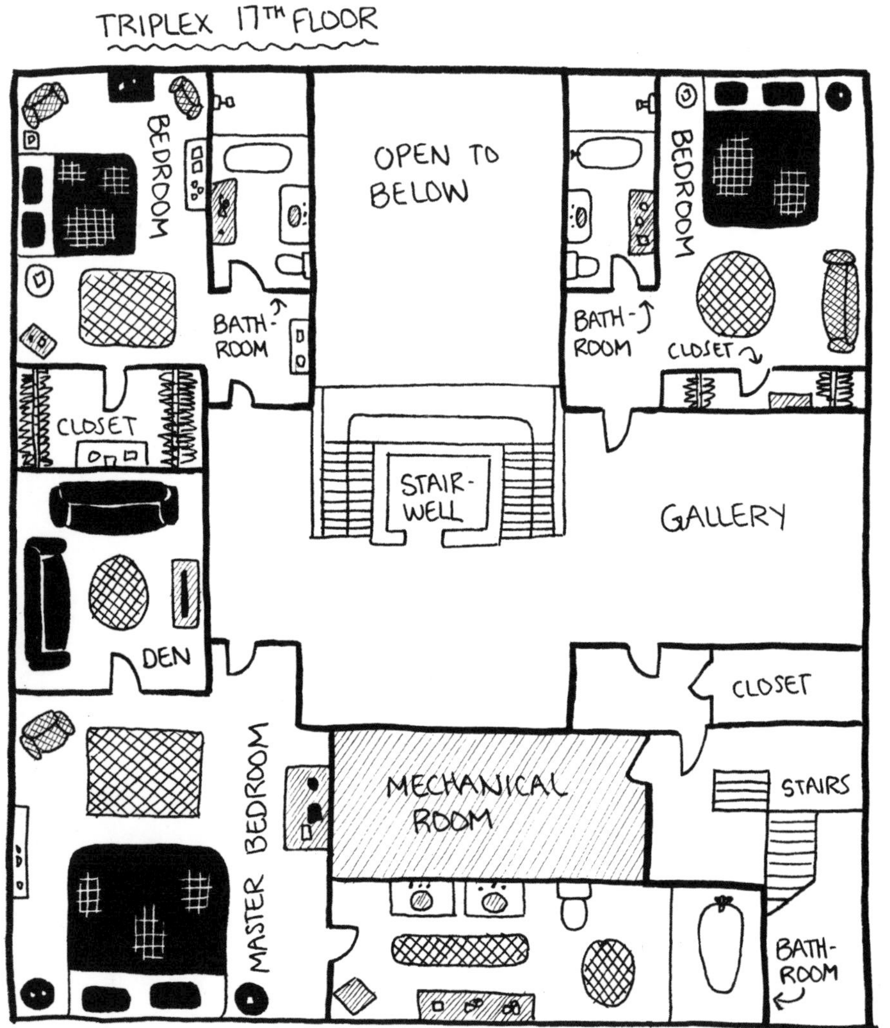

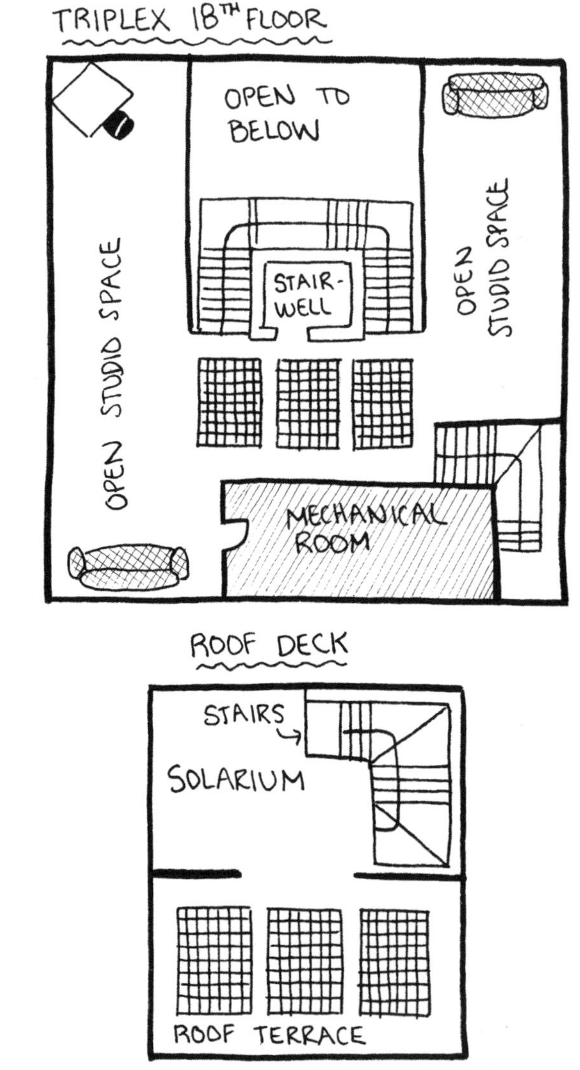

INTERIOR SCENES OF THE CLOCKTOWER PENTHOUSE. FOR THE RECORD, I'M NOT A FAN OF THIS APARTMENT. I FIND THE ELEVATOR -PLACED IN THE MIDDLE OF THE ROOM- TO BE INTRUSIVE, THE LOW WINDOWS ARE AWKWARD, AND NOTHING ABOUT IT IS CHARMING. BUT SUCH SUBJECTIVE DESIGN IS WHAT MAKES IT A GREAT EXAMPLE OF THE CITY'S EXPENSIVE MODERN PENTHOUSES, MANY OF WHICH ARE JUST CONFUSING AND UGLY.

TWO-STORY STAND-ALONE CARRIAGE HOUSE/FIREHOUSE
172 PACIFIC ST. COBBLE HILL, BROOKLYN

CARRIAGE HOUSES ARE STRUCTURES THAT USED TO HOUSE HORSES, BUT HAVE BEEN CONVERTED INTO RESIDENTIAL DWELLINGS. THIS COBBLE HILL CARRIAGE HOUSE WAS BUILT IN 1840, AND WAS ALSO USED AS A FIREHOUSE. IT HAS TWO FLOORS, FOUR BEDROOMS, FOUR BATHROOMS, AND A PERENNIAL GARDEN IN 2010 IT WAS FEATURED IN THE MOVIE *EAT, PRAY, LOVE*, AND WAS FOR SALE FOR ALMOST $8 MILLION. IN 2015, SINGER/SONGWRITER NORAH JONES PURCHASED THE HOUSE FOR $6.5 MILLION.

INTERIOR SCENES OF THE CARRIAGE HOUSE AS IT APPEAR CIRCA 2010

THE BACK OF THE CARRIAGE HOUSE, WHERE THE LARGE DOORS FOR THE HORSES AND FIRE TRUCKS ARE LOCATED.

FUN FACT: NORAH JONES PREVIOUSLY LIVED IN A DIFFERENT HISTORIC COBBLE HILL APARTMENT IN WHICH SHE HAD THE AUDACITY TO ADD WINDOWS TO A WINDOWLESS WALL, INCURRING THE WRATH OF THE COBBLE HILL ASSOCIATION. I'M ALL FOR PRESERVING HISTORY, BUT JONES'S WINDOW ADDITION WAS OF LITTLE CONCERN AND ACTUALLY MADE THE BUILDING NICER. BUT IF THERE'S ANYTHING NEW YORKERS UNANIMOUSLY LOVE COMPLAINING ABOUT, IT'S CHANGE OF ANY KIND.

PRE-WAR DUPLEX IN AN ART DECO LUXURY CO-OP
740 PARK AVE.
MANHATTAN, NEW YORK

740 PARK AVENUE IS A PRIME EXAMPLE OF A HISTORIC, MULTIDEFINITION RESIDENTIAL STRUCTURE. IT WAS DESIGNED BY ROSARIO CANDELA AND ARTHUR LOOMIS HARMON, AND BUILT IN 1929 BY JAMES T. LEE. THE ART DECO STYLE-BUILDING HAS 17 FLOORS AND 31 UNITS, AND IS OFTEN CITED AS NEW YORK'S RICHEST BUILDING, DUE TO ITS WEALTHY TENANTS WHO PAID AN AVERAGE OF $28 MILLION FOR THEIR APARTMENTS, WITH MAINTENANCE FEES OF AROUND $10,000 A MONTH. IN 2014, A DUPLEX SOLD FOR $71.3 MILLION, THE SECOND HIGHEST PRICE EVER PAID FOR A NYC CO-OP APARTMENT.

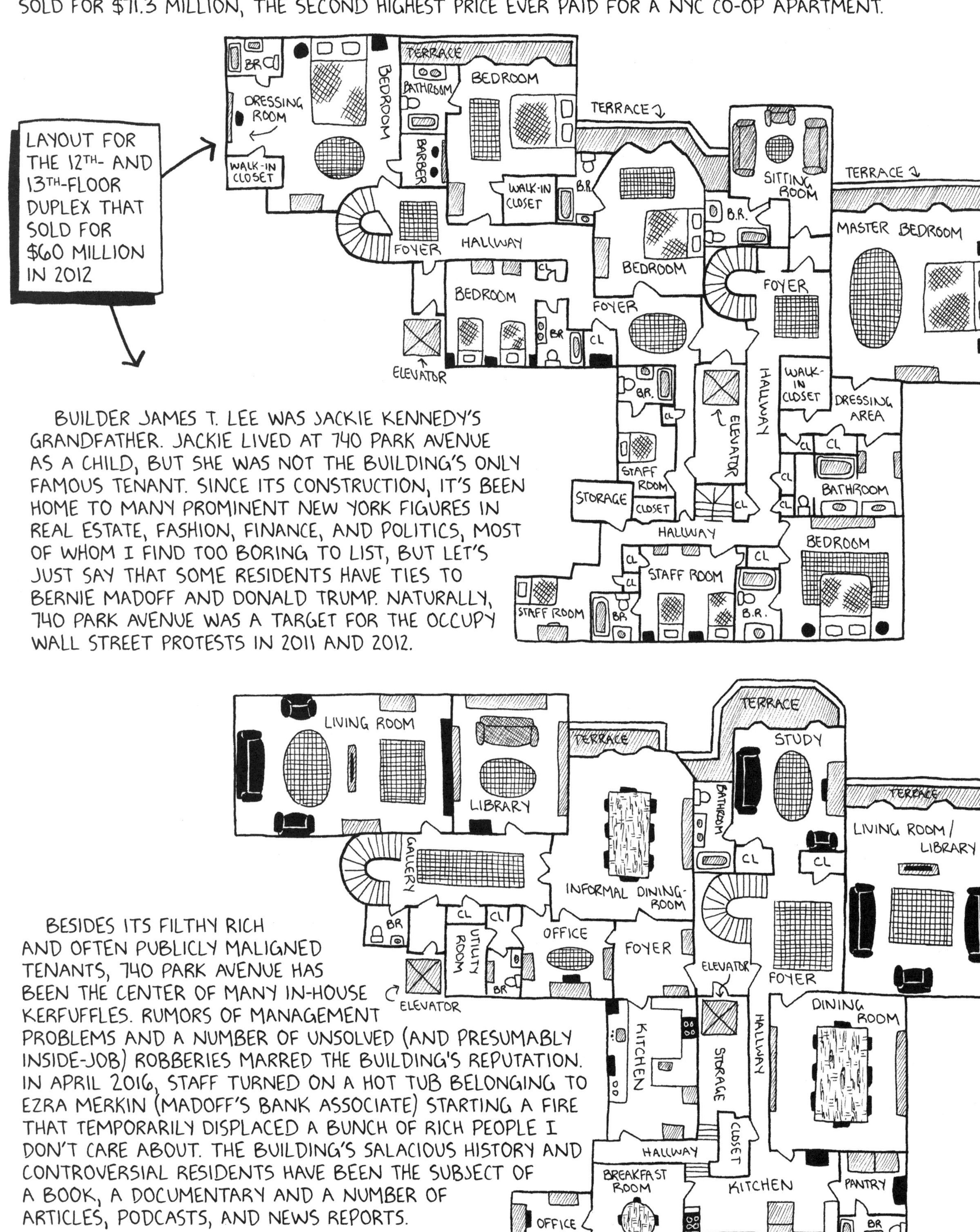

BUILDER JAMES T. LEE WAS JACKIE KENNEDY'S GRANDFATHER. JACKIE LIVED AT 740 PARK AVENUE AS A CHILD, BUT SHE WAS NOT THE BUILDING'S ONLY FAMOUS TENANT. SINCE ITS CONSTRUCTION, IT'S BEEN HOME TO MANY PROMINENT NEW YORK FIGURES IN REAL ESTATE, FASHION, FINANCE, AND POLITICS, MOST OF WHOM I FIND TOO BORING TO LIST, BUT LET'S JUST SAY THAT SOME RESIDENTS HAVE TIES TO BERNIE MADOFF AND DONALD TRUMP. NATURALLY, 740 PARK AVENUE WAS A TARGET FOR THE OCCUPY WALL STREET PROTESTS IN 2011 AND 2012.

BESIDES ITS FILTHY RICH AND OFTEN PUBLICLY MALIGNED TENANTS, 740 PARK AVENUE HAS BEEN THE CENTER OF MANY IN-HOUSE KERFUFFLES. RUMORS OF MANAGEMENT PROBLEMS AND A NUMBER OF UNSOLVED (AND PRESUMABLY INSIDE-JOB) ROBBERIES MARRED THE BUILDING'S REPUTATION. IN APRIL 2016, STAFF TURNED ON A HOT TUB BELONGING TO EZRA MERKIN (MADOFF'S BANK ASSOCIATE) STARTING A FIRE THAT TEMPORARILY DISPLACED A BUNCH OF RICH PEOPLE I DON'T CARE ABOUT. THE BUILDING'S SALACIOUS HISTORY AND CONTROVERSIAL RESIDENTS HAVE BEEN THE SUBJECT OF A BOOK, A DOCUMENTARY AND A NUMBER OF ARTICLES, PODCASTS, AND NEWS REPORTS.

740 PARK AVENUE APARTMENT IN THE 1930'S AND TODAY

740 PARK AVENUE BEDROOMS IN THE 1930'S AND TODAY

GARDEN BASEMENT STUDIO IN A VINYL SIDED ROW HOUSE
JEWEL ST. AND NASSAU AVE.
GREENPOINT, BROOKLYN

GREENPOINT, BROOKLYN IS KNOWN FOR ITS RESIDENTIAL ROW HOUSES COVERED IN VINYL SIDING. THE UBIQUITOUS VINYL IS SEEN AS A BLIGHT TO SOME, BUT OTHERS SEE IT AS A LAST REMAINING VESTIGE OF THE NEIGHBORHOOD'S WORKING CLASS ROOTS. WHEN I FIRST MOVED TO GREENPOINT, I HATED VINYL SIDING, BUT THE MORE I GOT TO KNOW WHAT IT MEANT, THE MORE I SAW IT AS A REMNANT OF THE AREA'S HARDWORKING POLISH RESIDENTS WHO WERE BEING PRICED OUT. AS A YOUNG, MIDDLE CLASS WHITE PERSON, I'D BE REMISS IF I FAILED TO ACKNOWLEDGE MY ROLE IN GENTRIFICATION. WHILE RENTING AN OLD BASEMENT STUDIO DIDN'T HAVE THE SAME IMPACT AS BUYING A NEW CONDO, IT STILL CONTRIBUTED TO THE OVERALL SHIFT IN THE NEIGHBORHOOD'S DEMOGRAPHIC. ANYONE IN SUCH A SITUATION WHO CLAIMS OTHERWISE IS AN ASSHOLE.

I LIVED IN THIS 300-SF GARDEN STUDIO FOR TEN YEARS BEFORE BEING UNCEREMONIOUSLY AND ILLEGALLY EVICTED. BUT BEFORE MY LANDLORD TURNED ON ME, HE ALLOWED ME TO PAY ONLY $800 FLAT A MONTH AS RENTS AROUND THE CITY SOARED. THAT ALLOWANCE WAS NOT OUT OF GENEROSITY, AS I DISCOVERED UPON MY EVICTION, BUT IT'S TOO INCRIMINATING A STORY TO MAKE PUBLIC. (IF YOU ASK ME PRIVATELY, I'LL TOTALLY TELL YOU ALL THE SALACIOUS DETAILS.) THE BOTTOM LINE IS DESPITE THE UGLY ENDING, I GOT AWAY WITH PAYING FAR BELOW MARKET VALUE FOR AN ENTIRE DECADE. GARDEN STUDIO DOES NOT ALWAYS MEAN ACCESS TO THE GARDEN (WHICH I DID NOT HAVE) BUT SOMETIMES SIMPLY MEANS GARDEN LEVEL, WHICH FOR THIS APARTMENT MEANT IT WAS A SUBBASEMENT STUDIO FACING THE BACKYARD.

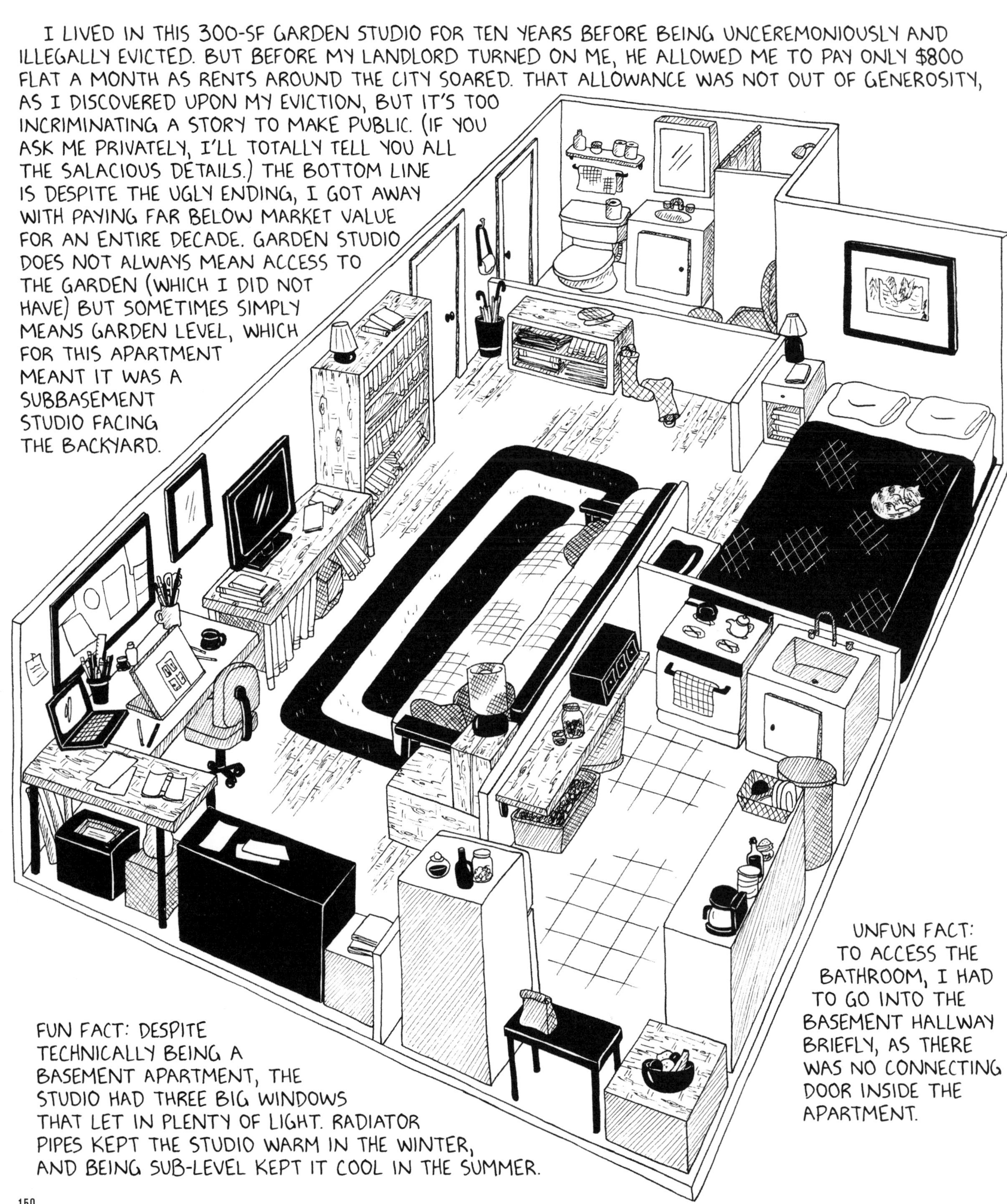

UNFUN FACT: TO ACCESS THE BATHROOM, I HAD TO GO INTO THE BASEMENT HALLWAY BRIEFLY, AS THERE WAS NO CONNECTING DOOR INSIDE THE APARTMENT.

FUN FACT: DESPITE TECHNICALLY BEING A BASEMENT APARTMENT, THE STUDIO HAD THREE BIG WINDOWS THAT LET IN PLENTY OF LIGHT. RADIATOR PIPES KEPT THE STUDIO WARM IN THE WINTER, AND BEING SUB-LEVEL KEPT IT COOL IN THE SUMMER.

INTERIORS OF MY STUDIO

NOTE: THIS IS A VERY CLEANED UP/DUMBED DOWN REPRESENTATION OF MY STUDIO, WHICH HAD WAY MORE STUFF IN IT, ESPECIALLY DURING MY URBAN EXPLORING YEARS. THIS IS WHAT I WISH IT LOOKED LIKE.

STAFF QUARTERS STUDIOS IN A MODERN RESIDENTIAL SKYSCRAPER
432 PARK AVE.
MIDTOWN, MANHATTAN

WHEN 432 PARK AVENUE WAS COMPLETED IN 2015, IT WAS MET WITH MIXED REVIEWS. AS THE SECOND TALLEST BUILDING IN THE CITY (AS OF 2016) IT CAST A THREE-QUARTER-MILE- LONG SHADOW OVER CENTRAL PARK. WHILE SOME PEOPLE PRAISED ITS SIMPLISTIC MODERN DESIGN, OTHERS THOUGHT THE BUILDING WAS UGLY AS HELL AND JOKED ABOUT ITS "TRASH CAN" DESIGN. MANY ALSO TOOK OFFENSE TO ITS ELITIST EXCLUSIVITY AND WASTE OF SPACE IN AN OVERCROWDED CITY IN NEED OF HOUSING. (OUT OF 400,000 SF OF AVAILABLE SPACE, THERE ARE ONLY 104 UNITS.)

DESIGNED BY ARCHITECT RAFAEL VIÑOLY, 432 PARK AVENUE STANDS 1,396 FEET TALL, WITH 96 STORIES. IT IS THE TALLEST RESIDENTIAL BUILDING IN THE WESTERN HEMISPHERE. THE UNITS RANGE FROM 350-SF "STAFF QUARTERS" STUDIOS TO A 8,255-SF PENTHOUSE WITH MONTHLY MAINTENANCE FEES OF NEARLY $33,000. IN 2016, SAUDI REAL ESTATE MAGNATE FAWAZ ALHOKAIR PURCHASED THE PENTHOUSE FOR $87.7 MILLION.

FOR THE PURPOSE OF APARTMENT VARIETY AND EVER-INCREASING BIAS AGAINST LUXURY HOUSING, I DREW THE LAYOUT OF ONE OF THE "STAFF QUARTERS" STUDIOS, WHICH WERE LISTED FOR $1.5 TO $2.8 MILLION. THE STUDIOS RANGE FROM 342 TO 615 SF, WHICH IN A MORE REASONABLE BUILDING IN THE CITY WOULD BE CONSIDERED A NORMAL APARTMENT.

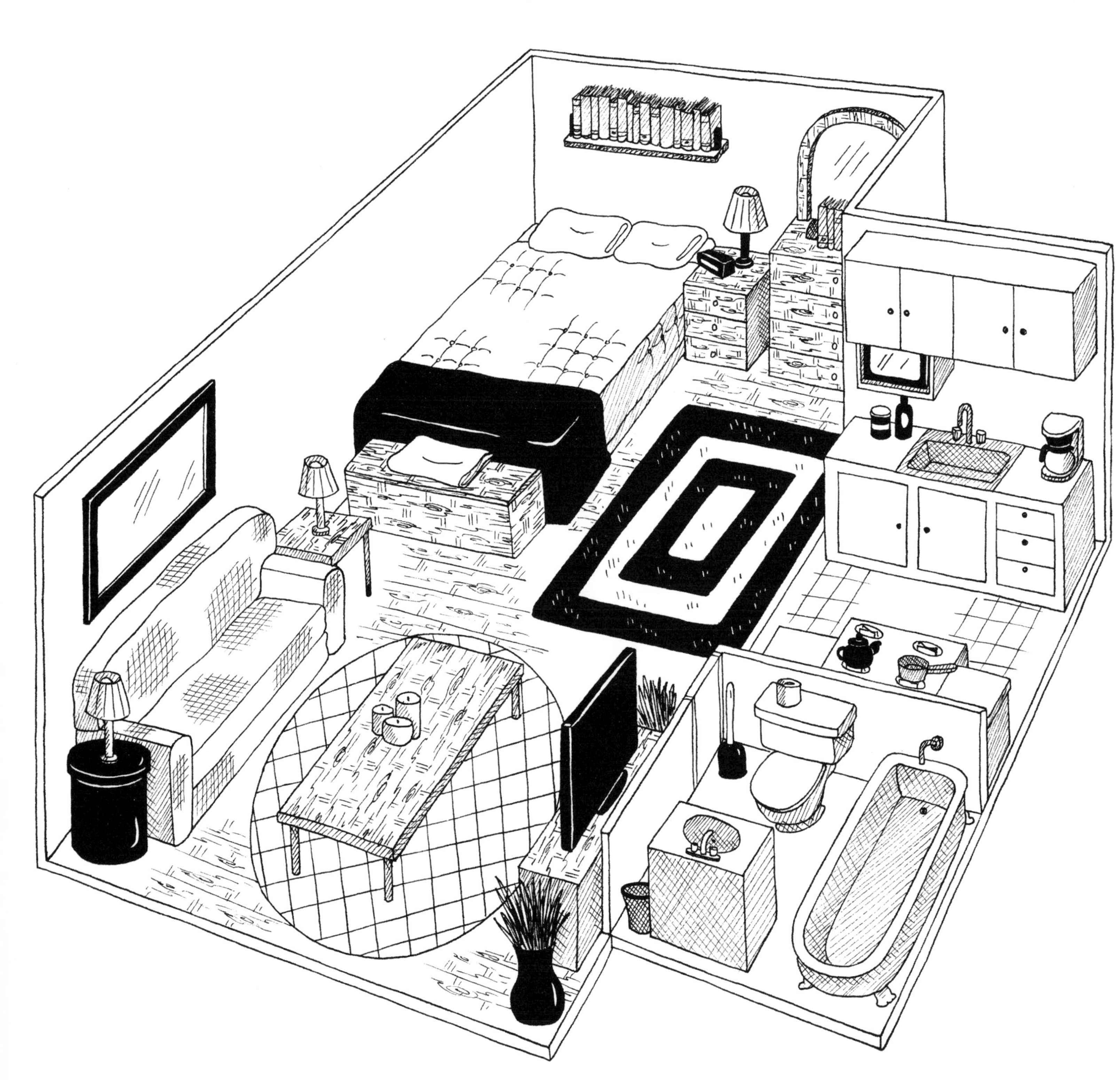

INTERIORS OF THE FIRST FINISHED LUXURY APARTMENT TO BE SHOWN IN THE BUILDING

THREE-BEDROOM APARTMENT IN A PREWAR GOTHIC VICTORIAN
CO-OP WITH NATIONAL HISTORIC LANDMARK STATUS
THE DAKOTA
1 W.72ND ST. UPPER WEST SIDE, MANHATTAN

THE DAKOTA, ONE OF THE MOST FAMOUS RESIDENTIAL BUILDINGS IN THE WORLD, IS AN ARCHITECTURAL AMALGAMATION OF STYLES INCLUDING GOTHIC REVIVAL, FRENCH RENAISSANCE, GERMAN RENAISSANCE, ENGLISH VICTORIAN, AND CHÂTEAUESQUE, TO NAME A FEW. IT WAS BUILT IN 1884 FOR SINGER SEWING MACHINE COMPANY FOUNDER EDWARD CLARK, WHO ORIGINALLY COMMISSIONED THE BUILDING TO HOUSE 60 FAMILIES. PURPORTEDLY, CLARK'S APARTMENT HAD STERLING SILVER FLOORS.

THE DAKOTA IS ARGUABLY MOST FAMOUS FOR BEING THE HOME AND ASSASSINATION SPOT OF JOHN LENNON. YOKO ONO STILL LIVES IN THE BUILDING, AND IT'S RUMORED THERE IS $30,000 HIDDEN BENEATH THE FLOORBOARDS IN THE MASTER BEDROOM OF THE APARTMENT THEY SHARED. ALTHOUGH MANY CELEBRITIES HAVE LIVED IN THE DAKOTA, I'M MORE AMUSED, AND SOMETIMES CONFUSED, BY WHO THE BUILDING'S CO-OP BOARD REJECTED, SUCH AS BILLY JOEL, JUDD APATOW, GENE SIMMONS, ANTONIO BANDERAS, AND MELANIE GRIFFITH.

JUDY GARLAND LIVED IN THE DAKOTA, AND I PICKED HER APARTMENT TO ILLUSTRATE BECAUSE AS A CHILD I WAS OBSESSED WITH THE *WIZARD OF OZ* BOOKS AND FILM. I EVEN MEMORIZED THE ENTIRE MOVIE SCRIPT. GARLAND'S APARTMENT, WHICH WAS RECENTLY ON THE MARKET FOR $16.7 MILLION, HAS 3 BEDROOMS, 2.5 BATHS, AND 7 FIREPLACES.

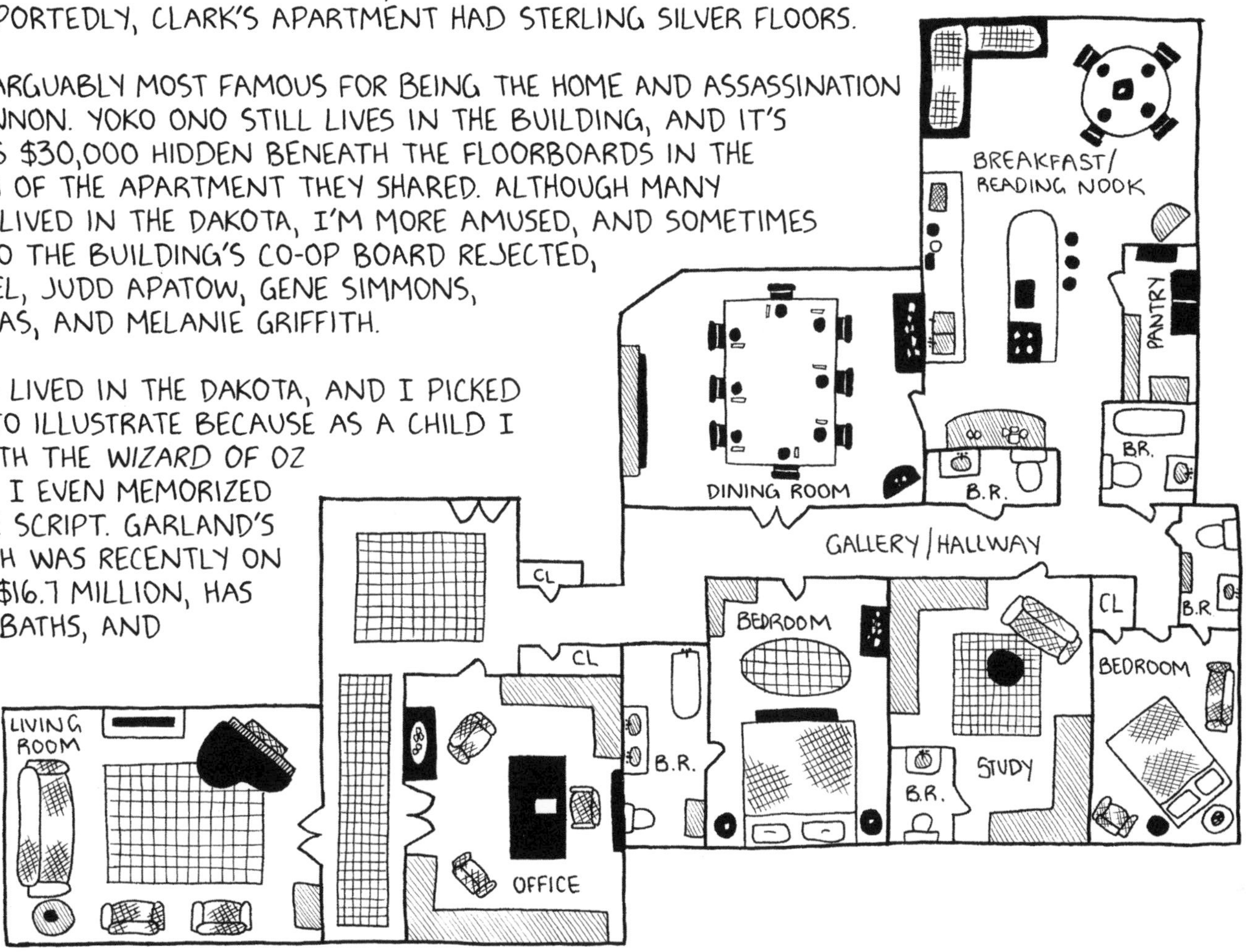

INTERIORS OF JUDY GARLAND'S APARTMENT. I WAS AMUSED TO NOTE THAT RECENT PHOTOS SHOWED THE BEDROOM FIREPLACE BEING USED TO DISPLAY AMETHYST GEODES.

THREE-ROOM RAILROAD APARTMENT IN A MULTI-FAMILY TENEMENT

THE TENEMENT MUSEUM*

97 ORCHARD ST., LOWER EAST SIDE, MANHATTAN

*THIS BUILDING IS PART OF THE MUSEUM, BUT THE VISITOR CENTER IS LOCATED AT 103 ORCHARD ST.

THE BEST HISTORICAL EXAMPLE OF A TENEMENT BUILDING IS IRREFUTABLY THE LOWER EAST SIDE'S TENEMENT MUSEUM. THE MUSEUM HAS PERFECTLY MAINTAINED THE 19TH-CENTURY TENEMENT APARTMENTS, FURNISHING THEM WITH ORIGINAL FURNITURE AND HOUSEHOLD ITEMS.

TENEMENTS WERE OCCUPIED BY POOR IMMIGRANT FAMILIES WHO PACKED THEMSELVES INTO THESE APARTMENTS IN NUMBERS THAT WOULD TODAY BE CONSIDERED ILLEGAL OCCUPATION. THE APARTMENTS WERE TYPICALLY RAILROAD-STYLE FLATS WITH WINDOWLESS ROOMS IN THE MIDDLE. TENEMENTS SPRANG UP IN THE CITY DURING THE INDUSTRIALIZATION OF THE 1800'S, WHEN IMMIGRANTS FLOODED THE CITY AND NEEDED CHEAP, FAST HOUSING. MANY ORIGINAL TENEMENT BUILDINGS STILL STAND, BUT HAVE BEEN RENOVATED AND ARE NO LONGER CALLED TENEMENTS.

LAYOUT OF ONE OF THE MUSEUM'S TENEMENT APARTMENTS. NOTE THE LACK OF BATHROOMS, AS PRIVIES WERE LOCATED IN THE BACKYARD.

INTERIORS OF 97 ORCHARD ST. AS THEY APPEAR TODAY AT THE TENEMENT MUSEUM

TENEMENT FLOOR PLANS FOR 97 ORCHARD ST., REIMAGINED AS MODERN APARTMENTS.

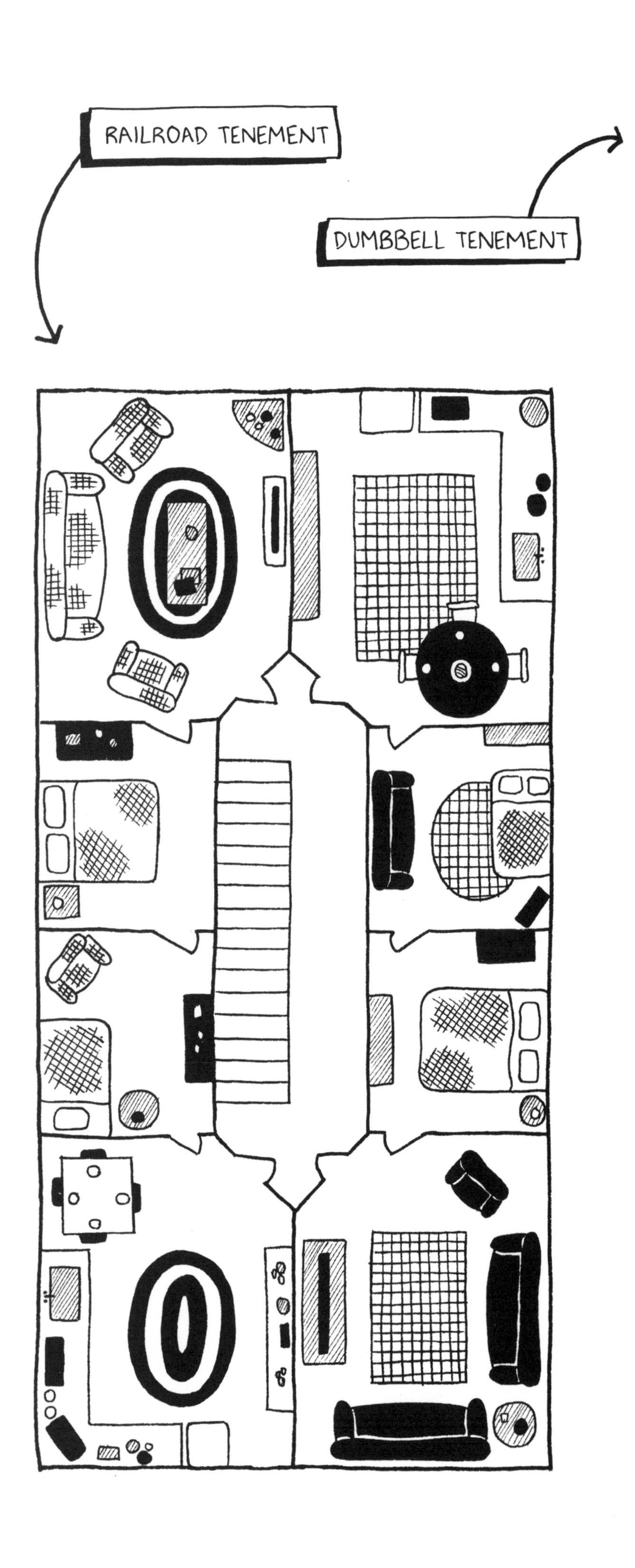

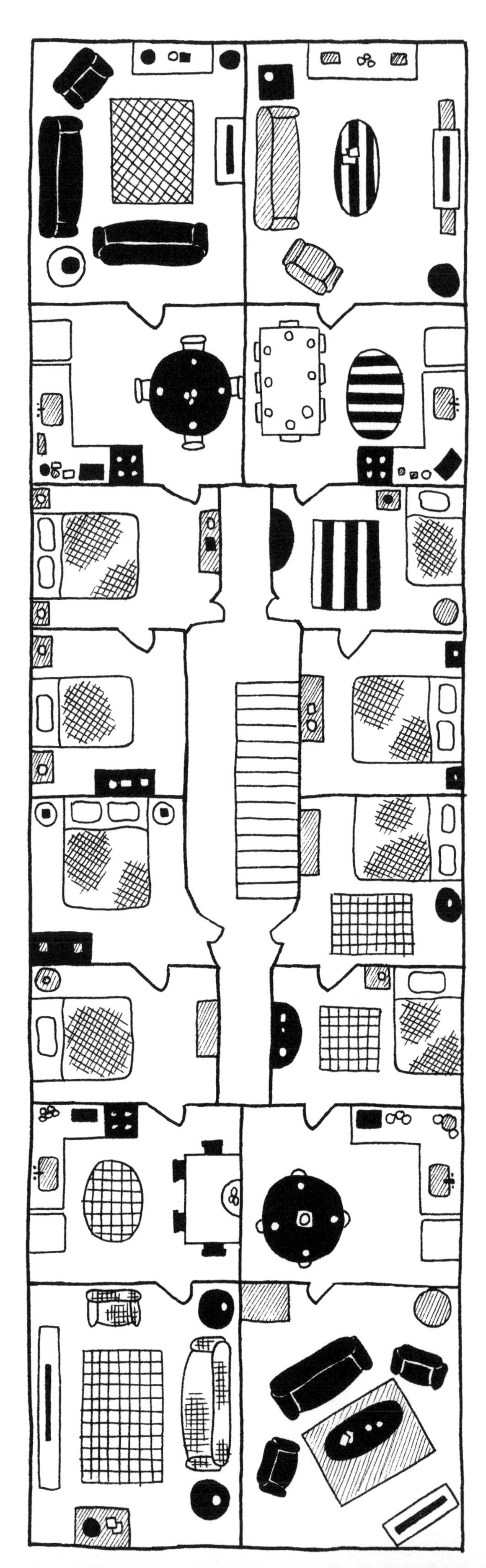

A TENEMENT BACKYARD, WHERE THE PRIVIES WERE LOCATED. MULTIPLE FAMILIES OFTEN SHARED A SINGLE, CRAMPED, FILTHY YARD. BATHROOMS WERE EXTREMELY LIMITED AND OFTEN DOUBLED AS TRASH RECEPTACLES.

MICRO-LIVING: REAL ESTATE'S BIGGEST SCAM

IN JANUARY 2013, NEW YORK CITY INTRODUCED THE FIRST LEGAL MICRO-UNIT APARTMENT BUILDING. THE UNITS RANGED FROM 265 SF TO 360 SF, AND RENTED FOR AROUND $3,000 PER MONTH. LOGICALLY, SUCH SMALL APARTMENTS SHOULD HAVE BEEN HALF THAT PRICE, BUT AS SOON AS THE BUILDING OPENED, IT WAS FILLED TO CAPACITY, AND NO ONE BALKED AT THE PRICE. SO HOW DID THAT HAPPEN?

AROUND THAT TIME, MICRO-LIVING WAS A HOT REAL ESTATE BUZZWORD AND TRENDY CULTURAL CONCEPT. GENERALLY DEFINED AS A LIVING SPACE OF 400 SF OR LESS, MICRO-APARTMENTS BECAME VERY POPULAR OVER THE LAST FIVE YEARS. THANKS TO THE CONCEPT OF MICRO-LIVING AS A LIFESTYLE, CRAMMING YOUR CRAP INTO A TINY CLOSET WAS ELEVATED TO AN ART FORM.

MICRO-LIVING HAS ECONOMIC, SOCIAL, AND OCCASIONALLY HISTORICAL BENEFITS. IN CROWDED CITIES, UNITS CAN BE QUICKLY ASSEMBLED INSIDE PREEXISTING STRUCTURES, PROVIDING FAST AND EFFICIENT HOUSING FOR LOW-INCOME FAMILIES. IT CAN ALSO HELP PRESERVE HISTORIC BUILDINGS BY SAVING THEIR FACADES WHILE CONSTRUCTING NEW HOUSING IN THE GUTTED INTERIOR.

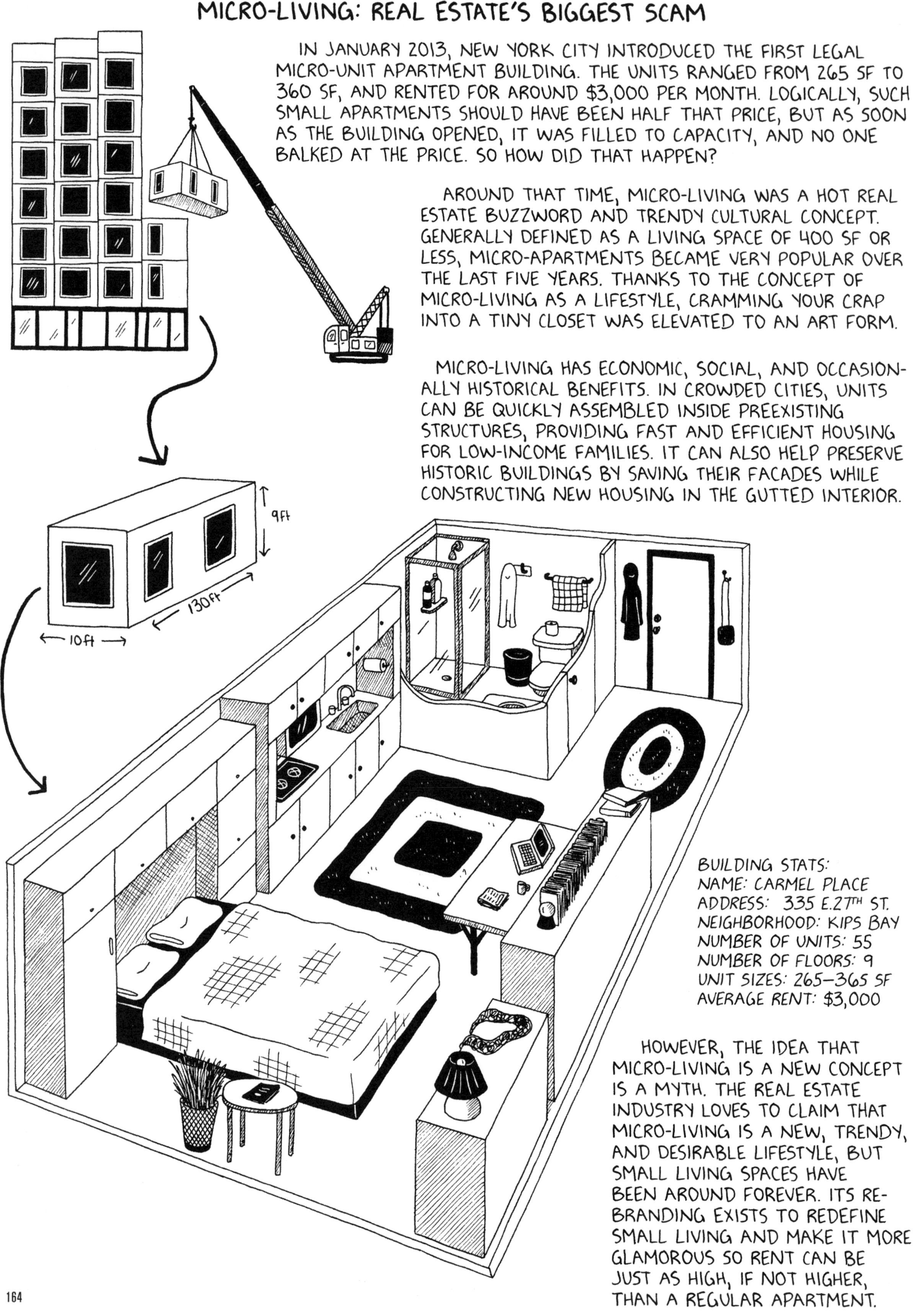

BUILDING STATS:
NAME: CARMEL PLACE
ADDRESS: 335 E.27TH ST.
NEIGHBORHOOD: KIPS BAY
NUMBER OF UNITS: 55
NUMBER OF FLOORS: 9
UNIT SIZES: 265–365 SF
AVERAGE RENT: $3,000

HOWEVER, THE IDEA THAT MICRO-LIVING IS A NEW CONCEPT IS A MYTH. THE REAL ESTATE INDUSTRY LOVES TO CLAIM THAT MICRO-LIVING IS A NEW, TRENDY, AND DESIRABLE LIFESTYLE, BUT SMALL LIVING SPACES HAVE BEEN AROUND FOREVER. ITS REBRANDING EXISTS TO REDEFINE SMALL LIVING AND MAKE IT MORE GLAMOROUS SO RENT CAN BE JUST AS HIGH, IF NOT HIGHER, THAN A REGULAR APARTMENT.

DESPITE SUDDEN POPULARITY, MICRO-LIVING IS NOT A NEW CONCEPT. IN FACT, ONE OF MANKIND'S EARLY DWELLINGS —CAVES— WERE THE ULTIMATE MICRO-UNITS.

INVISIBLE LINE HERE, YOU PLAY ROCK THERE.

IN SUBSEQUENT CENTURIES, SMALL HOUSES WERE OFTEN ALIGNED WITH LOW INCOME, WITH THE EXCEPTION OF PERSONAL TASTE. THEORETICALLY, ONE COULD SAY THE SHACKS OF A THIRD WORLD COUNTRY ARE A FORM OF MICRO-LIVING, BUT THEN YOU'D BE AN ASSHOLE.

WHEN NEW YORK WAS A BOOMTOWN IN THE 1800'S AND EARLY 1900'S, MICRO-LIVING WAS NOT A CONCEPT, IT WAS A REALITY. FAMILIES PACKED THEMSELVES INTO SMALL TENEMENTS, WHERE EACH PERSON HAD AN ESTIMATED AVERAGE OF 15 SQUARE FEET OF PERSONAL SPACE.

BOYS! IT'S SUPPER TIME! STOP FIGHTING AND GO GET YOUR FATHER!
ANNE, I'M HERE. YOU KNOW I'M HERE. I'M ALWAYS RIGHT.FUCKING.HERE.
HEY! GET OUT OF MY SPACE! YOU KNOW WHERE THE INVISIBLE LINE IS!
YEAH, IT'S RIGHT THERE, YA FOPDOODLE!

OVERCROWDED CITIES LIKE BEIJING AND TOKYO HAVE BEEN UTILIZING MICRO-UNITS FOR DECADES. IN LONDON, SMALL UNITS ARE KNOWN AS "A BEDSIT." IN NIGERIA THEY ARE CALLED "FACE-TO-FACE" APARTMENTS. IN THE USA THEY ARE KNOWN AS "SRO," FOR 'SINGLE ROOM OCCUPANCY.'

SRO LAYOUT COMMONLY SEEN OUTSIDE OF GOVERNMENT ASSISTANCE SRO BUILDINGS
BOARDING HOUSE STYLE SRO LAYOUT
BEDROOM
BATH-ROOM
SHARED KITCHEN
BEDROOM
BED-ROOM
BEDROOM
HALLWAY
BED-ROOM
BEDROOM
SHARED BATHROOM
SHARED KITCHEN

HOWEVER, REAL ESTATE AGENTS ARE QUICK TO POINT OUT THE DIFFERENCES BETWEEN AN SRO UNIT AND A MICRO-APARTMENT.

SRO UNITS USUALLY HAVE SHARED BATHROOMS AND KITCHENS, WHILE MOST MICRO-APARTMENTS ARE PRIVATE AND HAVE ALL THE REGULAR AMENITIES. WITH EXCEPTIONS, SRO UNITS ARE GENERALLY RESERVED FOR GOVERNMENT ASSISTANCE HOUSING, WHILE MICRO-APARTMENTS ARE GEARED MORE TOWARD THE MIDDLE AND UPPER CLASSES. AND SUCKERS.

BY THE 2000'S, NEW YORK CITY WAS OVERPOPULATED AND SHOWED NO SIGNS OF SLOWING GROWTH, AND REAL ESTATE WAS SCARCE. BUILDINGS WERE GETTING BIGGER AND APARTMENTS WERE GETTING SMALLER, BUT PRICES WERE SKYROCKETING, WHICH WAS A CHALLENGE FOR THE REAL ESTATE INDUSTRY.

BUILDINGS
APARTMENT SIZE
PRICE
1960 1970 1980 1990 2000 2010
THIS IS A DISASTER! HOW ARE WE SUPPOSED TO SELL THESE TINY, OVERPRICED APARTMENTS?
NO, THIS ISN'T A DISASTER, THIS IS A CLASSIC METROPOLITAN DILEMMA THAT WILL EQUAL HUGE PROFITS IF WE SPIN IT JUST RIGHT.

HMMMM....
OH MY GOD, I'VE GOT IT! AND IT'S *BRILLIANT*!

WE'RE GOING TO REBRAND THESE SHITTY, SMALL-ASS APARTMENTS AS "MICRO-LIVING" UNITS. WE'RE GOING TO SELL A HIP LIFESTYLE INSTEAD OF SPATIAL NIGHTMARE.
YOU'RE A GENIUS! ALL WE HAVE TO DO IS MAKE "TINY" COOL AND SEXY, AND THOSE RUBES WILL EAT IT UP!

THE PLAN WORKED, BECAUSE TURNING A SHIT SITUATION INTO A LIFESTYLE IS THE EASIEST WAY TO TRICK PEOPLE INTO PAYING MORE FOR LESS.

OKAY, HERE'S AN APARTMENT FOR $1,500 A MONTH AND, OH, WAIT, NO, THAT'S A CLOSET. THAT IS LITERALLY A CLOSET WITH A BED IN IT.
HM...WAIT, HERE'S SOMETHING- A "MICRO-APARTMENT" FOR $2,500.
OOOH, A MICRO-APARTMENT! I READ ABOUT THOSE IN *THE TIMES*! WE SHOULD DEFINITELY DO THAT, IT'D BE SO FUN!

THE TERM "MICRO-LIVING" CAUGHT ON FAST, BECOMING A POPULAR CULTURAL BUZZWORD.

WE'RE APARTMENT HUNTING RIGHT NOW, AND WE'VE SEEN A COUPLE OF SUPER SMALL PLACES.

OH, YEAH, THOSE ARE MICRO-UNITS. THEY'RE PUTTING THEM UP ALL OVER THE CITY. MICHAEL LIVES IN ONE ACTUALLY!

YUP, I HAVE A 270-SF PLACE IN THE LOWER EAST SIDE.

WELL MY APARTMENT IN ASTORIA IS ONLY 250 SF!

CURSE MY EXTRA 50 SF!

AS MICRO-LIVING GREW AS A CONCEPT, PREVIOUSLY EXISTING SMALL SPACES —SUCH AS JAPAN'S CAPSULE HOTELS— WERE REBRANDED AND ENJOYED A SURGE IN POPULARITY.
MANY NEW BUSINESSES POPPED UP, SPECIALIZING IN MICRO-SPACE ORGANIZATION.
WITH OUR NEW *CABINET WALL*, YOUR WALL IS ALSO YOUR BED, CLOSET, AND STORAGE SPACE!
CALL NOW 1-800-431-7291
CABINET WALL
$299.99

BY 2010, MICRO-LIVING HAD BECOME A HUGELY SUCCESSFUL INDUSTRY.
WITH THIS STYLISH CABINET WALL, YOU HAVE AMPLE STORAGE, PLUS THE TABLE AND BED FOLD UP INTO THE WALL!
WAIT, WHERE'S THE BED?
RIGHT HERE! THIS TABLE FOLDS OUT TO BECOME A FULL BED! NOTHING IS WHAT IT SEEMS, WHICH IS ONE OF THE MANY WONDERS OF TINY, I MEAN MICRO, APARTMENTS.
MICRO-LIVING BECAME THE INSPIRATION FOR MANY BLOGS, TV SHOWS, PODCASTS, AND COMEDIC SATIRE.*
WHERE'S THE BATHROOM?
WHERE ISN'T THE BATHROOM?
*SCENE FROM BROAD CITY
AS YOU PROBABLY KNOW, YOURS TRULY LIVED IN A 300-SF STUDIO FOR TEN YEARS. IT WAS WHERE THE MAJORITY OF THIS BOOK WAS MADE, AND IT WAS EVEN FEATURED ON CURBED NY AND THE LOCAL NEWS. YUP, I WAS ON THE NEWS ONCE, AND I NEVER STOPPED TALKING ABOUT IT!
WHEN ALL IS SAID AND DONE, IT WILL BE UP TO THOSE LIVING THE MICRO-LIFESTYLE TO DECIDE WHETHER OR NOT MICRO-LIVING IS PRACTICAL AND FUN, OR TOTAL FUCKING BULLSHIT.
I'M SO GLAD WE DECIDED TO GET RID OF ALL OUR THINGS AND DO THIS MICRO-LIFESTYLE THING!
YEAH, WE DIDN'T NEED ALL THAT SPACE! AND THE BATHROOM WAS SO FAR AWAY, I HATED GOING IN THE MIDDLE OF THE NIGHT.
ACTUALLY, I'M GOING TO THE BATHROOM RIGHT NOW! THE TOILET IS PART OF THE BED.
LOOK, I'M MAKING BREAKFAST IN BED, NOT JUST EATING IT. THIS IS THE AMERICAN DREAM!

WILLIAMSBURG & BUSHWICK THEN & NOW

GRAHAM AVE. AND METROPOLITAN AVE. IN 1937

GRAHAM AVE. AND METROPOLITAN AVE. IN 2015

THE WILLOUGHBY THEATER OPENED IN 1913 AND CLOSED IN 1951. FOR MANY YEARS IT ONLY SCREENED ITALIAN FILMS, TO CATER TO THE MOSTLY ITALIAN LOCAL COMMUNITY, BEFORE BRANCHING OUT.

KNICKERBOCKER AVE. AND WILLOUGHBY AVE. IN 1926

TWO YEARS AFTER CLOSING, THE WILLOUGHBY THEATER WAS TURNED INTO A DANCE AND CATERING HALL. CURRENTLY, IT IS HOME TO A BAPTIST CHURCH.

KNICKERBOCKER AVE. AND WILLOUGHBY AVE. IN 2016

THE RAINBOW THEATER WAS ONE OF THE FEW THEATERS BUILT IN THE CITY DURING THE DEPRESSION ERA. DUE TO FINANCIAL CONSTRICTIONS, IT WAS RARELY ADVERTISED, LEAVING ITS EXACT OPENING DATE TO SPECULATION. IT CLOSED IN THE LATE 1960'S.

FOR MANY YEARS, THE THEATER WAS HOME TO THE LOVE CHAPEL, A CHRISTIAN OUTREACH PROGRAM AND CHURCH. THE BUILDING WAS DEMOLISHED IN 2012 AND REPLACED WITH APARTMENTS.

GRAHAM AVE. AND CONSELYEA ST. IN 1935
J. LUICK
PRINTER
372
GRAHAM
CONSELYEA
GRAHAM AVE FLORIST
FLORIST
GRAHAM AVE. AND CONSELYEA ST. IN 2016
CONSELYEA
MESA COYOACAN
GRAHAM
CONSELYEA
MEI YING QIGONG TUI NA
TEL: 938-782-3093
ACU
CHO'S VARIETY 368
ONE WAY
FOOT RUB BACK RUB
FOOT RUB
ACUPUNCTURE BACK & FOOT RUB
OPEN
am NEW YORK
metro

27-29 BUSHWICK AVE. IN 1915. BUSHWICK, BROOKLYN

27-29 BUSHWICK AVE. IN 2016

STATEN ISLAND'S TRASH TROUBLE

FOR MORE THAN A CENTURY, STATEN ISLAND HAS BEEN NEW YORK CITY'S DUMPING GROUNDS FOR GARBAGE, BODIES, AND THE POOR AND HOMELESS. IN THE MID-1800'S, THE CITY OPENED FARM COLONY, WHERE IT SENT THE CITY'S POOR TO LIVE AND WORK ON FARMLAND. IN THE 1960'S, THE MARINE SCRAPYARD BECAME A GRAVEYARD OF RETIRED AND ABANDONED BOATS. TUBERCULOSIS PATIENTS WERE SENT TO SEAVIEW, WHERE THEY COULD REMAIN IN ISOLATION ON THE ISLAND. BUT FOR A LITTLE OVER 50 YEARS, THE CITY'S BIGGEST "CONTRIBUTION" TO STATEN ISLAND WAS TRASH.

IN 1947, FRESH KILLS LANDFILL WAS OPENED AND BEGAN RECEIVING BOATLOADS OF GARBAGE. BY 1985, IT HANDLED 90% OF THE CITY'S REFUSE. WITH THE CLOSING OF OTHER NEARBY LANDFILLS, FRESH KILLS WAS AT ONE POINT THE LARGEST LANDFILL IN THE WORLD. YEAH, THE WORLD. IN A CITY WHERE WE ALL LIVE ON TOP OF EACH OTHER, CRAM OUR BODIES INTO SUBWAY CARS, AND FIGHT FOR SPACE ON THE SIDEWALK, WE HAD ROOM FOR THE WORLD'S LARGEST PILE OF TRASH. AT ITS PEAK, IT WAS TALLER THAN THE STATUE OF LIBERTY. THE LANDFILL CLOSED IN EARLY 2001, WITH PLANS TO HAVE IT CAPPED AND TURNED IT INTO OPEN PARK SPACE FOR THE PUBLIC.

FRESH KILLS WOULD HAVE DROPPED OFF THE CULTURAL RADAR PERMANENTLY, WERE IT NOT FOR 9/11. WHEN THE TWIN TOWERS FELL, THEY CREATED A MASSIVE AMOUNT OF RUBBLE, WHICH THE CITY DID NOT HAVE ROOM FOR. SHIPPING CRATES WERE FILLED WITH DEBRIS AND STASHED AT FRESH KILLS LANDFILL WHICH TEMPORARILY REOPENED. THE STORY MIGHT HAVE ENDED THERE, HAD THE RUBBLE NOT CONTAINED HUMAN REMAINS. FOR YEARS, FORENSIC SPECIALISTS AND DETECTIVES COMBED OVER THE DEBRIS, RECOVERING 4,257 HUMAN REMAINS AND IDENTIFYING 300 BODIES.

EVENTUALLY THE SEARCH FOR REMAINS WAS CALLED OFF, MUCH TO THE DISMAY OF FAMILIES WHO STILL BELIEVE MORE HUMAN REMAINS ARE IN THE PILES OF DEBRIS. THEN THE CITY ANNOUNCED PLANS TO TURN THE LANDFILL INTO A PARK CALLED FRESHKILLS PARK, AND POSSIBLY 9/11 MEMORIAL, WHICH WOULD MEAN BURYING ALL THE UNSORTED REMAINS. PARK CONSTRUCTION BEGAN IN 2008, AND WAS GIVEN A COMPLETION DATE OF 2037. ALTHOUGH THE PARK PLAN IS SLOWLY PROGRESSING, THE BURYING OF THE 9/11 RUBBLE REMAINS A POLARIZING AND UNRESOLVED ISSUE.

STATEN ISLAND'S BOAT GRAVEYARD

JUST SOUTH OF THE FRESH KILLS LANDFILL IS THE STATEN ISLAND BOAT GRAVEYARD WHERE DOZENS OF SHIPS ARE SLOWLY DECOMPOSING. THE AREA IS KNOWN BY A NUMBER OF NAMES, THE ORIGINAL BEING THE WITTE MARINE SCRAPYARD. TODAY IT'S KNOWN AS THE DONJON IRON AND METAL SCRAP PROCESSING FACILITY.

THE GRAVEYARD IS MADE UP OF TWISTED, RUSTED METAL, AND DECOMMISSIONED BOATS—RANGING FROM WARSHIPS TO GIANT PASSENGER FERRIES TO DINGHIES—THAT LAY ROTTING IN A HIGHLY POLLUTED STRETCH OF RIVERBED ALONG THE ARTHUR KILL WATERWAY.

IN THE 1960'S, WITTE'S MARINE EQUIPMENT COMPANY BEGAN ACQUIRING DISCARDED BOATS FOR SALVAGE. AT ITS PEAK, THE WATERWAY HOUSED AROUND 400 BOATS, MANY OF WHICH WERE STILL INTACT, BY ORDER OF JOHN J. WITTE, WHO OWNED THE GRAVEYARD UNTIL HIS DEATH IN 1980. WHEN THE PROPERTY WAS TURNED OVER TO DONJON MARINE COMPANY, A WALL WAS ERECTED ALONG THE SHORE AND MOST OF THE BOATS WERE DISMANTLED, TO EITHER HAVE THEIR PARTS SALVAGED, OR TO BE SUNK IN THE RIVER. THE ESTIMATE FOR BOATS REMAINING TODAY IS A LITTLE OVER TWO DOZEN.

A FEW OF THE BOATS ARE FAMOUS, SUCH AS THE *ABRAM S. HEWITT* FIREBOAT. OPERATIONAL FROM 1903 TO 1958, THE BOAT'S CLAIM TO FAME WAS ASSISTING IN THE FAMOUS SHIPWRECK OF THE *PS. GENERAL SLOCUM* IN 1904. THE PASSENGER FERRY WAS MAKING ITS ANNUAL TREK TO A PICNIC SITE ON LONG ISLAND WHEN IT CAUGHT ON FIRE. A SERIES OF CARELESS MISHAPS SUCH AS ROTTED FIRE HOSES, MISPLACED FLAMMABLE LIQUIDS, CHEAP RESCUE EQUIPMENT, AND INACCESSIBLE LIFEBOATS LED TO THE DEATHS OF OVER 1,000 PASSENGERS, MOSTLY WOMEN AND CHILDREN. MANY VICTIMS' BODIES WASHED ASHORE ON NORTH BROTHER ISLAND.

THE BOAT GRAVEYARD IS A COMMONLY VISITED/PHOTOGRAPHED PLACE, AND MANY WEBSITES CLAIM IT'S DIFFICULT TO ACCESS, BUT THAT'S BULLSHIT. HERE ARE SOME INSTRUCTIONS: FIRST, YOU WALK THROUGH THE SLEIGHT FAMILY GRAVEYARD, WHICH YOU SHOULD STOP AND LOOK AT BECAUSE SOME OF THE GRAVES DATE BACK TO THE 1700'S. BEYOND THE GRAVEYARD IS A MOSTLY OBSCURED PATHWAY THAT YOU FOLLOW STRAIGHT OUT ONTO THE REEDY MARSHLANDS. WHEN FACING THE WATER, TO YOUR LEFT IS A SMALL CREEK AND SHRUBBERY-COVERED HILL, WHICH YOU CLIMB OVER/THROUGH, AND THEN YOU'LL BE AT THE MAIN PART OF THE BOAT GRAVEYARD. YOU CAN ALSO KAYAK THERE TO GET A CLOSER LOOK AT THE BOATS.

THE HILDA—A US NAVY RESCUE TUG FROM WWII

PILES OF DISCARDED RUSTY BOAT JUNK. VISIBILITY OF THIS AREA VARIES WITH THE TIDES, AS DOES MOST OF THE SCRAPYARD.

NEW YORK STATE PORT AUTHORITY PASSENGER FERRY.

THE BLOXOM- A 1944 TUGBOAT BUILT IN WEST VIRGINIA FOR THE US ARMY.

RUSTY BOAT ENGINES AND GEARS.

ONE OF THE NEWEST ADDITIONS—THE *JOHN B. CADDELL*, A 168 FOOT WATER TANKER THAT WAS PUSHED ONTO FRONT STREET DURING HURRICANE SANDY.

THE USS *SPARTAN*- A MINESWEEPER USED BY THE US NAVY FROM 1917-1919.

OLD WHEELHOUSE ON THE SHORE.

INSIDE THE WHEELHOUSE.

THEATERS OF STATEN ISLAND THEN & NOW

THE EMPIRE THEATRE OPENED IN 1916 AND OPERATED UNTIL 1978. SHORTLY BEFORE CLOSING, THE THEATER SCREENED ADULT FILMS, MUCH TO THE CHAGRIN OF ITS UPTIGHT NEIGHBORS.

THE YEAR THE EMPIRE CLOSED, IT WAS PURCHASED BY FARRELL LUMBER, WHO USED IT FOR STORAGE UNTIL 2012. IN 2013, RESCUE MINISTRIES CHURCH TOOK OVER THE BUILDING AND RENOVATED THE INTERIOR. THERE ARE PHOTOS OF THE RENOVATION ON THEIR WEBSITE.

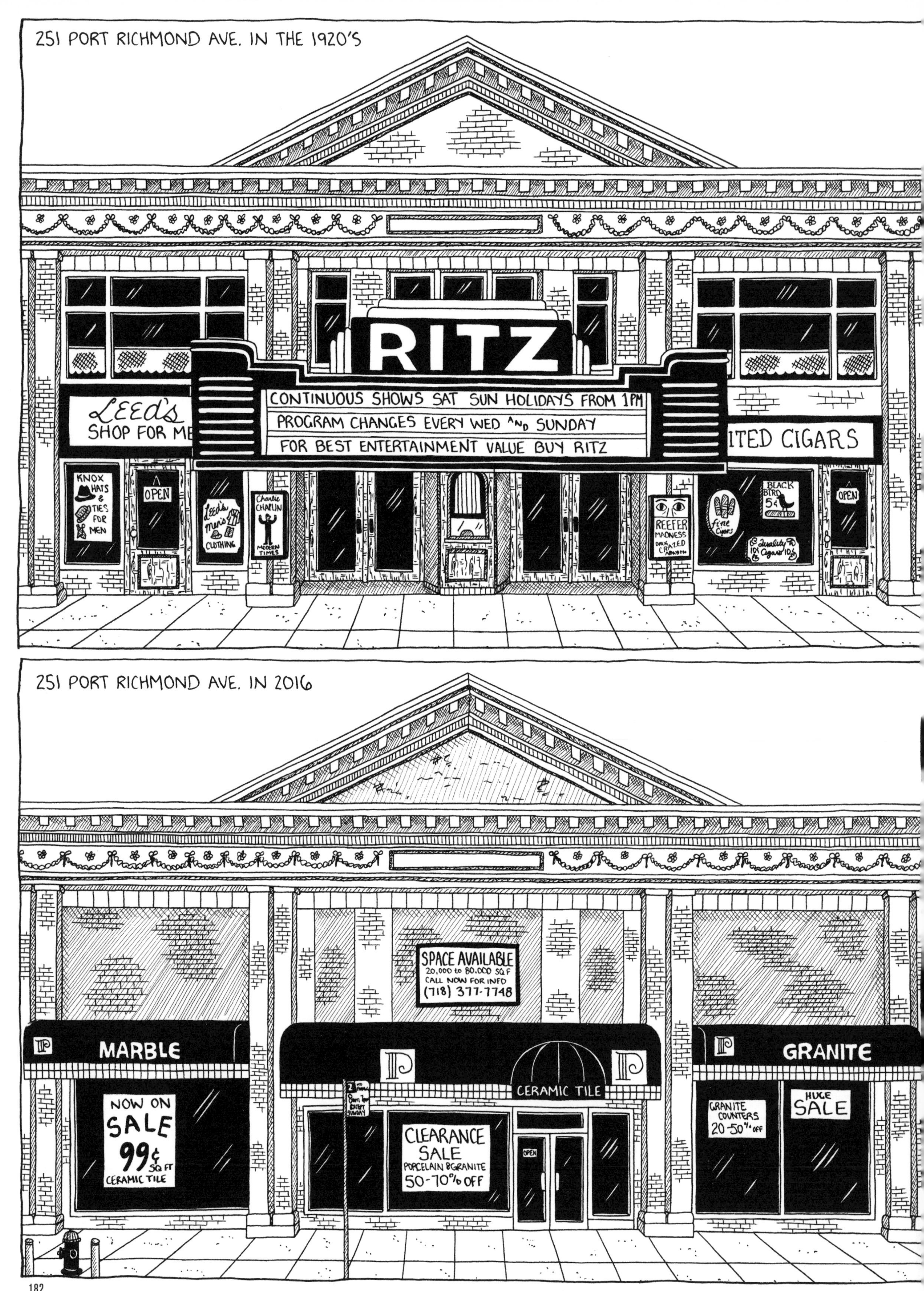
251 PORT RICHMOND AVE. IN THE 1920'S
RITZ
CONTINUOUS SHOWS SAT SUN HOLIDAYS FROM 1PM
PROGRAM CHANGES EVERY WED AND SUNDAY
FOR BEST ENTERTAINMENT VALUE BUY RITZ
LEED'S
SHOP FOR ME
ITED CIGARS
KNOX HATS & TIES FOR MEN
OPEN
Leed's Men's CLOTHING
Charlie CHAPLIN
MODERN TIMES
REEFER MADNESS
CRAZED
Fine Cigars
BLACK BIRD 5¢
Quality Cigars 10¢ 10¢
OPEN
251 PORT RICHMOND AVE. IN 2016
SPACE AVAILABLE
20,000 to 80,000 SQ F
CALL NOW FOR INFO
(718) 377-7748
MARBLE
CERAMIC TILE
GRANITE
NOW ON SALE 99¢ SQ FT CERAMIC TILE
CLEARANCE SALE
PORCELAIN & GRANITE
50-70% OFF
OPEN
GRANITE COUNTERS 20-50% OFF
HUGE SALE

168 NEW DORP LN. IN 1964
Lane
Lane
A HARD DAYS NIGHT
DR. STRANGELOVE
MATINEE MON-FRI 50¢
KARL EHMER
PRIME MEATS
HAM 59¢lb
Rolled BEEF ROAST 55¢lb
PORK ROAST 50¢lb
Roast CHICKEN 29¢lb +Sides
Broiler CHICKEN 45¢lb +SIDES
the Last Man on Earth
The Beatles
A Hard DAYS Night
Matinee EVERY MONDAY-FRIDAY 50¢
DELI
Cold Beer
Hot Coffee
168 NEW DORP LN. IN 2016
Lane
VILLA MONTE
PIZZERIA RESTAURANT
VILLA MONTE
PIZZERIA & RESTAURANT 718-663-0490
ITALIAN ICES
A
PIZZA
CROSSROADS CHURCH
BAGELS ON THE LA
HOT & COLD SANDWICHES
CATERING · CIGARETTES
OPEN
ATM
ATM
OPEN

THE AMBIGUOUS ORIGINS OF NEW YORK CITY'S FAMOUS
Egg Cream
FOX'S
u-bet
ORIGINAL
CHOCOLATE
FLAVOR SYRUP
NET WT 22 oz
WHOLE
MILK
CLASSIC EGG CREAM RECIPE:
-2 TABLESPOONS FOX'S U-BET CHOCOLATE SYRUP*
-1 1/2 OUNCES WHOLE MILK
-3/4 CUP SELTZER
-A FOUNTAIN GLASS
*YOU CAN USE ANY SYRUP YOU WANT, BUT EGG CREAM PURISTS SWEAR BY FOX'S U-BET
The Soda Fountain
Try our original
u-bet CHOCOLATE
Egg Cream
ALSO AVAILABLE IN
STRAWBERRY & VANILLA
5¢
Brooklyn, New York

WHAT IS AN EGG CREAM? IT'S A MIXTURE OF MILK, SELTZER WATER, AND CHOCOLATE (OR VANILLA AND STRAWBERRY) FLAVORED SYRUP. THERE IS NEITHER EGG NOR CREAM IN AN EGG CREAM. THE SWEET CONCOCTION WAS ONE OF THE MOST POPULAR DRINKS AT SODA FOUNTAINS FROM THE LATE 1800'S TO THE MID 1900'S. ALTHOUGH THE EGG CREAM WENT NATIONWIDE, ITS POPULARITY REMAINED MOSTLY AN EAST COAST THING, AND MAINLY IN NEW YORK CITY.

THE EXACT HISTORY OF THE EGG CREAM IS OF SOME DEBATE, BUT THE MOST POPULAR CLAIM IS THAT IT WAS CREATED IN THE 1890'S BY LOUIS AUSTER AT HIS BROOKLYN CANDY SHOP.

OTHERS BELIEVE IT WAS INVENTED BY BORIS THOMASHEFSKY, A FAMOUS YIDDISH ACTOR, AFTER HE DRANK A SIMILAR BEVERAGE IN PARIS.*

*I REJECT THIS THEORY, SINCE IT ONLY MEANS HE BROUGHT THE DRINK TO AMERICA, HE DIDN'T CREATE IT.

NO ONE KNOWS FOR SURE THE ORIGINS OF THE NAME "EGG CREAM." IT'S BEEN SUGGESTED IT WAS DERIVED FROM VERBAL MISUNDERSTANDINGS.

AUSTER'S CREATION WAS A HUGE SUCCESS, AND MANY SODA FOUNTAINS BEGAN SERVING EGG CREAMS, WHICH WERE ENJOYED BY EVERYONE.

AUSTER'S RECIPE WAS A CAREFULLY GUARDED SECRET.

IT WAS RUMORED THAT WHEN AUSTER TURNED DOWN AN OFFER FROM A MAJOR ICE CREAM COMPANY FOR HIS RECIPE, THE EXECUTIVE CALLED HIM A RACIAL SLUR, WHICH ONLY STRENGTHENED AUSTER'S RESOLVE.

POPULAR EGG CREAM RECIPE STYLES

THE ORIGINAL WAY, CIRCA LATE 1800'S, EARLY 1900'S. THE CLASSIC FOX'S U-BET CHOCOLATE EGG CREAM RECIPE WAS THE RECIPE OF CHOICE FOR MOST SODA FOUNTAINS.

THE ECONOMICAL WAY, CIRCA MID-1900'S TO TODAY. DURING THE SUBURBAN BOOM OF THE 40'S AND 50'S, ITEMS PREVIOUSLY ONLY AVAILALBE IN STORES BECAME AVAILABLE FOR HOMES, PROMPTING HOUSEWIVES ACROSS THE NATION TO BUY WHATEVER WAS CLOSEST AND CHEAPEST. PEOPLE ALSO KNEW PRETTY MUCH NOTHING ABOUT POLLUTION AND NUTRITION, SO EVERYTHING WAS MADE OF PAPER AND PLASTIC.

THE ARTISANAL WAY, CIRCA 1800'S AND 2000'S BUT NOT THE 1900'S SO MUCH. THE ARTISANAL, ORGANIC, HANDMADE EGG CREAM MADE A RESURGENCE IN THE EARLY 2000'S AND IS STILL AROUND TODAY. IT'S ALWAYS TOTALLY OVERPRICED, AND ALTHOUGH TASTY ENOUGH, IT'S A GOOD EXAMPLE OF WHY SOME SIMPLE THINGS SHOULD STAY SIMPLE.

A FEW PLACES TO GET A GOOD EGG CREAM TODAY

EDDIE'S SWEET SHOP
105-29 METROPOLITAN AVE.
FOREST HILLS, QUEENS

HINSCH
8518 5TH AVE.
BAY RIDGE, BROOKLYN
(NOW STEWART'S RESTAURANT)

PETER PAN DONUT & PASTRY SHOP
727 MANHATTAN AVE.
GREENPOINT, BROOKLYN

BROOKLYN FARMACY
& SODA FOUNTAIN
513 HENRY ST.
CARROLL GARDENS, BROOKLYN

NEIL'S COFFEE SHOP
961 LEXINGTON AVE.
UPPER EAST SIDE, MANHATTAN

TOM'S RESTAURANT
782 WASHINGTON AVE.
PROSPECT HEIGHTS, BROOKLN

RUSS & DAUGHTERS
179 E. HOUSTON ST.
LOWER EAST SIDE, MANHATTAN

KATZ'S DELICATESSEN
205 E. HOUSTON ST.
LOWER EAST SIDE, MANHATTAN

YONAH SCHIMMEL KNISH BAKERY
137 E. HOUSTON ST.
LOWER EAST SIDE, MANHATTAN

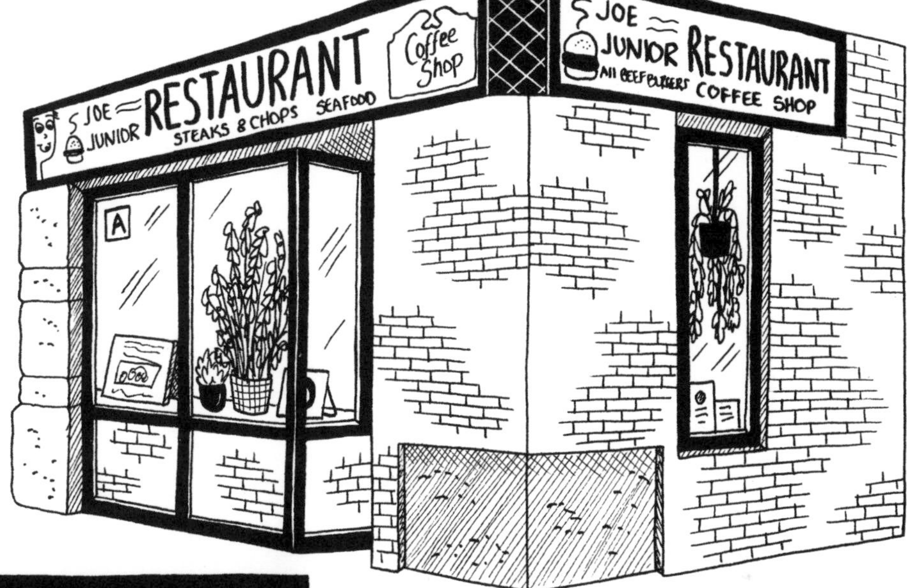

JOE JUNIOR RESTAURANT
167 3RD AVE.
GRAMERCY, MANHATTAN

EISENBERG'S SANDWICH SHOP
174 5TH AVE.
FLATIRON, MANHATTAN

ANOPOLI ICE CREAM PARLOR
AND FAMILY RESTAURANT
6920 3RD AVE.
BAY RIDGE, BROOKLYN

NEW YORK CITY
HOTEL KEYS OF YORE
HOTEL GREENWICH
132
180 BLEEKER
NYC
HOTEL
TAFT
573
NEW YORK
THE
CARLYLE
MADISON AVE AT 76TH ST
NEW YORK
WALDORF ASTORIA
ROOM
NO.
3
NEW YORK
The Plaza
THE BILTMORE NEW YORK
BILTMORE
HOTEL McALPIN
HOTEL
McALPIN
NEWYORK
1375
PENTHOUSE
15
RITZ
TOWERS
MILLS HOTE
945
7TH AVE & 36TH S
N.Y
THE WALDORF-ASTORIA NEW YORK
The Waldorf Astoria
NEW YORK
42B
WALDORF
W
74
Hotel
St-Regis
NewYork
1237

CARROLL GARDENS THEN & NOW

SMITH ST. AND DEGRAW ST. IN 1928

SMITH ST. AND DEGRAW ST. IN 2016

486 HENRY ST.
IN 1916
BEFORE THIS BUILDING WAS A THEATER, IT WAS THE PILGRIM CHAPEL, BUILT IN 1878. THE CHURCH HAD A TALL BELL TOWER, WHICH WAS DEMOLISHED WHEN THE BUILDING WAS REPURPOSED AS A THEATER IN 1916. THE ORIOLE THEATRE WAS SHORT-LIVED; IT CLOSED IN 1925. THERE IS NO DOCUMENTATION ABOUT THE BUILDING'S USE IN THE FOLLOWING FEW DECADES.
ORIOLE
CHARLIE CHAPLIN THE VAGABOND
WM S. HART HELL'S HINGES
20,000 Leagues UNDER THE Sea
SHERLOCK HOLMES
486 HENRY ST.
IN 2014
SOMETIME IN THE 1980'S, THE BUILDING BECAME A GROCERY STORE. IN THE FOLLOWING YEARS IT WAS A NUMBER OF DIFFERENT MARKETS, INCLUDING THE MET, AS ILLUSTRATED. IN 2015, IT BECAME A KEY FOODS.
Met
ONE WAY

MITH ST. AND DOUGLASS ST. IN 1928

MITH ST. AND DOUGLASS ST. IN 2013

A BRIEF HISTORY OF NEW YORK'S SUBWAY SYSTEM

NEW YORK'S FIRST PUBLIC UNDERGROUND SUBWAY OPENED IN 1904. PREVIOUSLY, THERE HAD BEEN PRIVATELY OWNED SUBWAY LINES SUCH AS THE ATLANTIC AVENUE TUNNEL RAILROAD, THE BROOKLYN RAPID TRANSIT COMPANY, AND OTHERS.

WHEN THE FIRST PUBLIC SUBWAY OPENED, IT WAS PART OF THE INTERBOROUGH RAPID TRANSIT COMPANY. THROUGHOUT THE FOLLOWING DECADES, THE IRT TOOK OVER PRIVATELY OWNED LINES, EVENTUALLY CREATING ONE MASSIVE SYSTEM THAT BECAME THE NEW YORK CITY TRANSIT AUTHORITY, A SUBSIDIARY OF THE METROPOLITAN TRANSIT AUTHORITY, OR MTA, AS IT IS KNOWN TODAY.

THE FIRST TIME I VISITED NEW YORK, PRIOR TO MOVING THERE, THE SUBWAY WAS MY FIRST EXPERIENCE OF THE CITY. I ARRIVED ON A RAINY AFTERNOON, AND PROMPTLY GOT LOST INSIDE PENN STATION, A CLASSIC TOURIST MOVE. I SOON BECAME A RESIDENT OF THE CITY, WHERE I WAS RELIEVED TO LEARN THAT EVEN LIFELONG NYC RESIDENTS STILL REFER TO THE MTA MAP TO NAVIGATE THE SUBWAY.

ALTHOUGH NEW YORKERS LOVE TO COMPLAIN ABOUT THE SUBWAY, I'VE ALWAYS BEEN FASCINATED BY BOTH ITS UNDERGROUND AND ABOVEGROUND ELEMENTS. UNDERGROUND, THE TRAINS ARE AN EXCELLENT PLACE TO PEOPLE-WATCH. ABOVEGROUND, YOU GET SPRAWLING VIEWS OF THE CITY. ALSO ABOVEGROUND ARE SOME OF THE LAST REMAINING ORIGINAL SUBWAY STATIONS.

REGARDLESS OF YOUR OPINION OF THE SUBWAY, IT'S UNDENIABLE IT'S AN IMPRESSIVE SYSTEM. THE NYC SUBWAY HAS 236 MILES OF TRACKS, MAKING IT THE WORLD'S FIFTH-LONGEST SUBWAY. IN THE FOLLOWING PAGES, I'LL COVER SOME LESSER KNOWN, MORE HISTORICAL ASPECTS OF THE SUBWAY, FROM THE SECRET MTA TOWNHOUSE TO PRESIDENT ROOSEVELT'S ABANDONED PRIVATE TRAIN CAR.

SUBWAY AND TRAIN TOKENS FROM THE CITY'S VARIOUS TRANSIT SYSTEMS. THE FIRST MTA SUBWAY TOKEN WAS INTRODUCED IN 1953, WHEN RIDES COST 15 CENTS. THE LAST TOKEN CAME OUT IN 1995, WHEN THE FARE WAS $1.50. TOKENS WERE DISCONTINUED IN 2003.

OTHER TOKENS FOR VARIOUS NEW YORK TRANSIT SYSTEMS.

HISTORIC SUBWAY ENTRANCES

ALTHOUGH MOST MODERN SUBWAY ENTRANCES HAVE A BLAND, UTILITARIAN LOOK TO THEM, THERE ARE MANY UNIQUE HISTORICAL ENTRANCES SCATTERED AROUND THE CITY. THESE STRUCTURES RANGE FROM ELABORATE STAND-ALONE BUILDINGS TO ORNATE GILDED AGE DOORWAYS. MOST OF THE ENTRANCES WERE BUILT WHEN THE SUBWAY SYSTEM WAS KNOWN AS THE INTERBOROUGH RAPID TRANSIT SUBWAY, OR IRT. MANY OF THEM STILL FUNCTION AS ACTIVE SUBWAY ENTRANCES, WHILE OTHERS REMAIN ONLY IN FACADE. (NOTE: MOST OF THESE ARE ORIGINAL, BUT A FEW ARE REPRODUCTIONS, AND ARE NOTED ACCORDINGLY.)

THE ATLANTIC AVENUE SUBWAY STATION WAS BUILT IN 1908 AS ONE OF THE ORIGINAL FARE CONTROL STATIONS. IT EVENTUALLY CLOSED AND WAS CONVERTED INTO A NEWSSTAND, BEFORE BEING ABANDONED ALTOGETHER AND BECOMING SUBJECT TO GRAFFITI, VANDALISM, AND DISREPAIR. IN 1980, IT WAS ADDED TO THE NATIONAL REGISTRY OF HISTORIC PLACES.

ON THE BROADWAY SIDE OF THE FULTON STREET STATION IS A GILDED AGE SUBWAY ENTRANCE. IT'S TUCKED INTO A BUILDING THAT USED TO BE THE HEADQUARTERS OF AMERICAN TELEPHONE AND TELEGRAPH AND WESTERN UNION, WHICH RECEIVED THE FIRST TRANSATLANTIC PHONE CALL FROM LONDON TO NYC IN 1927.

THE 190TH STREET OVERLOOK TERRACE SUBWAY STATION WAS ONE OF MANY SUBWAY STATIONS DESIGNED BY PAINTER, POET, AND ARCHITECT, SQUIRE J. VICKERS. FROM 1906 TO 1943, VICKERS DESIGNED AROUND 300 STATIONS AND EVEN DID SOME OF THE INTERIOR TILE WORK HIMSELF. (NOTE: THIS IS THE BACK ENTRANCE, I JUST LIKED IT MORE THAN THE FRONT.)

A FEW BLOCKS DOWN FROM THE 190TH STREET ENTRANCE IS THE WEST 181ST STREET AT OVERLOOK TERRACE SUBWAY ENTRANCE. BUILT IN 1932, THE ART DECO STRUCTURE WAS ANOTHER ONE OF VICKERS'S MANY DESIGNS.

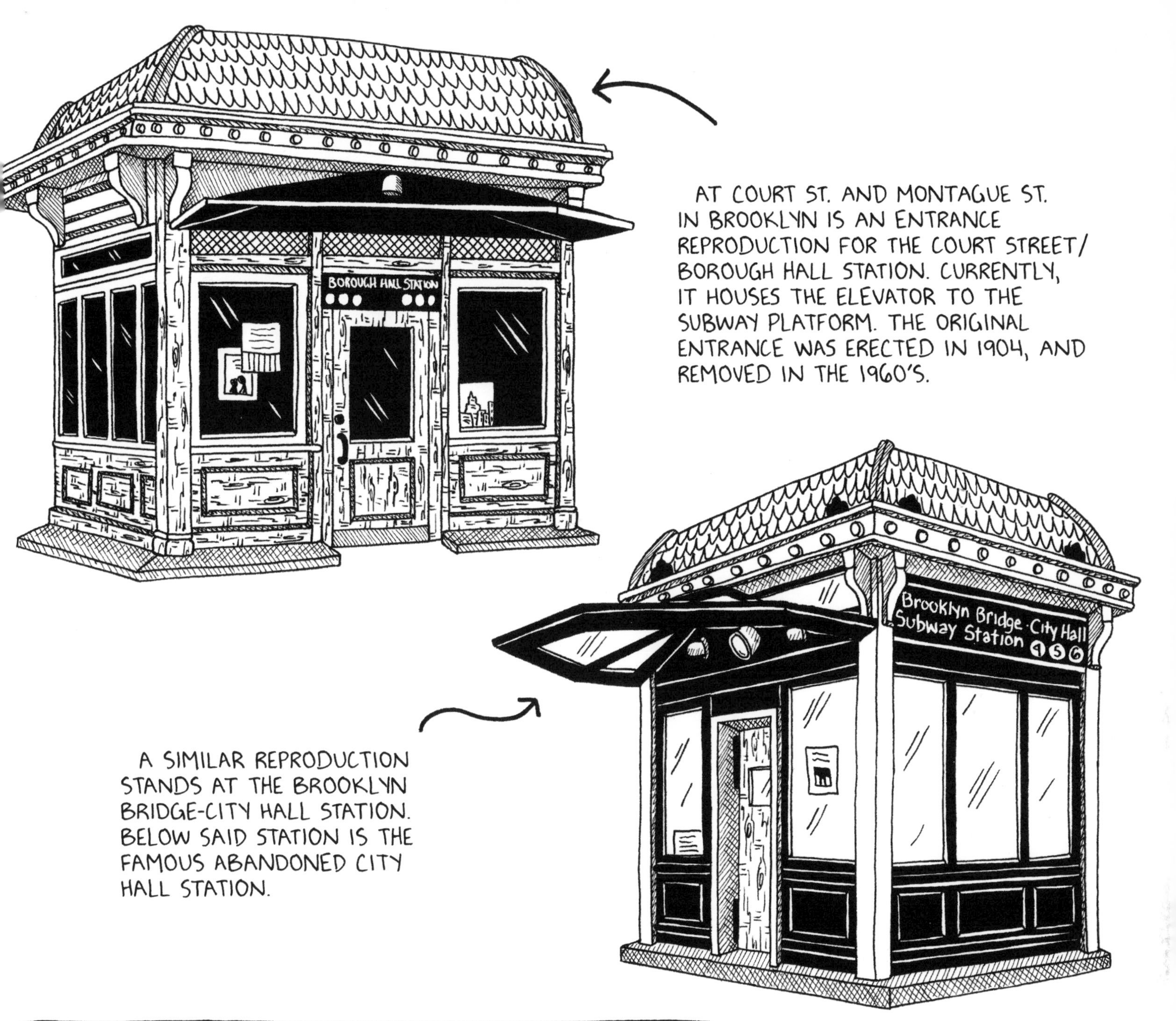

AT COURT ST. AND MONTAGUE ST. IN BROOKLYN IS AN ENTRANCE REPRODUCTION FOR THE COURT STREET/ BOROUGH HALL STATION. CURRENTLY, IT HOUSES THE ELEVATOR TO THE SUBWAY PLATFORM. THE ORIGINAL ENTRANCE WAS ERECTED IN 1904, AND REMOVED IN THE 1960'S.

A SIMILAR REPRODUCTION STANDS AT THE BROOKLYN BRIDGE-CITY HALL STATION. BELOW SAID STATION IS THE FAMOUS ABANDONED CITY HALL STATION.

AT 111 BROADWAY, THE TRINITY BUILDING SUBWAY ENTRANCE IS NO LONGER FUNCTIONAL, AND IS NOW HOME TO A SUBWAY SANDWICH SHOP. THE ENTRANCE MIRRORS THE GOTHIC ARCHITECTURE OF THE TRINITY BUILDING, WHICH FINISHED CONSTRUCTION IN 1907. ORIGINALLY, THE ENTRANCE LED TO THE WALL STREET STATION.

THE BOWLING GREEN SUBWAY STATION WAS DESIGNED BY HEINS & LAFARGE AND DATES TO 1905. IT WAS ONE OF THE ORIGINAL CONTROL HOUSE STATIONS FOR THE IRT. CONTROL HOUSE STATIONS WERE LARGER THAN KIOSK ENTRANCES AND WERE DESIGNED TO CONTROL AND EASE PASSENGER FLOW. THEY OFTEN HAD WAITING AREAS, BATHROOMS, BAGGAGE STORAGE, AND/OR NEWSSTANDS INSIDE THE HISTORIC STRUCTURES.

THE 72ND STREET CONTROL HOUSE WAS ONCE THE ONLY ENTRANCE TO THE 72ND STREET SUBWAY STATION, WHICH OPENED IN 1904. THE INTERIOR WAS RENOVATED TO WIDEN THE ORIGINAL STAIRS.

SECRET SUBWAY

MY FAVORITE (AND WORST-KEPT) SUBWAY SECRET IS A BUILDING AT 58 JORALEMON ST. IN BROOKLYN HEIGHTS. ALTHOUGH THE THREE-STORY GREEK REVIVAL TOWN HOUSE BLENDS IN WITH ITS NEIGHBORS, IT IS NOT WHAT IT SEEMS FROM THE OUTSIDE.

BUILT IN 1847 AS A PRIVATE RESIDENCE, IT WAS TAKEN OVER BY THE INTERBOROUGH RAPID TRANSIT COMPANY IN 1908 TO SERVE AS AN ELABORATE HIDDEN VENTILATOR FOR THE SUBWAY BELOW. IT ALSO SERVES AS AN EMERGENCY EXIT, MAKING IT THE ONLY TIME I EVER WISHED FOR A SUBWAY EVACUATION—JUST SO I COULD SEE IT.

IN ORDER TO KEEP UP WITH THE EVER-CHANGING NEIGHBORHOOD, THE BUILDING UNDERGOES PERIODIC EXTERIOR RENOVATIONS. EARLY ON, THE WINDOWS COULD OPEN AND SHUT, AND OCCASIONALLY NEIGHBORS WOULD COMPLAIN ABOUT SMOKE POURING OUT OF THE HOUSE THROUGH THE OPEN WINDOWS. IN 1999 THE OLD FANS AND GENERATORS WERE REPLACED AND THE WINDOWS WERE SEALED. TUNNEL AIR NOW ESCAPES THROUGH A ROOF VENTILATION SYSTEM. IF THE TOWN HOUSE WAS A FUNCTIONING RESIDENTIAL APARTMENT BUILDING, IT WOULD BE WORTH AN ESTIMATED $3 MILLION.

MY SECOND-FAVORITE POORLY KEPT SECRET IS THE WALDORF-ASTORIA'S TRACK NUMBER 61, A SEMI-ABANDONED TRAIN PLATFORM FOR A PRIVATE SUBWAY CAR USED BY FRANKIN D. ROOSEVELT AND OTHER IMPORTANT POLITICAL FIGURES. IT WAS REPORTED THAT EVERYTHING IN THE STATION WAS BUILT LARGER THAN THE PUBLIC STATIONS IN ORDER TO ACCOMMODATE ROOSEVELT'S ARMOR-PLATED LIMOUSINE, WHICH WOULD DRIVE ONTO AND OFF OF HIS PRIVATE TRAIN, AND WOULD EVEN GO IN THE ELEVATOR. ALTHOUGH ROOSEVELT'S SUBWAY CAR REMAINS ABANDONED, THE REST OF THE STATION IS USED FOR STORAGE, AND REPORTEDLY WAS SOMETIMES STILL USED BY OTHER PRESIDENTS AS LATE AS 2003, ALTHOUGH THE REPORTS ARE UNCONFIRMED.

THE ABANDONED CITY HALL SUBWAY STATION WAS BUILT IN 1904 AND CLOSED IN 1945. IT CAN BE ACCESSED A NUMBER OF WAYS. THERE ARE OCCASIONAL GUIDED TOURS, OR IF YOU'RE ON THE 6 TRAIN AND DON'T GET OFF AT THE BROOKLYN BRIDGE/CITY HALL STATION, THE LAST STOP, THE TRAIN WILL MAKE A RETURN LOOP. YOU WON'T BE ABLE TO GET OFF, BUT YOU WILL BRIEFLY GET A GLIMPSE OF THE CITY HALL STATION. I ALSO KNOW EXPLORERS WHO WALK THE TRACKS TO GET THERE, BUT I DON'T RECOMMEND IT, BECAUSE WALKING ACTIVE SUBWAY LINES IS FUCKING STUPID.

THE HISTORIC AVENUE H STATION HOUSE IS LOCATED AT 802 E.16TH ST. IN FLATBUSH, BROOKLYN. BUILT IN 1906, IT WAS ORIGINALLY PART OF THE BROOKLYN, FLATBUSH & CONEY ISLAND RAILROAD. IT WAS THE CITY'S ONLY STATION THAT HAD PREVIOUSLY BEEN A WOOD COTTAGE THAT WAS HOME TO THOMAS BENTON ACKERSON'S REAL ESTATE OFFICE. IT CURRENTLY SERVES THE B AND Q LINES. THE BUILDING WAS LANDMARKED IN 2002.

SECRETS OF THE ASTOR PLACE SUBWAY STATION

THE ASTOR PLACE STATION IS AN EAST VILLAGE SUBWAY STOP THAT OPENED IN 1904 AND HOSTS THE 4 AND 6 TRAIN LINES. ALTHOUGH THE ASTOR PLACE STATION IS LISTED AS ONE OF THE CITY'S REGISTERED HISTORIC PLACES, THE UPTOWN ENTRANCE, OFTEN INCORRECTLY CITED AS BEING ORIGINAL, IS IN FACT A REPRODUCTION.

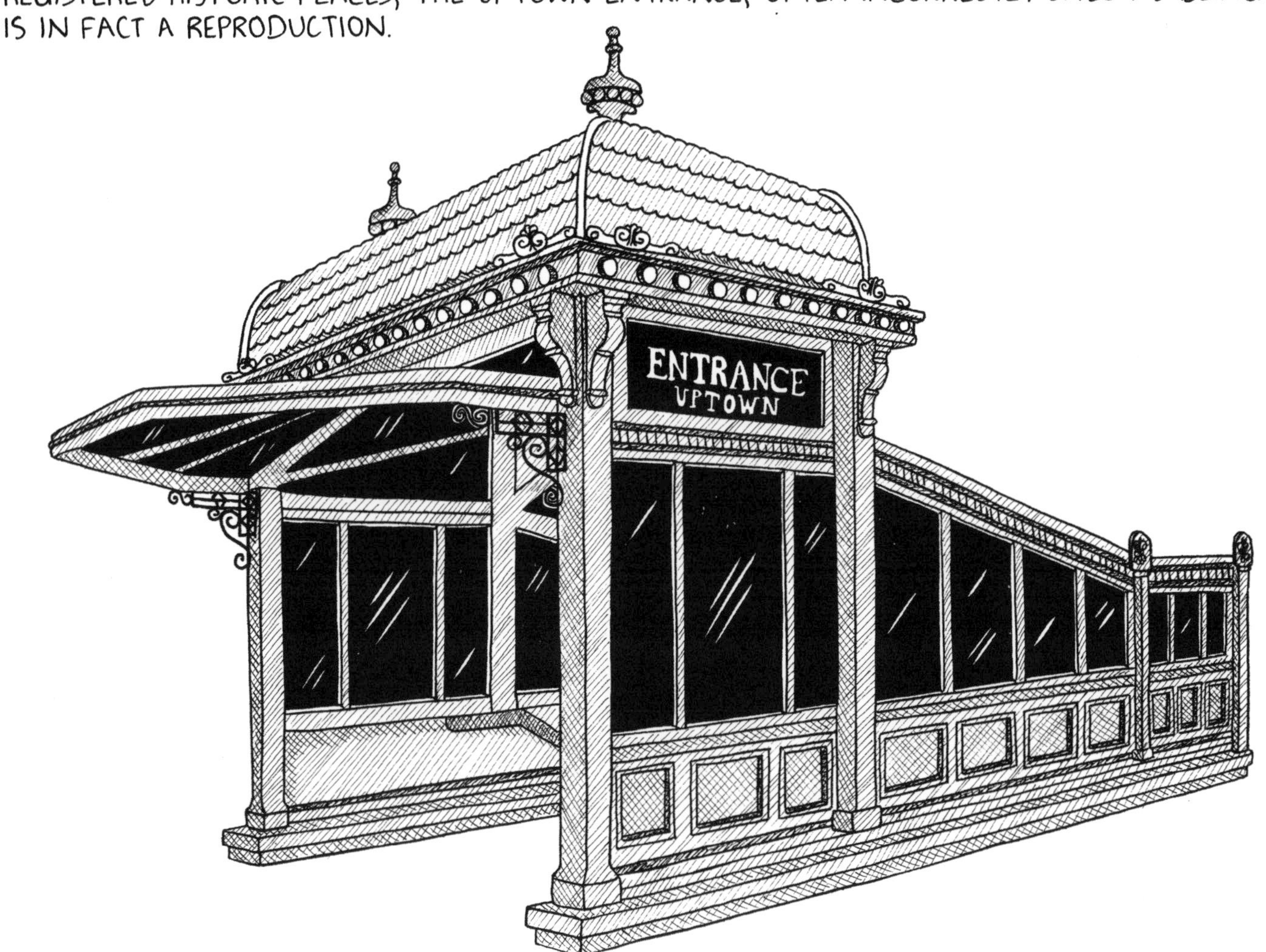

THE STATION UNDERWENT A SERIES OF RENOVATIONS THAT DESTROYED SOME OF THE ORIGINAL DETAILS. HOWEVER, A FEW HAVE BEEN PRESERVED. SOME PARTS OF THE ORIGINAL TILE ARTWORK ALONG THE WALLS OF THE PLATFORM FEATURE BEAVERS, A NOD TO THE AREA'S NAMESAKE, JOHN JACOB ASTOR, WHO MADE HIS FORTUNE SELLING BEAVER PELTS.

ON THE SOUTHBOUND PLATFORM, THERE IS A BRICKED-OVER DOORWAY, ADORNED WITH A BRASS PLAQUE THAT SAYS "CLINTON HALL." WHEN THE STATION WAS COMPLETED IN 1904, CLINTON HALL—PREVIOUSLY KNOWN AS THE ASTOR PLACE OPERA HOUSE, WHICH WAS FAMOUS FOR BEING THE LOCATION OF THE 1849 SHAKESPEARE RIOT—SAT DIRECTLY ABOVE.

THE OPERA HOUSE WAS TORN DOWN IN 1890 AND REPLACED WITH CLINTON HALL, WHICH GOT ITS OWN SUBWAY ENTRANCE IN 1904. THE ENTRANCE WAS BRICKED UP IN THE 1940'S, AND CLINTON HALL WAS CONVERTED TO CONDOS IN 1995.

THE PLATFORM WALLS ALSO FEATURE A NUMBER OF PORCELAIN MURALS BY MILTON GLASER, WHICH WERE INSTALLED DURING A RENOVATION IN 1986.

THE BELOWGROUND ENTRANCE TO KMART USED TO BE THE ENTRANCE TO WANAMAKER'S DEPARTMENT STORE. BEFORE THAT, IT WAS AN A.T. STEWART'S.

IN THE EARLY 1900'S, WHEN PEOPLE ACTED MORE CIVILIZED, MANY SUBWAY STATIONS HAD PUBLIC BATHROOMS. THAT LUXURY FELL OUT OF FAVOR AS PEOPLE GREW INCREASINGLY DISGUSTING, AND THE ASTOR PLACE BATHROOMS WERE EVENTUALLY CONVERTED INTO A CANDY AND MAGAZINE STAND.

VINTAGE SUBWAY ETIQUETTE ADS

IN 2013, THE TERM "MANSPREADING" WAS COINED TO REFER TO MEN WHO SIT WITH THEIR LEGS WIDELY OPEN WHILE RIDING THE SUBWAY, OBLIVIOUSLY TAKING UP TOO MUCH SPACE ON CROWDED TRAINS. HOWEVER, MANSPREADING IS NOT A NEW CONCEPT. SUBWAY ETIQUETTE HAS ALWAYS BEEN AN ISSUE, ONE THE INTERBOROUGH RAPID TRANSIT COMPANY ATTEMPTED TO ADDRESS THROUGH ADS TARGETING BAD SUBWAY BEHAVIOR IN 1918.

THE ADS FEATURED A SERIES OF CARTOONS DEPICTING VARIOUS TRANSGRESSIONS A PERSON MIGHT COMMIT ON THE TRAINS. KNOWN AS THE "SUBWAY SUN" ADS, THEY WERE DESIGNED TO LOOK LIKE NEWSPAPERS, AND DEPICTED MEN AND WOMEN IN VARIOUS STATES OF UNACCEPTABLE BEHAVIOR. ARTIST FRED COOPER CREATED THE ADS, WHICH WERE TAKEN OVER IN THE 1940'S BY AMELIA OPDYKE JONES, KNOWN AS "OPPY," WHOSE ADS I HAVE RE-CREATED HERE.

CURRENT SUBWAY ETIQUETTE ADS

SHORTLY AFTER MANSPREADING BECAME PART OF THE CULTURAL VERNACULAR, THE MTA BEGAN THEIR "COURTESY COUNTS" CAMPAIGN. THE ADS WERE THEMATICALLY SIMILAR TO THE "SUBWAY SUN," FEATURING A MAIN OFFENDER CARRYING OUT VARIOUS MISDEEDS AMONG MORE COURTEOUS RIDERS.

THE SUCCESS OF THE ADS IS SUBJECTIVE. PRIOR TO THE "COURTESY COUNTS" CAMPAIGN, THE MTA WAS RELUCTANT TO POST ETIQUETTE ADS, SKEPTICAL OF THEIR EFFECT. WHEN ASKED BY GOTHAMIST IF THERE WERE ANY PLANS FOR ADS, MTA SPOKESPERSON ADAM LISBERG SAID, "YOU CAN GO BACK IN HISTORY AND SEE OLD EXAMPLES OF ETIQUETTE POSTERS HERE AND ELSEWHERE. PEOPLE LITERALLY NEVER LEARN. IF SYSTEMS ALL OVER THE WORLD HAVE BEEN TRYING AND FAILING TO CURB BAD BEHAVIOR FOR DECADES, WHY DO WE THINK WE WOULD SUDDENLY DISCOVER THE MAGIC BULLET TO GET PEOPLE TO CHANGE?"

WHILE THE ADS THEMSELVES MIGHT NOT BE VERY EFFECTIVE, THEY DO HELP RAISE AWARENESS TO THE PUBLIC, WHO MIGHT HOLD THE PROVERBIAL MAGIC BULLET ON THEIR PHONES. THE HASHTAG #MANSPREADING IS HUGELY POPULAR, ACCOMPANIED BY HUNDREDS OF PHOTOS FEATURING UNSUSPECTING MEN SITTING WITH KNEES SPLAYED, ABSENTMINDEDLY TAKING UP TWO SEATS. ALTHOUGH MORALLY QUESTIONABLE, PUBLIC SHAMING IS A MORE EFFECTIVE TOOL THAN POSTER ADS.

Dude... Stop the Spread, Please

It's a space issue.

Don't Be A Pole Hog

Leave room for others to hold
In other words, share the pole

Poles Are For Your Safety, Not Your Latest Routine

Hold the pole, not our attention
A subway car is no place for showtime.

Clipping? Primping?

Everybody wants to look their best but it's a subway car, not a restroom.

It's A Subway Car, Not A Dining Car

It may be take-out, but please, don't eat here.

Keep Your Stuff To Yourself

Be a space saver. The less space your things take up, the more room for everyone.

DISCLAIMER: ALTHOUGH MANSPREADING HAS GOTTEN MUCH ATTENTION LATELY, BAD SUBWAY BEHAVIOR IS CERTAINLY NOT LIMITED TO MEN. I'VE SEEN WOMEN DO SOME WEIRD, GROSS SHIT ON THE SUBWAY, INCLUDING THROWING A USED TAMPON ON THE GROUND, FILING THEIR NAILS AND PEEING INTO EMPTY CUPS. EVEN I HAVE COMMITTED A FEW SUBWAY BLUNDERS AS WELL, SUCH AS EATING FOOD AND PUTTING MY BAGS ON THE SEAT. MY APOLOGIES TO ANY RIDERS I MIGHT HAVE INCONVENIENCED OR DISGUSTED.

SIX TYPES OF FORCED PHYSICAL CONTACT ON A NEW YORK CITY SUBWAY

1) THE OBLIVIOUS BUTT BUMP, NOT THAT BAD BECAUSE BUTTS ARE NO BIG DEAL REALLY. (ALTHOUGH BUTT TO BUTT FEELS HELLA WEIRD.)

2) THE DUBIOUSLY ACCIDENTAL BOOB GRAZE, SOMETIMES UNCOMFORTABLE FOR BOTH PARTIES, BUT ONLY IF TRULY AN ACCIDENT.

3) THE SLIGHT KNEE-KNOCK, MAYBE ONE OF THE MOST TOLERABLE AS LONG AS EVERYONE IS WEARING PANTS. NO FLESH ON FLESH!

4) THE SWEATY ARMPIT AMBUSH. EVEN IF CONTACT DOESN'T OCCUR, IF THE SMELL OFFENDS YOUR OLFACTORY, YOUR PERSONAL SPACE HAS BEEN VIOLATED.

5) THE UNAVOIDABLE BODY AGAINST BODY ON A PACKED TRAIN. ABSOLUTE FUCKING NIGHTMARE.

6) THE NONCHALANT, LIGHTLY-LINGERING HAND TOUCH ON THE POLE, INDISPUTABLY THE WORST BECAUSE IT'S SO INTIMATE.

THE OLDEST BARS IN NEW YORK CITY

NO ONE SEEMS TO AGREE ON WHICH NYC BARS ARE THE OLDEST, DUE TO UNOFFICIAL CLAIMS, NAME CHANGES, AND PROHIBITION-ERA COMPLICATIONS. I TALLIED UP THE BARS AND NARROWED THEM DOWN TO THE TOP 10 OLDEST, ALTHOUGH I KNOW MY LIST WILL BE AS INCOMPLETE AS A BUZZFEED OR UNTAPPED CITIES LIST, SINCE LISTS OF THIS NATURE ARE UNVERIFIABLE.

WHEN PROHIBITION BEGAN IN 1920, MANY OF THESE ESTABLISHMENTS CONTINUED OPERATIONS, EITHER SERVING ALCOHOL DISCREETLY, OR OPENLY SERVING "NEAR BEER," AS McSORLEY'S DID. NEAR BEER WAS HEAVILY WATERED-DOWN ALE THAT STILL TECHNICALLY DEFIED THE RULES OF PROHIBITION, BUT VARIOUS HISTORICAL ACCOUNTS CLAIM AUTHORITY MOSTLY TURNED A BLIND EYE, IN SEARCH OF MORE FLAGRANT DEFIANCE SUCH AS BASEMENT SPEAKEASIES. WHEN PROHIBITION WAS LIFTED, NEW BARS SPRUNG UP ALL OVER THE CITY, AND WOULD CONTINUE TO BE ONE OF THE FASTEST GROWING INDUSTRIES OVER THE FOLLOWING CENTURY. CURRENTLY, NYC HAS OVER 2,000 BARS TO CHOOSE FROM, BUT IF IT'S HISTORY YOU'RE LOOKING FOR, THE FOLLOWING BARS ARE A GOOD START.

FRAUNCES TAVERN, 54 PEARL ST. FINANCIAL DISTRICT, MANHATTAN. OPEN SINCE 1762

MCSORLEY'S OLD ALE HOUSE
15 E.7TH ST.
EAST VILLAGE, MANHATTAN
OPEN SINCE 1854

OLD TOWN BAR
& RESTAURANT
45 E.18TH ST.
FLATIRON, MANHATTAN
OPEN SINCE 1892

MULBERRY STREET BAR, 176 MULBERRY ST. LITTLE ITALY, MANHATTAN. OPEN SINCE 1908

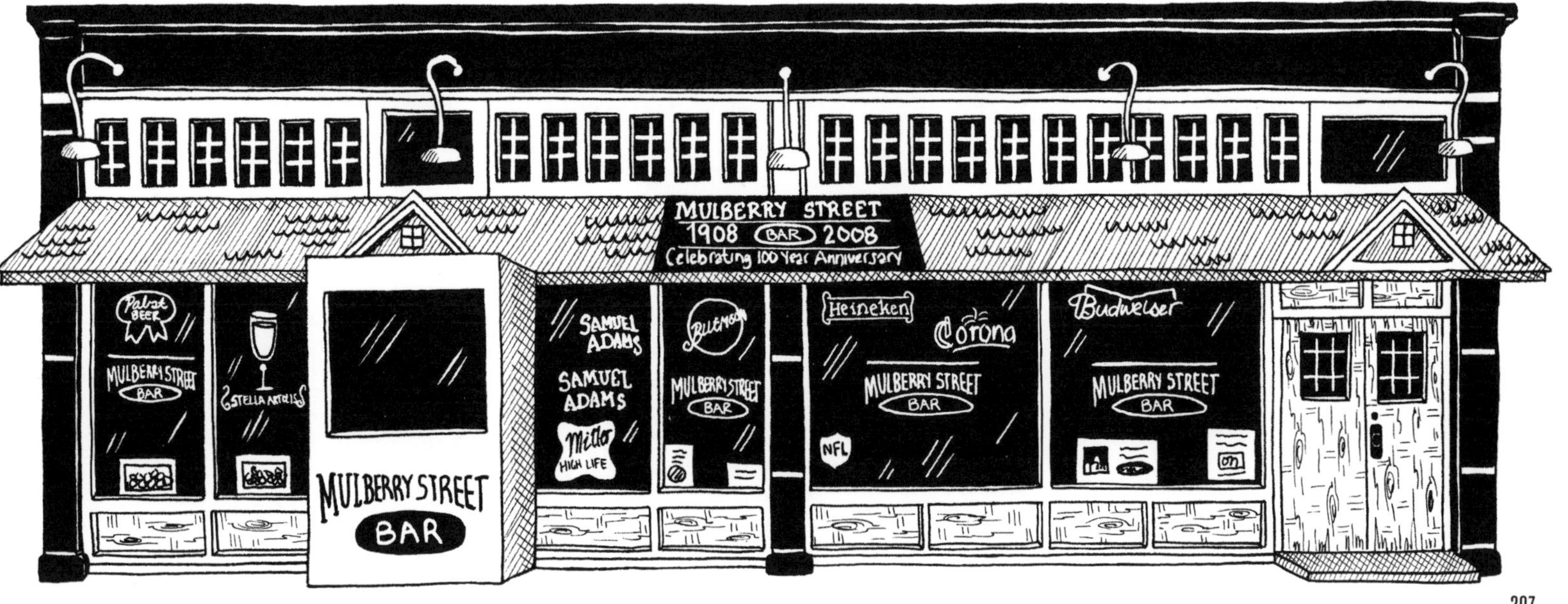

NEIR'S TAVERN, 87-48 78TH ST. WOODHAVEN, QUEENS. OPEN SINCE 1829

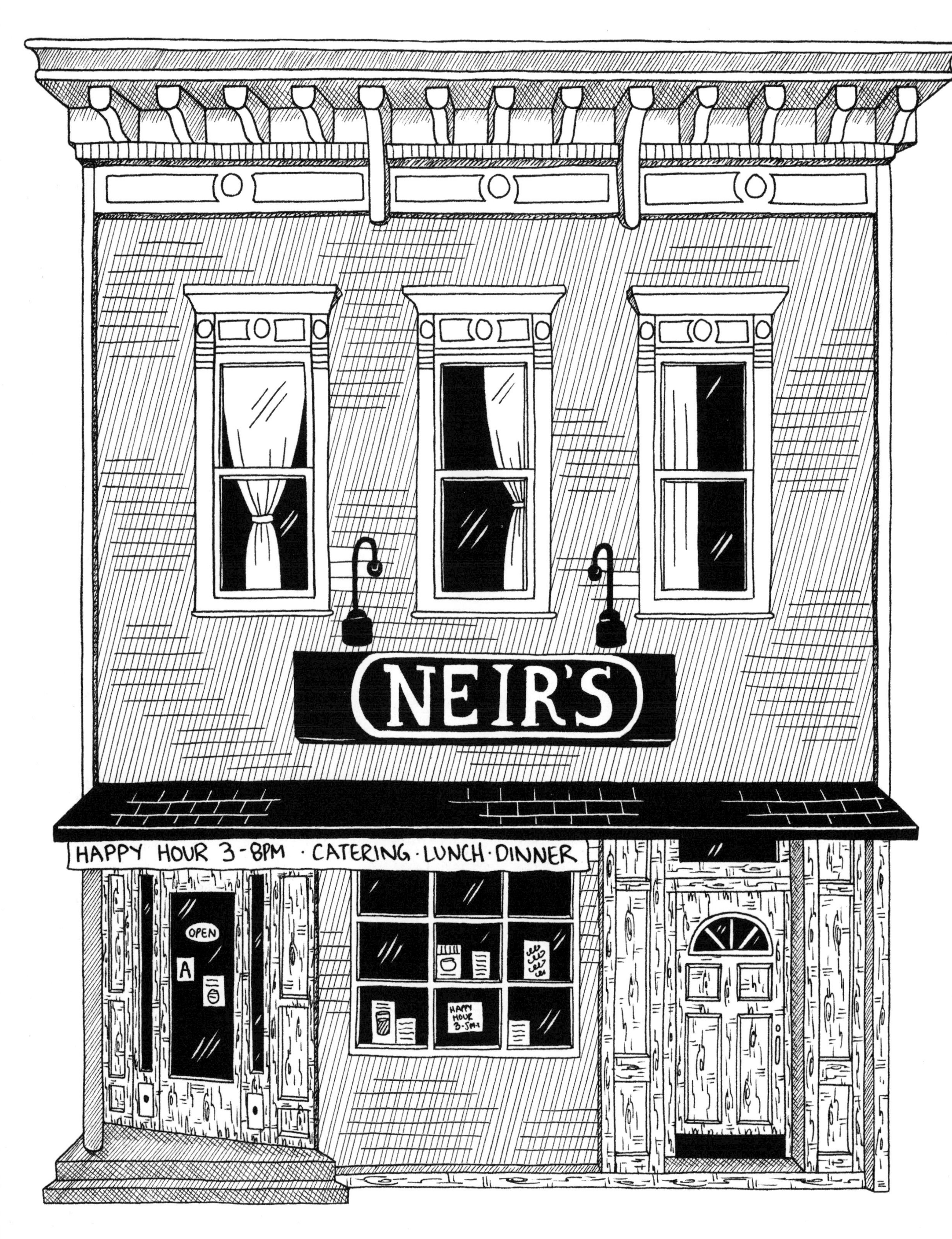

BRIDGE CAFE, 279 WATER ST. FINANCIAL DISTRICT, MANHATTAN. 1794-?

THE BRIDGE CAFE WAS FORCED TO CLOSE AFTER SUSTAINING DAMAGE IN HURRICANE SANDY. ALTHOUGH THE OWNER STATED PLANS TO RE-OPEN, IT WAS STILL CLOSED IN 2016 WHEN I FINISHED THIS BOOK.

CHUMLEY'S, 86 BEDFORD ST. WEST VILLAGE, MANHATTAN. OPEN SINCE 1922

HONORABLE MENTIONS:
P.J. CLARKE'S, 915 3RD AVE. MIDTOWN, MANHATTAN. OPEN SINCE 1884
WHITEHORSE TAVERN, 567 HUDSON ST. WEST VILLAGE, MANHATTAN. OPEN SINCE 1880
PETE'S TAVERN, 129 E.18TH ST. GRAMERCY, MANHATTAN. OPEN SINCE 1864
THE EAR INN, 326 SPRING ST. SOHO, MANHATTAN. OPEN SINCE 1817

HIDDEN BARS OF NEW YORK CITY

IN A CITY FILLED WITH THOUSANDS OF DRINKING ESTABLISHMENTS, MOST BARS STRUGGLE TO STAND OUT AMIDST MASSIVE COMPETITION. SO INSTEAD OF EMPLOYING THE USUAL PUBLICITY TACTICS AND ADVERTISEMENTS, A HANDFUL OF BARS HAVE MADE THEMSELVES KNOWN SIMPLY BY HIDING IN PLAIN SIGHT, RELYING ON THEIR LACK OF PUBLICITY TO BE THEIR PUBLICITY. (IRONICALLY, MANY "SECRET" BARS ARE ON VERY PUBLIC LISTS, SINCE NOTHING IS ACTUALLY SECRET ANYMORE.)

HIDDEN BARS WERE POPULARIZED DURING PROHIBITION, WHEN SPEAKEASIES HID THEIR ESTABLISHMENTS BEHIND STOREFRONTS, AND/OR USED HARD-TO-FIND, PASSWORD-PROTECTED DOORWAYS. ONCE PROHIBITION WAS LIFTED, MOST BARS REVERTED BACK TO PUBLIC DRINKING SPACES. HOWEVER, A FEW BARS MAINTAINED THEIR SECRECY, MORE OR LESS AS A PUBLICITY GIMMICK.

WHEN THE SPEAKEASY AESTHETIC RETURNED TO NEW YORK IN THE 2000'S, NEW BARS POPPED UP WITH THE INTENTION OF REMAINING SECRETIVE AND HARD TO FIND, WHICH, IN THE AGE OF GOOGLE, IS A MOSTLY FUTILE ENDEAVOR. BUT FUCK IT, THEY'RE STILL FUN TO CHECK OUT, EVEN IF YOU'RE LIKE ME AND LOATHE THE IDEA OF PAYING TOO MUCH MONEY FOR SMALL DRINKS WHILE CONSTANTLY ASKING EVERYONE WHAT THEY JUST SAID BECAUSE YOU CAN'T HEAR SHIT OVER THE LOUD MUSIC. ALTHOUGH I'M NOT A BAR PERSON, I APPRECIATE A GOOD PSEUDO-SECRET, SO HERE ARE A FEW OF MY FAVORITE "HIDDEN" BARS THAT ARE WORTH CHECKING OUT.

PLEASE DON'T TELL, 113 ST. MARK'S PL. EAST VILLAGE, MANHATTAN

INSIDE CRIF DOGS IS AN UNASSUMING OLD WOODEN PHONE BOOTH, WHICH IS THE ENTRANCE TO PLEASE DON'T TELL. INSIDE THE BOOTH, DIAL "1" AND WAIT FOR THE HOST TO EITHER LET YOU IN OR GIVE YOU AN ESTIMATED WAITING TIME. THIS IS THE LEAST SECRET HIDDEN BAR, SO GO DURING AN OFF-HOUR OR YOU'LL FEEL LIKE A TOTAL CHUMP STANDING AROUND WAITING WITH ALL THE OTHER TOURISTS WHO READ ABOUT IT IN *TIME OUT NEW YORK* OR ON SOMEONE'S BLOG. .

ATTABOY
134 ELDRIDGE ST.
LOWER EAST SIDE, MANHATTAN

KNOCK ON THE DOOR NEXT TO THE WINDOW THAT SAYS "TAILORS M&H ALTERATIONS" AND YOU'LL BE LET INTO A SMALL, PACKED BAR THAT HAS NO MENUS AND (AS OF 2016) A FLAT PRICE OF $17 PER DRINK, EFFECTIVELY PRICING OUT ANYONE I'D WANT TO HANG OUT WITH. BEFORE ATTABOY, THE SPACE WAS HOME TO MILK & HONEY, A POPULAR SPEAKEASY COCKTAIL BAR. AFTER IT MOVED, TWO MILK & HONEY BARTENDERS OPENED ATTABOY AND CONTINUED THE TRADITION OF FLAMBOYANT MIXOLOGY, A SKILL THAT IS SADLY LOST ON ME AS A NON-DRINKER AND A NO-FUCKS GIVER.

THE BACK ROOM
102 NORFOLK ST.
LOWER EAST SIDE, MANHATTAN

THE BACK ROOM IS ONE OF MY FAVORITES, SIMPLY BECAUSE OF THE WAY ONE GETS TO THE BAR. WHEN FACING THE LOWER EAST SIDE TOY COMPANY STOREFRONT, LOOK TO THE LEFT TO FIND A GATE (NOT ILLUSTRATED) THAT LEADS DOWN THE STAIRS TO AN UNMARKED DOOR. PASS THROUGH THE DOOR AND DOWN THE ALLEY, THEN UP MORE STAIRS, AND A BOUNCER WILL LET YOU IN. ON THEIR WEBSITE, THE BACK ROOM CLAIMS TO BE ONE OF TWO CURRENTLY OPERATING PROHIBITION-ERA SPEAKEASIES IN NEW YORK, ALTHOUGH DUE TO THE SECRETIVE NATURE OF SPEAKEASIES, SUCH A CLAIM IS UNVERIFIABLE. ALSO, A SPEAKEASY WITH A WEBSITE IS SOMETHING OF AN OXYMORON.

THE BLIND BARBER
339 E.10TH ST.
EAST VILLAGE, MANHATTAN

DURING THE DAY, THE BLIND BARBER FUNCTIONS AS AN OLD-TIMEY BARBERSHOP THAT SERVES FREE DRINKS WITH THEIR HAIRCUTS. BUT AT NIGHT, IF YOU GO THROUGH THE SHOP'S BACK DOOR, YOU'LL FIND A QUAINT SPEAKEASY LOUNGE WITH COZY BOOTHS. THE BAR IS NAMED AFTER A 1934 DETECTIVE NOVEL BY JOHN DICKSON CARR. SUPPOSEDLY THE BAR BECOMES MORE RAUCOUS IN THE LATE NIGHT WHEN THE DJ TAKES OVER, BUT I'VE PROBABLY NEVER BEEN AWAKE THAT LATE, SO I CAN'T VOUCH FOR IT. JUST A HEADS-UP.

APOTHÉKE, 9 DOYERS ST. CHINATOWN, MANHATTAN

TUCKED AWAY ON THE ONCE INFAMOUS DOYERS STREET, APOTHÉKE IS AN APOTHECARY-THEMED BAR LOCATED IN WHAT USED TO BE A CHINATOWN OPIUM DEN. TO FIND THE BAR, LOOK FOR A SMALL "CHEMISTS" SIGN ABOVE AN UNASSUMING STOREFRONT NEAR THE HISTORIC NOM WAH TEA PARLOR. THE BAR IS NAUSEATINGLY GIMMICKY WITH ITS CHEMISTRY THEME, BUT IT'S WORTH IT JUST TO SEE THE LOVELY ORIGINAL PRESSED TIN CEILING, WHICH WAS DISCOVERED DURING A REMODEL WHEN THE CRAPPY MODERN DROP CEILING WAS REMOVED.

BEAUTY AND ESSEX, 146 ESSEX ST. LOWER EAST SIDE, MANHATTAN

BEAUTY AND ESSEX HAS ONE OF MY FAVORITE STOREFRONT FACADES. THE BUILDING USED TO BE HOME TO M. KATZ & SONS FINE FURNITURE (AS IT STILL SAYS ON THE REMAINING VERTICAL SIGN) SO THE BAR IS HUGE. TO GET TO IT, YOU HAVE TO PASS THROUGH THE FULLY FUNCTIONAL PAWN SHOP PACKED WITH GUITARS AND RANDOM TRINKETS AND TREASURES. (FUN FACT: KATZ & SONS FURNITURE, WHICH STARTED IN 1906, IS STILL AROUND, AND STILL A FAMILY-RUN BUSINESS. THEY'RE NOW LOCATED AT 20 ORCHARD STREET.) AS MUCH AS I LIKE THE AESTHETICS OF BEAUTY AND ESSEX, IT ISN'T A BAR I'D CHOOSE TO HANG OUT IN SIMPLY BECAUSE IT'S LARGE AND LOUD AND IRRITATING, AND I AM SMALL AND QUIET AND EASILY ANNOYED.

EMPLOYEES ONLY, 510 HUDSON ST. WEST VILLAGE, MANHATTAN

TO ENTER EMPLOYEES ONLY, LOOK FOR A NEON SIGN IN THE WINDOW THAT SAYS "PSYCHIC" AND PROCEED INTO THE BAR. INSIDE, A TAROT CARD READER IS ON HAND TO SWINDLE ALL THE SUCKERS WHO ONLY BELIEVE IN THE RACKET ONCE THEY'RE DRUNK.

THE SHIP
158 LAFAYETTE ST.
SOHO, MANHATTAN

FULL DISCLOSURE: I'VE NEVER BEEN TO THE SHIP, BUT THEIR MISLEADING WAREHOUSE EXTERIOR IS ONE OF MY FAVORITES. TO BE HONEST, NONE OF THE BARS IN THIS PIECE APPEAL TO ME AS MUCH AS THEIR SECRET FACADES DO. SO DON'T HEED MY BAR SUGGESTIONS, SINCE I MOSTLY HAVE NO IDEA WHAT I'M TALKING ABOUT.

NEW YORK CITY BARS THEN & NOW

490 8TH AVE. IN 1949. MIDTOWN WEST, MANHATTAN

490 8TH AVE. IN 2016

WHITEHALL ST. IN THE 1960'S. FINANCIAL DISTRICT, MANHATTAN

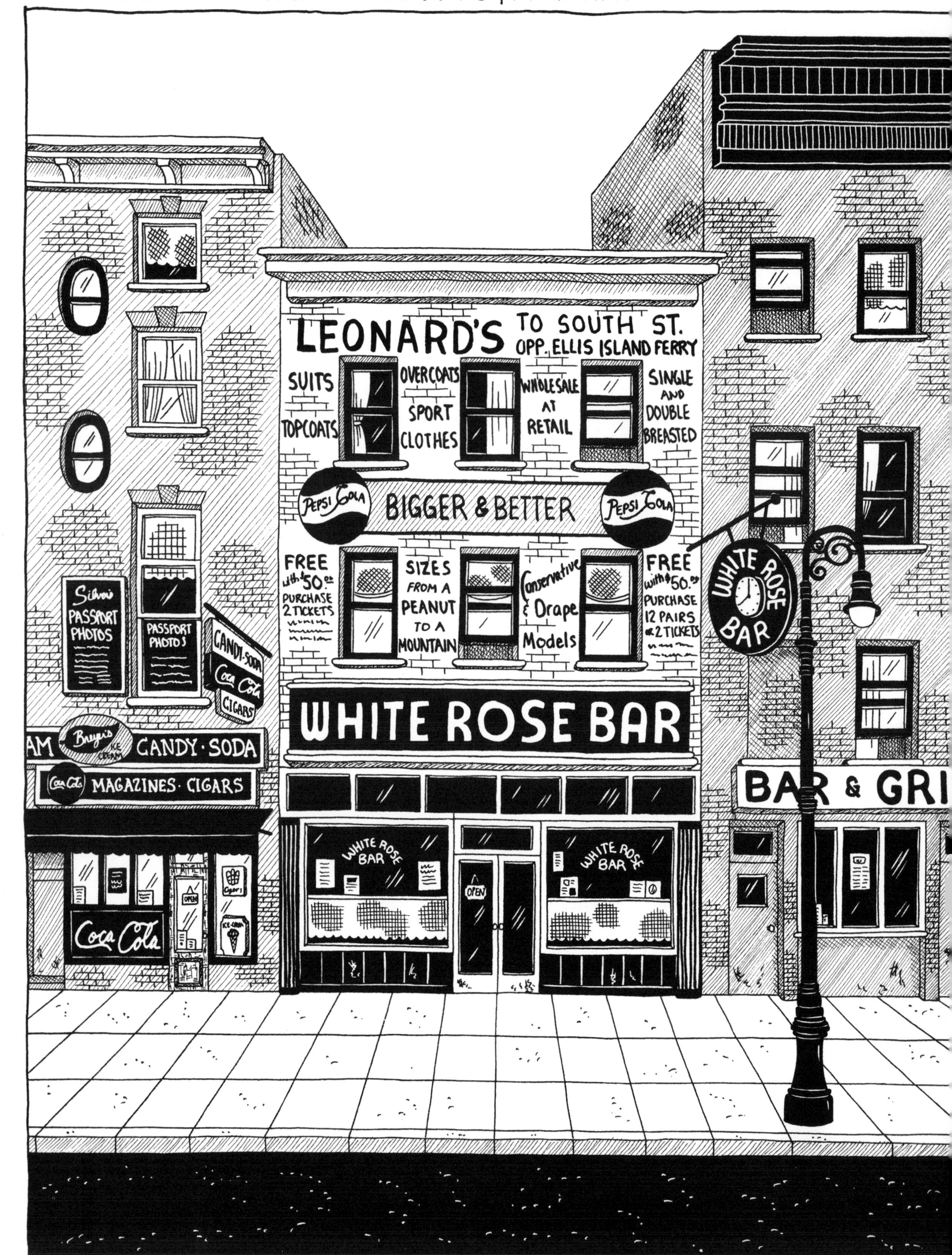

WHITEHALL ST. IN 2016

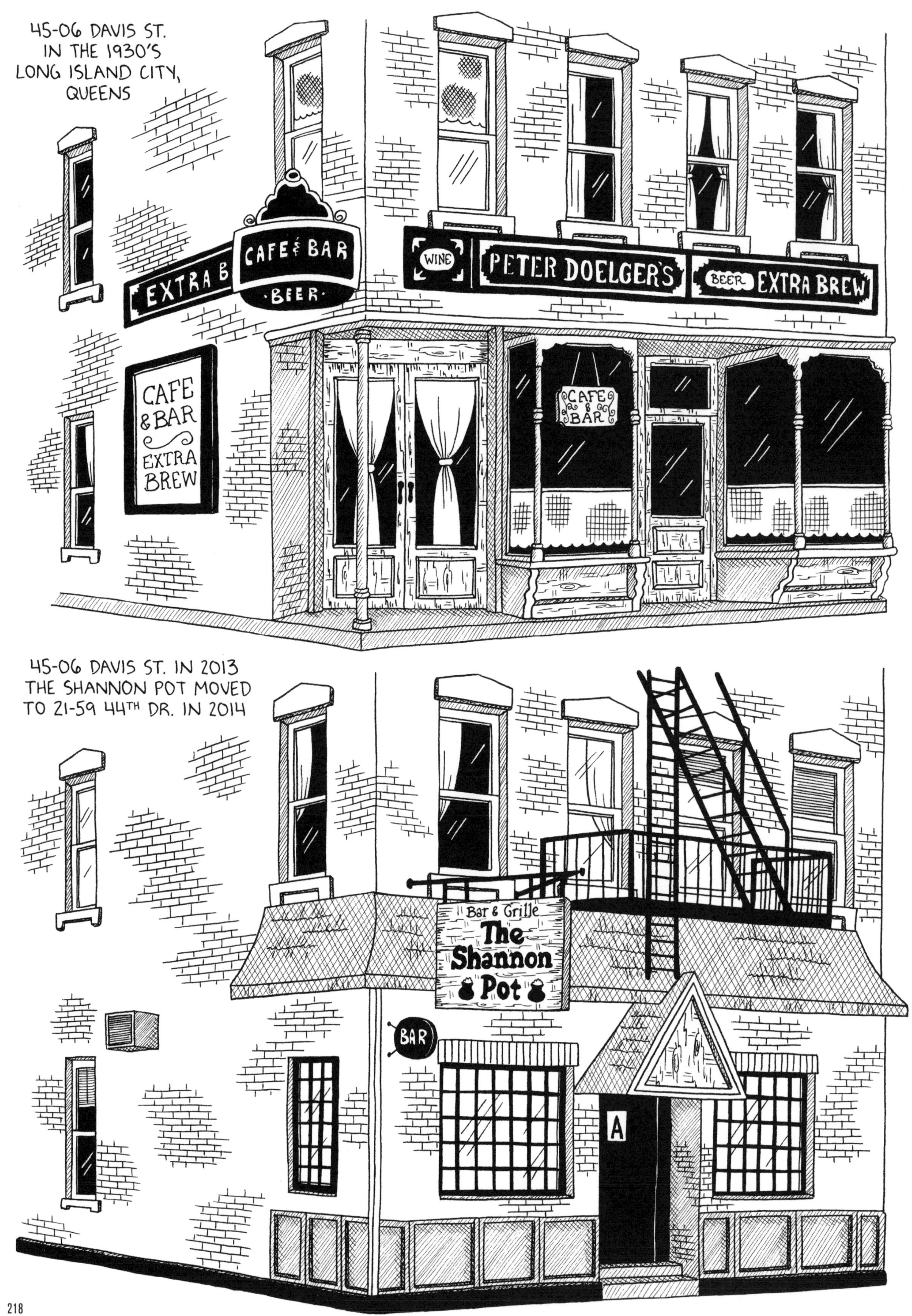
45-06 DAVIS ST.
IN THE 1930'S
LONG ISLAND CITY,
QUEENS
EXTRA B
CAFE & BAR
BEER
WINE
PETER DOELGER'S
BEER
EXTRA BREW
CAFE & BAR
EXTRA BREW
CAFE & BAR
45-06 DAVIS ST. IN 2013
THE SHANNON POT MOVED
TO 21-59 44TH DR. IN 2014
Bar & Grille
The Shannon Pot
BAR
A

TYPHOID MARY: THE INFECTIOUS COOK

BORN MARY MALLON IN 1869 IN IRELAND, TYPHOID MARY GOT HER NAME FROM SPREADING TYPHOID THROUGH HER COOKING DURING HER YEARS AS A COOK AND MAID IN NEW YORK CITY. SHE WAS THE FIRST PERSON IDENTIFIED AS AN IMMUNE CARRIER OF TYPHOID, A SCIENTIFIC MARVEL STILL BEING STUDIED TODAY.

AROUND AGE 14, MALLON EMIGRATED TO AMERICA, WHERE SHE EVENTUALLY WORKED AS A COOK IN MAMARONECK, NEW YORK. SHE ONLY WORKED THERE FOR TWO WEEKS BEFORE SEVERAL RESIDENTS FELL ILL WITH TYPHOID FEVER. MALLON, NOT A SUSPECTED CARRIER AT THE TIME, MOVED TO MANHATTAN WHERE SHE BEGAN WORKING FOR SEVERAL DIFFERENT FAMILIES, MANY OF WHOM FELL ILL.

FROM 1900 TO 1907, MALLON FREQUENTLY JOB-HOPPED AND NAME-CHANGED, SPREADING TYPHOID FEVER THROUGH HER FOOD, WHICH SHE MADE USING HER DIRTY, INFECTIOUS, UNWASHED HANDS. WHEREVER MALLON WORKED, PEOPLE SOON FELL ILL AND MANY DIED. THE STATISTICS AREN'T CONCRETE, BUT IT'S ESTIMATED SHE CAUSED AROUND 50 TYPHOID FEVER FATALITIES.

IN 1906, AN INVESTIGATION WAS LAUNCHED, IN WHICH RESEARCHER GEORGE SOPER BEGAN LOOKING INTO MALLON'S WORK HISTORY AND THE ILLNESSES THAT FOLLOWED HER FROM JOB TO JOB. WHEN CONFRONTED BY SOPER, MALLON REFUSED TO COOPERATE, CLAIMING SHE DIDN'T BELIEVE SHE WAS A CARRIER OF TYPHOID, AND SHE DIDN'T BELIEVE IN PERSONAL HYGIENE WHILE IN THE KITCHEN. MALLON JUST FLAT OUT REFUSED TO WASH HER FILTHY FUCKING HANDS.

WOMAN "TYPHOID FACTORY" HELD AS A PRISONER

Hospital Officials Isolate Mary Ilverson as a Menace.

Mary Ilverson, a cook, large and robust and buxom, is a prisoner in Roosevelt Hospital, adjudged by Sanitary Superintendent Walter O. Bensal, a menace to the community, in that she scatters typhoid germs unconciously.

1907 NEWSPAPER ARTICLE IN *THE EVENING WORLD*, DOCUMENTING MALLON'S FIRST QUARANTINE ON NORTH BROTHER ISLAND

1909 NEWSPAPER ILLUSTRATION OF MARY MALLON AND HER VIRULENT COOKING METHODS

BY 1907, SOPER HAD AMASSED ENOUGH EVIDENCE AGAINST MALLON FOR THE HEALTH DEPARTMENT TO HAVE HER ARRESTED AND QUARANTINED ON NORTH BROTHER ISLAND, WHERE SHE REMAINED FOR THREE YEARS.

UPON HER RELEASE, WHICH WAS CONTINGENT ON HER NEVER WORKING AS A COOK AGAIN, THE DEFIANT MALLON CHANGED HER NAME AND RESUMED HER WORK AS A COOK, WHICH INEVITABLY RESUMED THE SPREADING OF TYPHOID. SOPER, STILL ON THE CASE, WAS UNABLE TO TRACK MALLON BECAUSE SHE CHANGED JOBS SO FREQUENTLY.

FAMOUS PHOTO OF MALLON DURING HER FIRST QUARANTINE AT RIVERSIDE HOSPITAL ON NORTH BROTHER ISLAND

IN 1915, MALLON CAUSED A LARGE OUTBREAK OF TYPHOID AT THE SLOANE HOSPITAL FOR WOMEN, WHERE SHE WAS WORKING AS A COOK ONCE AGAIN. MALLON WAS ARRESTED AND RETURNED TO QUARANTINE ON NORTH BROTHER ISLAND ON A PERMANENT BASIS, WHERE SHE SPENT THE REST OF HER DAYS ISOLATED IN A QUAINT COTTAGE.

MALLON DIED OF PNEUMONIA IN 1938. HER ASHES WERE BURIED IN ST. RAYMOND'S CEMETERY IN THE BRONX.

BUSINESS SIGNS OF YORE & TODAY

McCARTYS
BILLIARD
PARLOR
452

KEYS MADE
GLASS
Cut to size
ALLIED
BUILDERS
HARDWARE
PLUMBING SUPPLIES
PAINTS
ELECTRICAL SUPPLIES

PAINTS
HARDWARE
PLUMBING
WARSHAW
EST. 1928
AIR CONDITIONING - SALES - SERVICE
JANITOR SUPPLIES
LOCKSMITH
ELECTRICIAN

ŁOMŻYNIANKA
RESTAURACJA

French GARMENT CLEANERS Co.

A TRUNCATED HISTORY OF *THE VILLAGE VOICE*

SINCE THE ADVENT OF PRINT, NEW YORK CITY HAS HOSTED COUNTLESS NUMBERS OF ALTERNATIVE WEEKLIES COVERING ART, CULTURE, POLITICS, CURRENT AFFAIRS, AND MORE. INARGUABLY, THE MOST FAMOUS WEEKLY IS *THE VILLAGE VOICE*, THE OLDEST AND MOST WIDELY DISTRIBUTED PAPER OF ITS TYPE IN THE UNITED STATES. IT'S NEARLY IMPOSSIBLE TO WRITE A CONCLUSIVE HISTORY OF A 60-YEAR-OLD, HUGELY INFLUENTIAL PAPER, SO PLEASE FORGIVE ANY GLARING OMISSIONS.
THE VOICE WAS CREATED IN A GREENWICH VILLAGE APARTMENT BY NORMAN MAILER, ED FANCHER, JOHN WILCOCK, AND DAN WOLF. THE FIRST ISSUE LAUNCHED IN OCTOBER OF 1955, WITH A FOCUS ON LOCAL EVENTS, CULTURE, AND POLITICS.
the Village Voice
coffee
the village Voice
5¢
THE 'VOICE' NUMBER 1
VILLAGE TRUCKER SUES COLUMBIA
MAILER, IN HIS MID-20'S AT THE TIME, WAS THE MORE RADICAL ONE, AND FREQUENTLY AT ODDS WITH HIS CO-CREATORS. MAILER'S OUTLANDISH COLUMNS DEFINED THE EARLY YEARS OF THE PAPER. HE DUBBED HIMSELF "GENERAL MARIJUANA," AND WROTE PASSIONATELY ABOUT HIS EXPLOITS, AS WELL AS OTHER MORE CONTROVERSIAL CULTURAL IDEOLOGY. HIS ECCENTRICITY CLASHED WITH FANCHER AND WOLF, WHO REJECTED MANY OF MAILER'S IDEAS ABOUT HOW TO DEVELOP *THE VOICE*. DESPITE INTERNAL DISAGREEMENTS, THE MEN PLODDED ON, PUTTING OUT NEW ISSUES EVERY WEEK.
EVEN FROM THE START, *THE VOICE'S* REACH EXTENDED BEYOND THE PAPER. A YEAR AFTER THE FIRST ISSUE WAS RELEASED, ED FANCHER CREATED THE OBIE AWARDS, FOR EXCELLENCE IN OFF-BROADWAY SHOWS, AS DECIDED BY THEATER CRITIC JERRY TALLMER. EVENTUALLY THE AWARDS BECAME ELIGIBLE FOR OFF-OFF-BROADWAY SHOWS, MEANING ANY PLAY ANYWHERE IN THE CITY COULD BE CONSIDERED FOR AN AWARD.
the Village Voice
the village Voice
IN THE 1960'S, *THE VOICE* MOVED TO SHERIDAN SQUARE, WHERE IT CONTINUED TO GROW, BECOMING A HIGHLY RESPECTED INDEPENDENT WEEKLY PAPER. AT THAT TIME IT WAS NOT FREE, AN ELEMENT THAT WOULD DEFINE THE PAPER'S LATER YEARS.

THE VOICE CYCLED THROUGH MULTIPLE COLUMNS, MANY OF WHICH BECAME LONG RUNNING AND HIGHLY LAUDED, SUCH AS HOWARD SMITH'S "SCENES," WHICH COVERED THE 1960'S AND 70'S COUNTERCULTURE. SMITH, ALONG WITH A HANDFUL OF OTHER JOURNALISTS AT THE TIME (E.G., HUNTER THOMPSON) FORGED A NEW TYPE OF IMMERSIVE JOURNALISM BY WRITERS WHO ACTUALLY LIVED THE LIVES THEY WROTE ABOUT, AS OPPOSED TO WRITING ABOUT LIVES THEY MERELY OBSERVED.

AS MORE WEEKLY PAPERS POPPED UP AS COMPETITION, *THE VOICE* MAINTAINED ITS STRONG SALES AND RELIABLE REPUTATION AS A GO-TO FOR RADICAL JOURNALISM AND LOCAL EVENTS. IT WAS ALSO NOTORIOUS FOR HAVING MORE INFLAMMATORY ADULT CONTENT THAN ITS COMPETITORS, INCLUDING SEX ADVICE COLUMNS AND BACK-PAGE ESCORT SERVICE ADS.

IN THE MID-1970'S, *THE VOICE* MOVED ITS OFFICES TO 80 UNIVERSITY PLACE.

A SMALL SAMPLING OF THE MANY NYC PAPERS OF THE 20TH CENTURY

THE PAPER RAN (AND MADE FAMOUS) MANY CARTOONISTS SUCH AS R. CRUMB, MATT GROENING, LYNDA BARRY, STAN MACK, MARK ALAN STAMATY, TED RALL, TOM TOMORROW, WARD SUTTON, RUBEN BOLLING, AND M. WARTELLA, WHO WENT ON TO FOUND DREAM FACTORY. BY 2000, CONTRIBUTORS TERESA CARPENTER, JULES FEIFFER, AND MARK SCHOOFS HAD SNAGGED THREE PULITZER PRIZES FOR THEIR WORK IN THE PAPER.

THE VOICE HAS BEEN A LONGTIME SUPPORTER OF LGBT RIGHTS. IN THE 50'S, THEY WERE THE ONLY PAPER TO INTENTIONALLY HIRE OPENLY GAY WRITERS. HOWEVER, IN THE LATE 60'S, SOME OF THEIR COVERAGE OF THE STONEWALL RIOTS WAS PERCEIVED AS HOMOPHOBIC, DUE TO REPEATED USE OF THE WORDS "FAGGOTS" AND "DYKES." IRONICALLY, THE PAPER ALSO DID NOT ALLOW GAY CLUBS TO RUN ADS IN THE CLASSIFIEDS, CITING THE WORD "GAY" AS BEING DEROGATORY, WHICH IS HILARIOUS CONSIDERING THE LANGUAGE ALLOWED IN THEIR ARTICLES. THE POLICY WAS EVENTUALLY ERADICATED. BUT FOR THE MOST PART, *THE VOICE* STRONGLY SUPPORTED (AND STILL SUPPORTS) GAY RIGHTS. IN 1982, THEY BECAME THE SECOND ORGANIZATION IN THE UNITED STATES TO OFFER EMPLOYEE BENEFITS TO SAME-SEX COUPLES IN DOMESTIC PARTNERSHIPS.

IN THE 1990'S, *THE VOICE* MOVED TO ITS CURRENT LOCATION AT 36 COOPER SQUARE, WHERE IT CONTINUED TO RUN POPULAR COLUMNS LIKE THE "PAZZ & JOP" MUSIC POLL, RUN BY ROBERT CHRISTGAU. (IT STILL RUNS TODAY.) IN 1996, *THE VOICE* DITCHED ITS COVER PRICE AND BECAME A FREE WEEKLY PAPER.

IN 2005, THE PAPER WAS BOUGHT BY NEW TIMES MEDIA, MUCH TO THE CHAGRIN OF MANY READERS WHO CONSIDERED THE MOVE A SELL-OUT. THE PAPER WAS PLAGUED WITH PROBLEMS FROM THE MINUTE THEY WERE ACQUIRED. THE NEW ADMINISTRATION FIRED MANY WELL-KNOWN, LONGTIME COLUMNISTS, INCITING INTERNAL AND PUBLIC BACKLASH. THE PAPER TOOK ON A NOTICEABLY MORE MAINSTREAM ANGLE, WHICH SEEMED LIKE IT MIGHT WORK, BUT BY 2008, HALF OF *THE VOICE'S* STAFF WAS GONE.

STAFFING ISSUES WERE NOT THE ONLY PROBLEM THE PAPER GRAPPLED WITH. THE RISE IN ONLINE MEDIA WAS HAVING A HUGELY NEGATIVE IMPACT ON PRINT MEDIA. AD REVENUE, *THE VOICE'S* FINANCIAL MAINSTAY, SHARPLY DECLINED. TO STAY RELEVANT, THE PAPER GOT ONLINE, AND REDUCED THEIR PHYSICAL CIRCULATION.

IN 2015, *THE VOICE* WAS PURCHASED BY PETER D. BARBEY, AN AFFLUENT FIGURE OF MUCH DEBATE, DUE TO HIM SAYING GROSS SHIT, LIKE CLAIMING THE PAPER WAS "ONE OF AMERICA'S GREAT NEWSPAPER BRANDS IN TERMS OF POTENTIAL BY THE POUND... THERE'S GREAT VALUE IN *THE VILLAGE VOICE* BRAND." DESPITE BARBEY'S CONTROVERSIAL INFLUENCE, *THE VOICE* HAS RECENTLY DONE A GREAT JOB OF EMPLOYING CARTOONISTS, AND PAYING THEM WELL, WHICH IS PRETTY UNHEARD OF IN THE COMICS INDUSTRY, SO THEY GET KUDOS FOR THAT.

THERE HAS NOT BEEN ENOUGH TIME TO ACCURATELY ASSESS HOW BARBEY'S OWNERSHIP HAS AFFECTED THE PAPER, OR IF IT CAN REGAIN THE ALTERNATIVE CREDIBILITY IT ONCE HAD. BUT REGARDLESS OF THE DIFFERING OPINIONS OF WHAT *THE VILLAGE VOICE* HAS BECOME, IT IS UNDENIABLE THAT IT WAS ONE OF THE MOST IMPORTANT AND INFLUENTIAL WEEKLIES OF THE 20TH CENTURY.

60 E.161ST ST. IN 1941. CONCOURSE VILLAGE

60 E.161ST ST. IN 2016

E. KINGSBRIDGE RD. BETWEEN E. FORDHAM RD. AND COLE LN. IN THE 1930'S

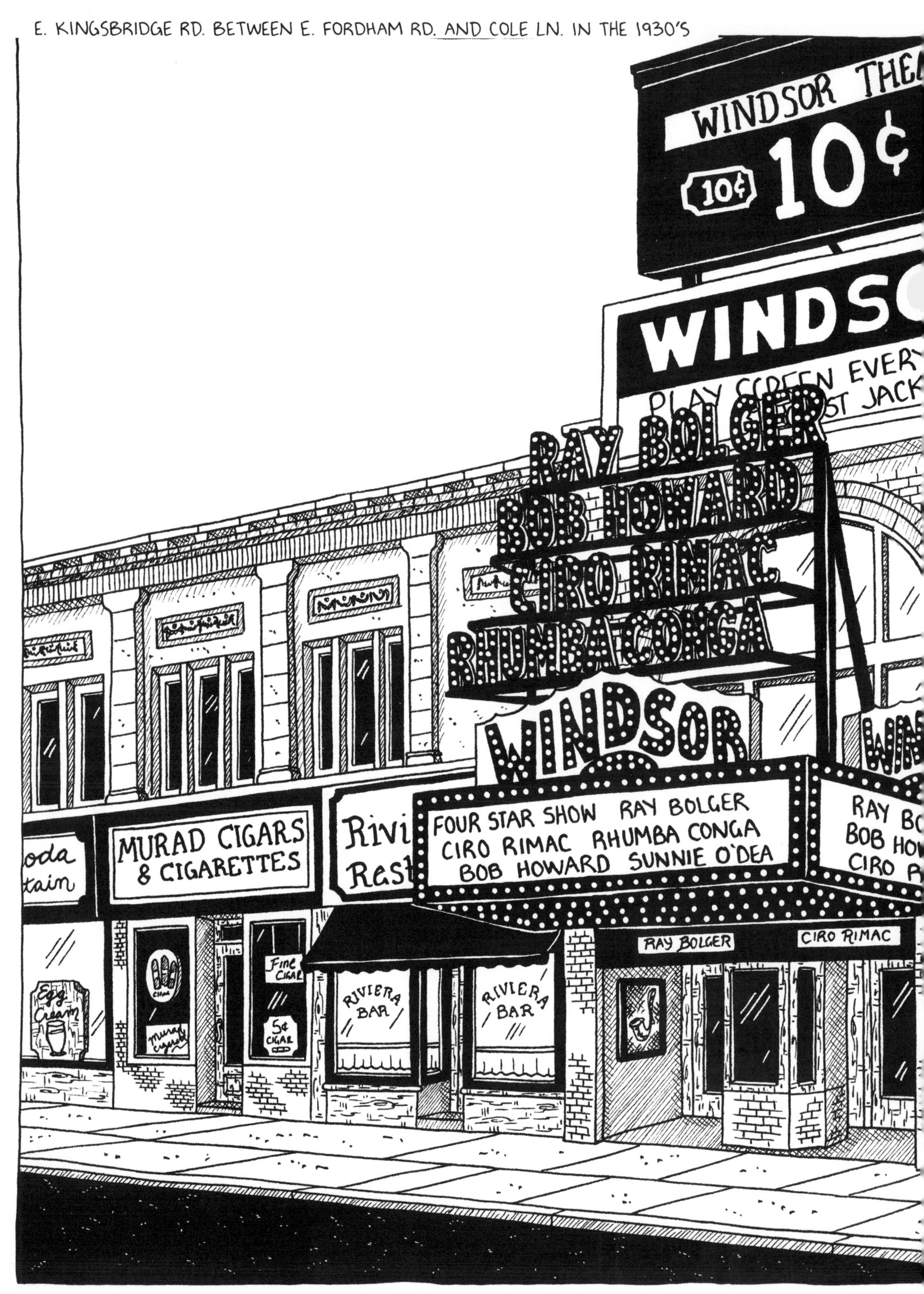

LUCKY STRIKE
Be Happy, Go Lucky!
fine
LUCKY STRIKE TOBACCO
WINDSOR BEAUTY SALON
WINDSOR
BEAUTY
DR. HALL DENTIST
JEWELRY CASH BUYER OLD GOLD & SILVER
GOLD
SHEILS CAFE
&BAR
MAR
10¢

E. KINGSBRIDGE RD. BETWEEN E. FORDHAM RD. AND COLE LN. IN 2014

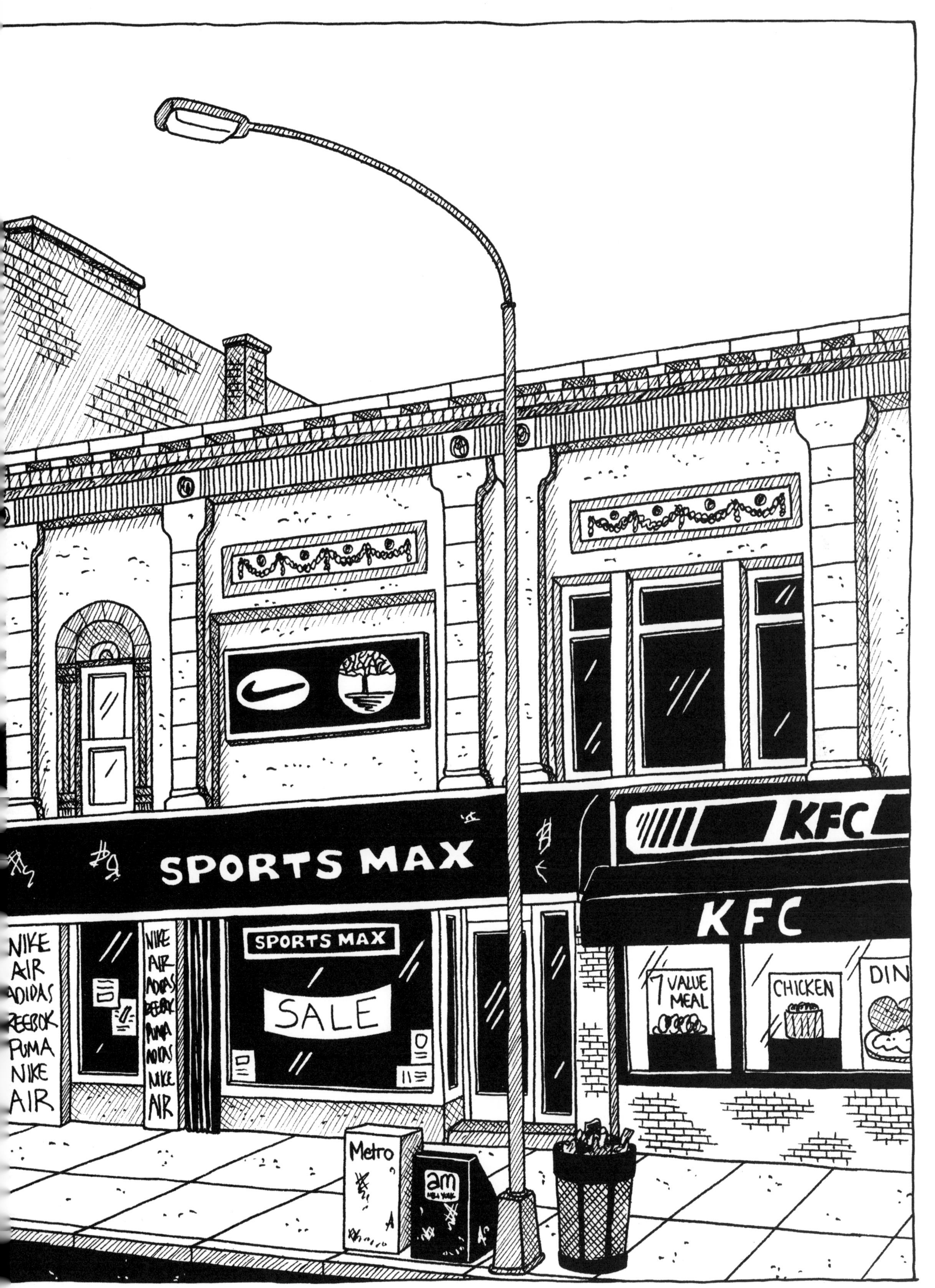

KFC
SPORTS MAX
KFC
NIKE
AIR
ADIDAS
REEBOK
PUMA
NIKE
AIR
NIKE
AIR
ADIDAS
REEBOK
PUMA
ADIDAS
NIKE
AIR
SPORTS MAX
SALE
7 VALUE MEAL
CHICKEN
DIN
Metro
am

NEW YORK CITY'S OLDEST BAKERIES STILL OPEN TODAY

FERRARA BAKERY & CAFE, 195 GRAND ST. LITTLE ITALY, MANHATTAN. OPEN SINCE 1892

GLASER'S BAKE SHOP
1670 1ST AVE.
UPPER EAST SIDE, MANHATTAN
OPEN SINCE 1902

EGIDIO PASTRY
622 E.187TH ST.
BELMONT, BRONX
OPEN SINCE 1912

PARISI BAKERY
198 MOTT ST.
NOLITA, MANHATTAN
OPEN SINCE 1903

CAPUTO'S BAKE SHOP
329 COURT ST.
CARROLL GARDENS, BROOKLYN
OPEN SINCE 1904

VENIERO'S PASTRY SHOP
342 E. 11TH ST.
EAST VILLAGE
OPEN SINCE 1894

CAFFÉ ROMA PASTRY
385 BROOME ST.
LITTLE ITALY, MANHATTAN
OPEN SINCE 1891

BAKERIES OF NYC THEN & NOW

AMSTERDAM AVE. AND W. 167TH ST. IN THE 1930'S
UPPER WEST SIDE, MANHATTAN

AMSTERDAM AVE. AND W.167TH ST. IN 2014
AMSTERDAM
Lofts & Condos
realtor.COM
BUSINESS, RESIDENTUAL, CO-OP HOUSING, HOMES, BROWNSTONES & MORE
NATIONAL ASSOCIATION OF REALTORS
COLUMBIA UNIVERSITY MEDICAL CENTER
AMSTERDAM
W. 167TH ST
AHEAD
2172
GROCERY
SANDWICHES · SODA · BEER · ATM
ATM
LAS REYNAS
RESTAURANT
LAS REYNAS
LAS REYNAS
LAS REYNAS
RESTAURANT
OPEN
LAS REYNAS
LAS REYNAS
RES
REAL TASTE
ZERO SUGAR
IT'S POSSIBLE!
Coca Cola
ZERO
OPEN HAPPINESS

fresh Bread
BAKERY
BAKERY
BAKERY
4123 8TH AVE. IN 1915
SUNSET PARK, BROOKLYN

NEW YORK LOTTERY
PLAY HERE
LOTTO·SCRATCH
Mini Market
777
4123
Mini Market
NEW 777
WE ACCEPT FOOD STAMPS
718-633-5866
LOTTERY·BEER·SODA·CANDY·
NEW YORK LOTTERY
BREAKFAST
OPEN
OPEN
NEW YORK LOTTERY
WE ACCEPT EBT & WIC
Budweiser
Blue Moon
WE APPRECIATE YOUR BUSINESS
LUNCH SPECIAL
ATM
4123 8TH AVE. IN 2016

LIZZIE HALLIDAY: THE FORGOTTEN SERIAL KILLER ARSONIST

LIZZIE HALLIDAY, ORIGINALLY NAMED ELIZA MARGARET MCNALLY, WAS BORN IN 1859 IN IRELAND, AND EMIGRATED TO NEW YORK AS A CHILD. HER CLAIM TO FAME IS BEING A MOSTLY FORGOTTEN SERIAL KILLER AND ARSONIST. *THE NEW YORK TIMES* DUBBED HER THE "WORST WOMAN ON EARTH."

LIZZIE'S FIRST HUSBAND/VICTIM WAS CHARLES HOPKINS, WHOM SHE MARRIED IN 1877. HOPKINS WAS DEAD BY 1879. NEXT, SHE MARRIED ARTEMUS BREWER, WHO DIED LESS THAN A YEAR LATER. THESE DEATHS WOULD NOT BECOME SUSPICIOUS UNTIL MANY YEARS LATER, WHEN IT WAS PRESUMED LIZZIE POISONED THEM. LIZZIE THEN TRIED TO COURT A MAN NAMED HIRAM PARKINSON, BUT HE FLED, PERHAPS HAVING SENSED HIS IMPENDING UNTIMELY DEMISE AT HER HAND. UNDETERRED, LIZZIE MARRIED GEORGE SMITH, WHO WAS A FRIEND OF HER MURDERED SECOND HUSBAND. SHE TRIED TO POISON HIM TOO, BUT WHEN SHE FAILED, SHE FLED TO VERMONT, WHERE SHE MARRIED CHARLES PLAYSTEL. LIZZIE ALMOST IMMEDIATELY DISAPPEARED (WITHOUT MURDERING PLAYSTEL) AND REAPPEARED IN PHILADELPHIA.

IN PHILADELPHIA, LIZZIE LIVED WITH THE McQUILLAN FAMILY; A HUSBAND, WIFE AND THEIR LITTLE GIRL. LIZZIE OPENED A LITTLE SHOP, WHICH SHE PROMPTLY BURNED DOWN FOR THE INSURANCE MONEY. AROUND THE SAME TIME, TWO OF THE McQUILLANS DISAPPEARED, LEAVING ONLY THE HUSBAND. LIZZIE WAS ARRESTED FOR THE FIRST TIME, AND SERVED TWO YEARS IN PRISON FOR ARSON, BUT NOT MURDER, AS THERE WERE NO BODIES YET DISCOVERED.

SHORTLY AFTER HER RELEASE, LIZZIE WENT TO WORK AS A MAID FOR A SULLIVAN COUNTY MAN NAMED PAUL HALLIDAY. PAUL EVENTUALLY MARRIED LIZZIE, ALTHOUGH IT WAS RUMORED THAT HE DID IT ONLY TO AVOID PAYING HER FOR HER MAID SERVICES. PERHAPS UNDERSTANDABLY, LIZZIE EVENTUALLY FLED WITH A NEIGHBOR AND A FLEET OF HORSES. ONCE THEY REACHED NEWBURGH, THE NEIGHBOR DESERTED HER AND SHE WAS ARRESTED FOR THEFT OF THE HORSES. SHE PLEADED INSANITY, AND WAS SENT TO AN ASYLUM.

AT THE ASYLUM, LIZZIE RECONCILED WITH PAUL, WHO SECURED HER RELEASE, AND RETURNED TO HIS HOUSE, WHICH SHE PROMPTLY BURNED DOWN. THE FIRE CONSUMED PAUL'S HOUSE, BARN, AND A NEARBY MILL, AND KILLED ONE OF HIS SONS. AFTER THE FIRE, PAUL DISAPPEARED.

WHEN PAUL DID NOT RESURFACE, HIS PROPERTY WAS SEARCHED, AND THE BODIES OF THE MISSING McQUILLAN FAMILY WERE DISCOVERED BURIED UNDER A HAYSTACK. THEY HAD BEEN SHOT. LIZZIE WAS ARRESTED AND IMPRISONED AGAIN. A FEW DAYS LATER, PAUL'S BODY WAS DISCOVERED UNDER THE FLOORBOARDS OF THE BURNED-OUT HOUSE. HE HAD BEEN HOGTIED AND SHOT. LIZZIE WAS CHARGED WITH ALL THREE MURDERS.

DURING HER TIME IN CONFINEMENT, LIZZIE WAS A DIFFICULT PRISONER. SHE FREQUENTLY REUSED TO EAT, SHE LIT HER BEDCLOTHES ON FIRE, TRIED TO HANG HERSELF, TRIED TO STRANGLE THE SHERIFF'S WIFE, AND EVEN SLASHED HER THROAT AND ARMS WITH BROKEN GLASS. SHE WAS CHAINED TO THE PRISON FLOOR FOR THREE MONTHS DUE TO THIS BEHAVIOR.

WHILE IN PRISON, LIZZIE BECAME A NATIONAL SENSATION WHEN DOZENS OF NEWSPAPERS AGGRANDIZED HER STORY. FAMOUS JOURNALIST NELLIE BLY WAS GRANTED A RARE FACE-TO-FACE INTERVIEW WITH LIZZIE FOR *THE NEW YORK WORLD.*

She did not raise her head when told to do so, but commenced shaking her skirt and rubbing her hand over the arm of the constable standing before her. She made no reply as her name, residence, occupation and religious instruction were asked, nor did she seem to hear the questions. After she had taken her seat, the shaking of her head and hands which had previously marked her conduct in the court room began. She also, as on other occasions, slapped the hand holding the handkerchief against her mouth quite hard. When asked if she had any legal reasons to show why sentence should not be pronounced she made no reply.

MURDER BY A MANIAC

Lizzie Halliday, Ex-Gypsy, Adds a Seventh Victim to Her List.

STABS NURSE WITH SHEARS

Horrible Crime of Crazy Woman in Hospital For Insane Criminals at Matteawan, N.Y.

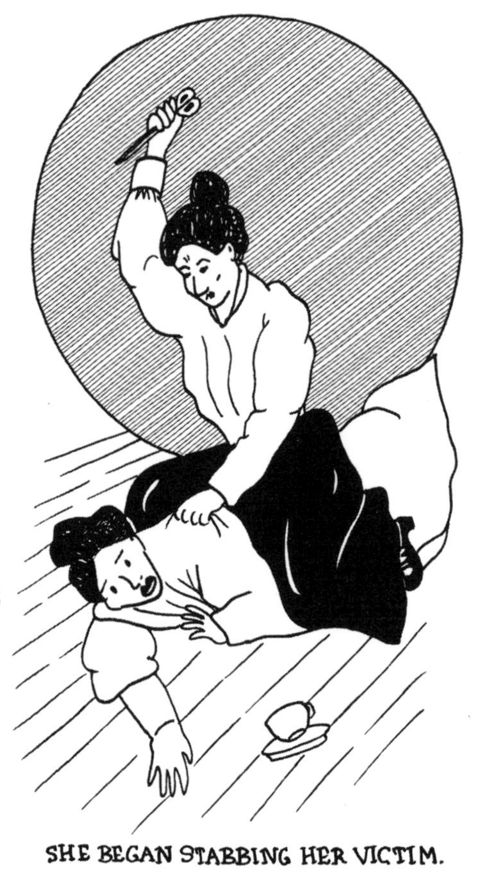

SHE BEGAN STABBING HER VICTIM.

WITH SENSATIONALIZED AND SOMETIMES ERRONEOUS FACTS FLYING AROUND, LIZZIE WAS BRIEFLY ACCUSED OF BEING LONDON'S INFAMOUS SERIAL KILLER JACK THE RIPPER. WHEN ASKED ABOUT IT, LIZZIE REPLIED, "DO YOU THINK I AM AN ELEPHANT? THAT WAS DONE BY A MAN."

WHEN LIZZIE WENT TO TRIAL, HER BEHAVIOR IN COURT WAS ERRATIC. SHE WAS CONVICTED OF THE McQUILLAN MURDERS AND SENTENCED TO DEATH. SHE AGAIN MADE NEWS AS THE FIRST WOMAN IN THE NATION TO BE SENTENCED TO DEATH ROW, ALTHOUGH SHE DID NOT REMAIN THERE LONG.

LIZZIE ESCAPED HER COURT-MANDATED FATE WITH A VERY CONVINCING INSANITY PLEA. INSTEAD OF BEING EXECUTED, HER SENTENCE WAS DEFERRED AND SHE WAS SENT TO MATTEAWAN HOSPITAL FOR THE CRIMINALLY INSANE IN DUCHESS COUNTY. WHILE IN THE ASYLUM, LIZZIE CLAIMED HER LAST VICTIM, A NURSE NAMED NELLIE WICKES, WHOM LIZZIE STABBED 200 TIMES WITH A PAIR OF SCISSORS.

LIZZIE SPENT THE REST OF HER LIFE IN THE ASYLUM, WHERE SHE FINALLY DIED OF KIDNEY DISEASE IN 1918. BY THE TIME OF HER DEATH, LIZZIE HAD FIVE PROVEN MURDERS AGAINST HER, ALTHOUGH MANY SOURCES THINK SHE GOT AWAY WITH A LOT MORE. SHE WAS BURIED IN THE MATTEAWAN PATIENT CEMETERY IN AN UNMARKED GRAVE.

LIZZIE HALLIDAY DEAD

Guilty of Five Murders and Described as 'Worst Woman on Earth.'

Special to The New York Times.

BEACON, N.Y. June 28.- Lizzie Halliday, described as the "worst woman on earth" after she had killed five persons, her husband, a step-son, two women friends, and then a nurse who attended her in Matteawan Asylum, died at the State Hospital today. She was convicted and then adjudged insane, but there was a strong suspicion that she had murdered several others, including a former husband and an itinerant peddler.

NEIGHBORHOOD SHOPPING & DINING THEN & NOW

W.131ST ST. AND LENNOX AVE. IN 1938. HARLEM, MANHATTAN

W.131ST ST. AND LENNOX AVE. IN 2010

SUTTER AV
WILLIAMS ST
ONE WAY
Coffee

SUTTER AVE. AND WILLIAMS AVE. IN 1942. BROWNSVILLE, BROOKLYN

SUTTER AVE. AND WILLIAMS AVE. IN 2014
SUTTER AV
WILLIAMS ST
ONE WAY

Zino's
BEAUTY SALON
DOMINICAN STYLE
OPEN
Mens Styles
15.

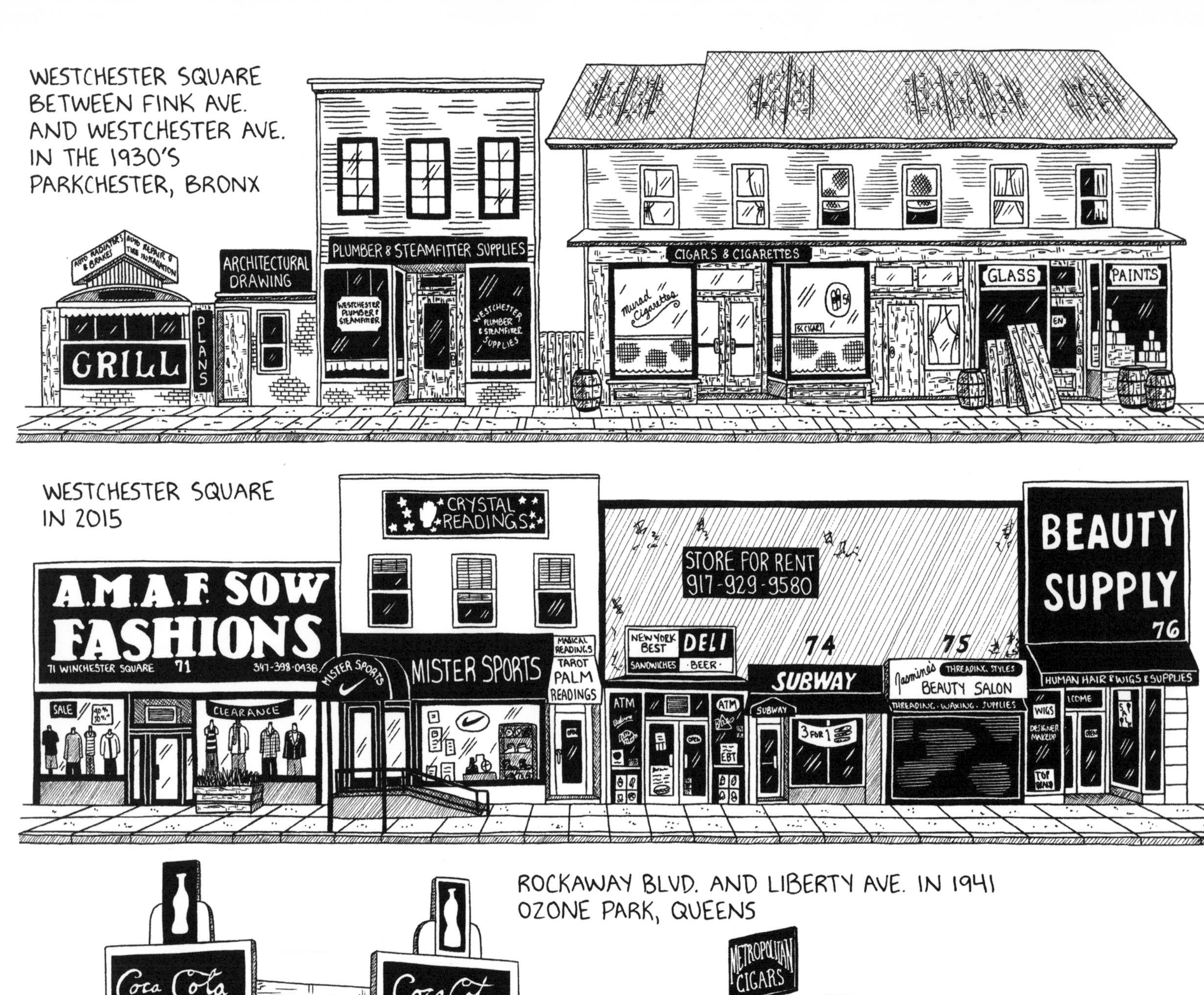
WESTCHESTER SQUARE
BETWEEN FINK AVE.
AND WESTCHESTER AVE.
IN THE 1930'S
PARKCHESTER, BRONX
GRILL
PLANS
ARCHITECTURAL DRAWING
PLUMBER & STEAMFITTER SUPPLIES
CIGARS & CIGARETTES
Murad Cigarettes
GLASS
PAINTS
WESTCHESTER SQUARE
IN 2015
A.M.A.F. SOW
FASHIONS
71 WINCHESTER SQUARE 71 347-398-0438
SALE
CLEARANCE
CRYSTAL READINGS
MISTER SPORTS
MAGICAL READINGS
TAROT
PALM READINGS
STORE FOR RENT
917-929-9580
NEW YORK BEST DELI
SANDWICHES · BEER ·
ATM
74
SUBWAY
3 FOR 1
75
Jasmine's THREADING STYLES
BEAUTY SALON
THREADING · WAXING · SUPPLIES
BEAUTY
SUPPLY
76
HUMAN HAIR & WIGS & SUPPLIES
WIGS

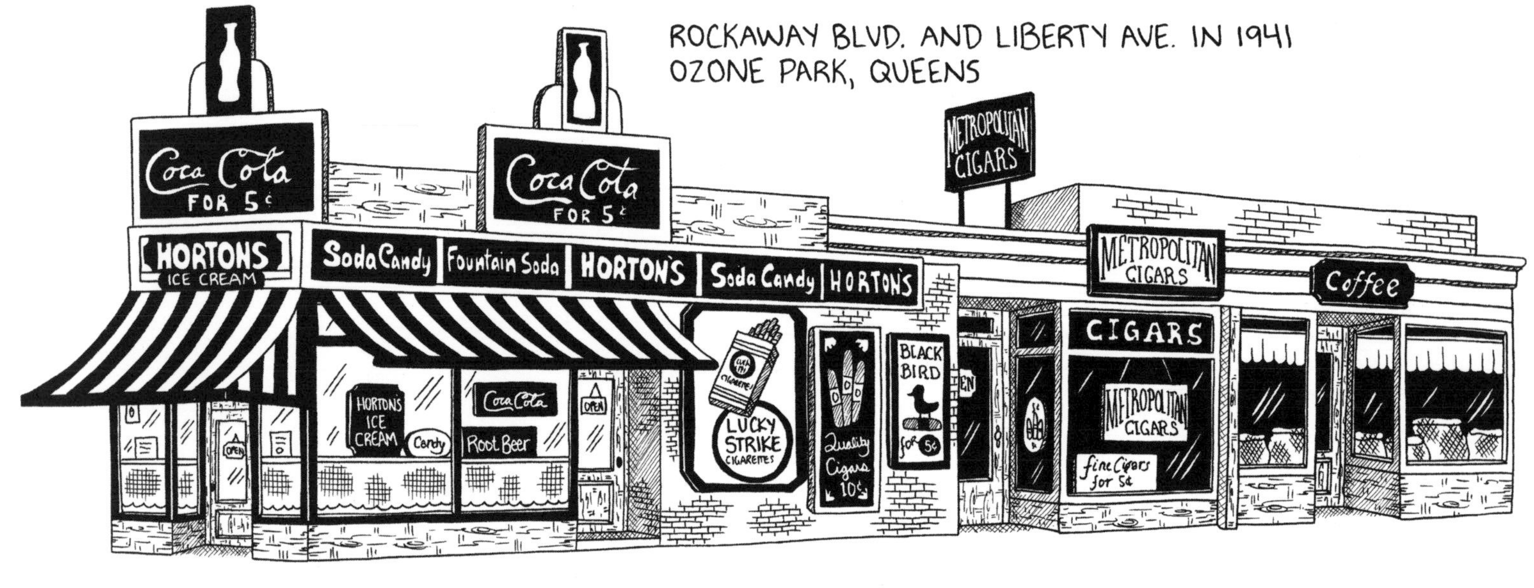
ROCKAWAY BLVD. AND LIBERTY AVE. IN 1941
OZONE PARK, QUEENS
Coca Cola
FOR 5¢
HORTONS
ICE CREAM
Soda Candy | Fountain Soda | HORTON'S | Soda Candy | HORTON'S
HORTONS ICE CREAM
Candy
Coca Cola
Root Beer
OPEN
LUCKY STRIKE
CIGARETTES
Quality Cigars 10¢
BLACK BIRD
for 5¢
METROPOLITAN
CIGARS
CIGARS
METROPOLITAN CIGARS
fine Cigars for 5¢
Coffee

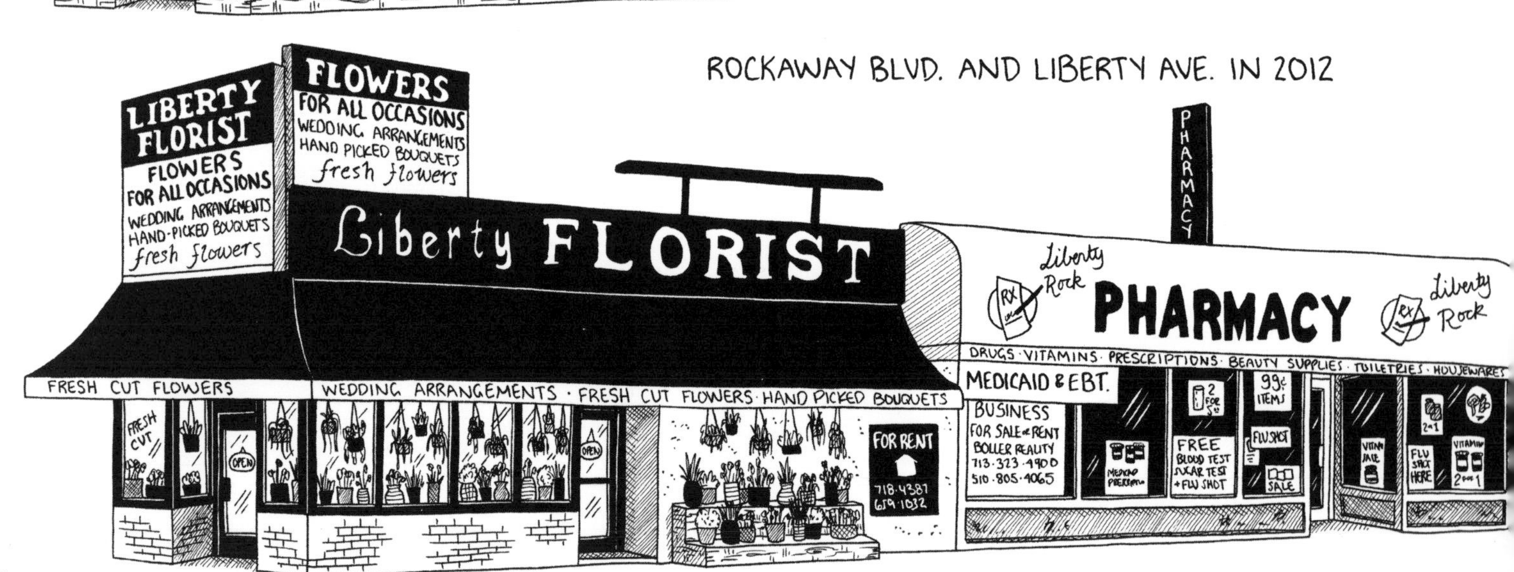
ROCKAWAY BLVD. AND LIBERTY AVE. IN 2012
LIBERTY FLORIST
FLOWERS
FOR ALL OCCASIONS
WEDDING ARRANGEMENTS
HAND-PICKED BOUQUETS
fresh flowers
FLOWERS
FOR ALL OCCASIONS
WEDDING ARRANGEMENTS
HAND PICKED BOUQUETS
fresh flowers
Liberty FLORIST
FRESH CUT FLOWERS
WEDDING ARRANGEMENTS · FRESH CUT FLOWERS · HAND PICKED BOUQUETS
FRESH CUT
OPEN
FOR RENT
718-4387
619-1032
PHARMACY
Liberty Rock
PHARMACY
Liberty Rock
DRUGS · VITAMINS · PRESCRIPTIONS · BEAUTY SUPPLIES · TOILETRIES · HOUSEWARES
MEDICAID & EBT.
BUSINESS
FOR SALE or RENT
BOLLER REALTY
713-323-4900
510-805-4065
99¢ ITEMS
FREE
BLOOD TEST
SUGAR TEST
+ FLU SHOT
FLU SHOT
SALE
FLU SHOT HERE

VANISHING NEW YORK CITY

THE FOLLOWING SIX STORES WERE DRAWN FOR A *NEW YORK TIMES* PIECE BY JAYNE MERKEL, CALLED "NEW YORK'S DISAPPEARING STOREFRONTS," ABOUT VANISHING INDEPENDENT BUSINESSES. IT WAS ESPECIALLY HEARTBREAKING FOR ME TO SEE NEW YORK CENTRAL ART SUPPLY CLOSE IN 2016, THE SAME YEAR I LEFT THE CITY. THE STORE HAD BEEN A FAVORITE OF MANY ARTISTS, MYSELF INCLUDED. I USED TO BUY MOLESKINE NOTEBOOKS THERE, THEN WALK AROUND THE CITY AND FILL THEM WITH SKETCHES THAT EVENTUALLY BECAME THIS BOOK.

NEW YORK CENTRAL ART SUPPLY
62 3RD AVE.
EAST VILLAGE, MANHATTAN
1905–2016

EMPIRE DINER, 210 10TH AVE. CHELSEA, MANHATTAN
OPEN 1946–2016*
*MAYBE. THE DINER HAS OPENED AND CLOSED MANY TIMES THROUGHOUT THE YEARS.

ROCCO'S CALAMARI
6408 FORT HAMILTON PKWY.
DYKER HEIGHTS, BROOKLYN
1981–2016

TEKSERVE, 119 W.23RD ST. CHELSEA, MANHATTAN. 1987–2016

KRUP'S KITCHEN & BATH
11 W.18TH ST.
FLATIRON, MANHATTAN
CLOSED IN 2016

THE CITY QUILTER
133 W.25TH ST.
CHELSEA, MANHATTAN
1997–2016

THE NEXT 20 STOREFRONTS I DREW SIMPLY BECAUSE I WANTED TO. THEY'RE NOT CONNECTED TO *THE TIMES* PIECE, EXCEPT IN SPIRIT. I WAS ABLE TO FIND OPENING AND CLOSING DATES FOR THE MAJORITY OF THESE STORES, BUT SOME OF THAT INFORMATION HAS BEEN LOST TO HISTORY. IT SHOULD ALSO BE NOTED THAT DUE TO THE UNRELIABLE NATURE OF THE INTERNET, IT'S POSSIBLE SOME OF MY INFORMATION IS INCORRECT, SO IF YOU, KIND READER, KNOW SOMETHING I DO NOT, OR NOTICE ANY ERRORS I'VE MADE, PLEASE LET ME KNOW. ALTHOUGH MOST OF THE FOLLOWING STORES ARE CLOSED, A FEW ARE STILL OPEN, AND WILL HOPEFULLY REMAIN THAT WAY FOR MANY MORE YEARS.

RAY'S CANDY STORE
113 AVENUE A
EAST VILLAGE, MANHATTAN
OPEN SINCE 1974

TONY'S LUNCHEONETTE
7206 NEW UTRECHT AVE.
BENSONHURST, BROOKLYN
CLOSED IN 2013

KATY'S CANDY STORE
125 TOMPKINS AVE.
BED-STUY, BROOKLYN
1969–2007

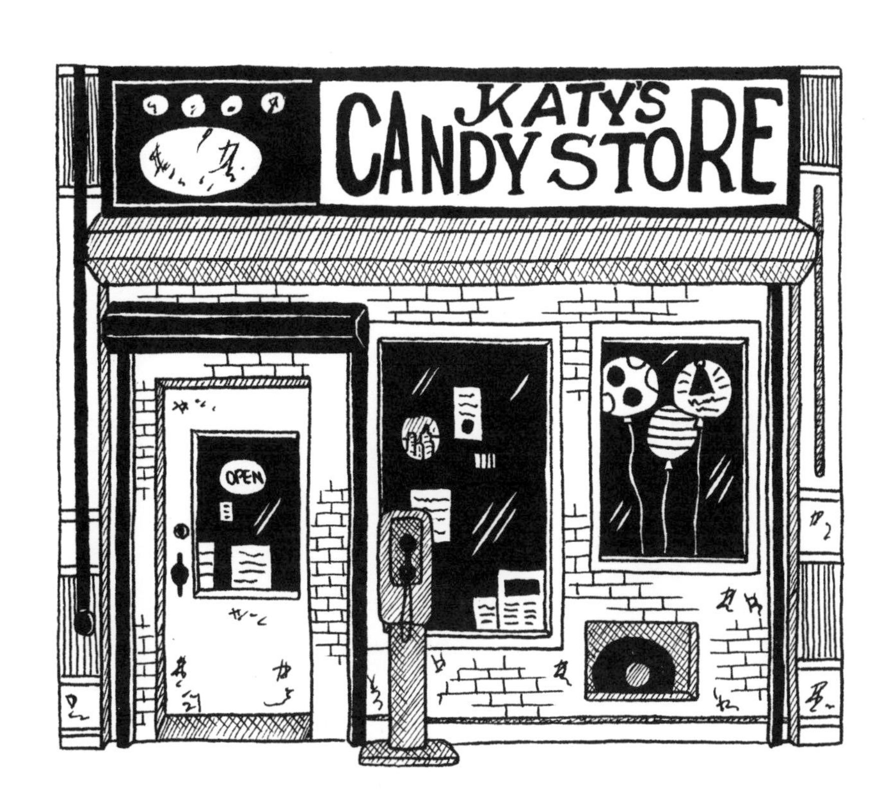

CLAREMONT WINE
& LIQUOR STORE
3826 3RD AVE.
MORRISANIA, BRONX
STILL OPEN, BUT THE
OLD SIGN HAS BEEN
REPLACED

SCHUMER'S WINE & LIQUORS
59 E.54TH ST.
MIDTOWN, MANHATTAN
OPEN SINCE THE 1970'S

BRAND'S WINE & LIQUOR
550 W.145TH ST.
HARLEM, MANHATTAN
STILL OPEN, BUT HAS
A NEW SIGN

CONCOURSE MUSIC CENTER
2366 GRAND CONCOURSE
FORDHAM HEIGHTS, BRONX
CLOSED CIRCA 2007

OTHER MUSIC
15 E. 4TH ST.
EAST VILLAGE,
MANHATTAN
1995–2016

MUSIC INN
169 W. 4TH ST.
WEST VILLAGE, MANHATTAN
OPEN SINCE 1958

LUDLOW GUITARS
164 LUDLOW ST.
LOWER EAST SIDE,
MANHATTAN
1999–2010*
*THIS LOCATION
CLOSED IN 2010 WHEN
THE STORE RELOCATED
TO 189 FRONT ST.

BLEECKER BOB'S
RECORDS
118 W. 3RD ST.
GREENWICH VILLAGE,
MANHATTAN
1968–2013

ZIG ZAG RECORDS
2301 AVE. U
SHEEPSHEAD BAY, BROOKLYN
1976–2011

ASCIONE'S PHARMACY
2268 1ST AVE.
HARLEM, MANHATTAN
CLOSED IN 2013. CURRENTLY IT'S A DOLLAR STORE, BUT THE OLD SIGN STILL EXISTS BENEATH IT.

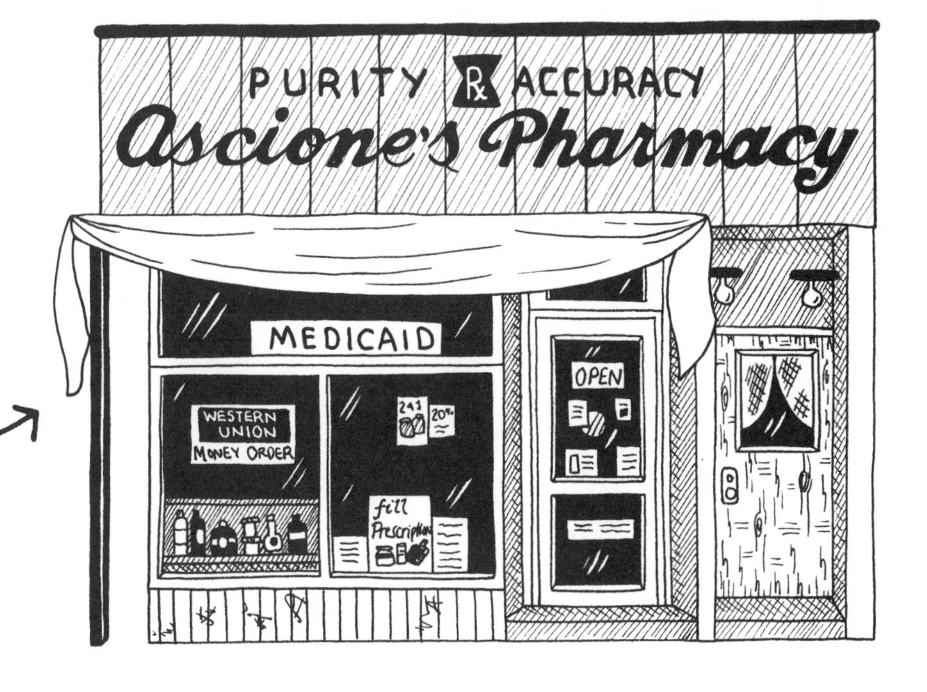

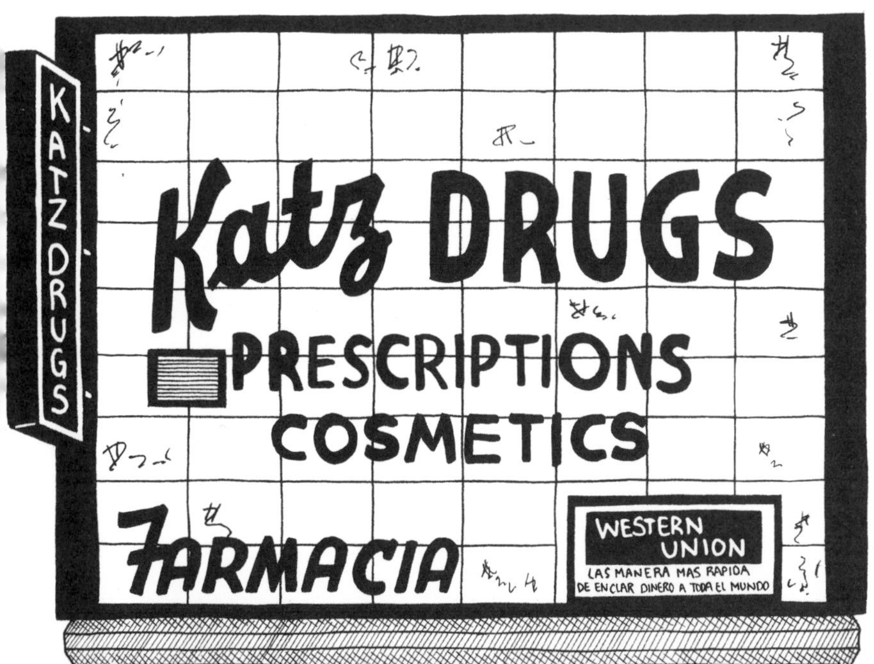

KATZ DRUGS
76 GRAHAM AVE.
EAST WILLIAMSBURG, BROOKLYN
OPEN SINCE 1956

BLOCK DRUG STORES
101 2ND AVE.
EAST VILLAGE, MANHATTAN
OPEN SINCE 1885

M&G DINER
383 W.125TH ST.
HARLEM,
MANHATTAN
1968–2008

DELIGHTFUL
RESTAURANT
2258 1ST AVE.
HARLEM,
MANHATTAN
CLOSED IN 2003

ALDO'S COFFEE SHOP
241 S.4TH ST.
WILLIAMSBURG,
BROOKLYN
CLOSED IN 2011

IDEAL DINETTES
329 KNICKERBOCKER AVE.
BUSHWICK, BROOKLYN
1953–2008

IDEAL HOSIERY, 339 GRAND ST. LOWER EAST SIDE, MANHATTAN. 1965– ?

IDEAL HOSIERY MERITS EXTRA ATTENTION, AS THE WHOLE BUILDING IS SOMETHING OF A MYSTERY. THE LANDMARKED ROW HOUSE WAS BUILT IN 1832-1833, AND THE LAST RENOVATION WAS DONE IN 1932. THE STOREFRONT WAS ADDED IN 1965 WHEN IDEAL HOSIERY OPENED, BUT REPORTEDLY, NOTHING ELSE HAS CHANGED SINCE THE RENOVATION. BUILDINGS THAT OLD HAVE USUALLY BEEN PRESERVED OR RENOVATED. IT'S PRETTY UNCOMMON TO SEE ONE THAT LOOKS TOTALLY UNTOUCHED BY THE CHANGING CITY. BEFORE IT WAS IDEAL HOSIERY, IT WAS A STOVE STORE AND MATTRESS SHOP. THE INTERIOR OF THE BUILDING IS A MYSTERY. IT WAS SUPPOSEDLY APARTMENTS AT ONE TIME, BUT IN THE LATER YEARS, YOU COULD SEE TOWERING PILES OF OLD BOXES IN THE WINDOWS, FILLING ALL THE ROOMS.

THE LONG WALK

DURING MY DECADE IN THE CITY, I OFTEN ESCHEWED THE SUBWAY AND WENT ON LONG WALKS THROUGH MULTIPLE BOROUGHS. MY FAVORITE WALK WENT THROUGH BROOKLYN, MANHATTAN, AND QUEENS. IT STARTED AT HOME IN GREENPOINT, THEN WENT THROUGH WILLIAMSBURG, ACROSS THE WILLIAMSBURG BRIDGE, THROUGH THE LOWER EAST SIDE, CHINATOWN, SOHO, THE BOWERY, GREENWICH VILLAGE, THE EAST VILLAGE, UNION SQUARE, GRAMERCY, KOREATOWN, MIDTOWN, THE UPPER WEST SIDE, CENTRAL PARK, THE UPPER EAST SIDE, ACROSS THE QUEENSBORO BRIDGE, THROUGH LONG ISLAND CITY, AND BACK TO GREENPOINT.

IF MY WALK WAS ENTERTAINMENT BASED, I'D SEE A MOVIE AT THE SUNSHINE CINEMA, THE ANGELIKA, THE 3RD AVENUE AMC, OR EAST VILLAGE CINEMA. IF MY WALK WAS FOOD BASED, I'D EITHER GET AREPAS AT CARACAS, COOKIES AT CITY BAKERY, OR FALAFEL ON ST. MARKS, AND I'D SIT AND EAT AND PEOPLE-WATCH IN TOMPKINS SQUARE PARK OR WASHINGTON SQUARE PARK. THEN I'D GET ICE CREAM AT BIG GAY ICE CREAM, ODDFELLOWS, OR THE CHINATOWN ICE CREAM FACTORY. THE WALK WAS USUALLY ABOUT 15 MILES, GIVE OR TAKE, SINCE I DID A LOT OF ZIG-ZAGGING THROUGH VARIOUS NEIGHBORHOODS. WALKING IS NOT A TIME-EFFICIENT WAY TO GET ANYWHERE, BUT IT'S THE BEST WAY TO TRULY EXPERIENCE THE CITY, AND TO BE REMINDED OF YOUR PLACE IN IT.

ONE OF MANY VARIATIONS OF MY LONG CITY WALKS:

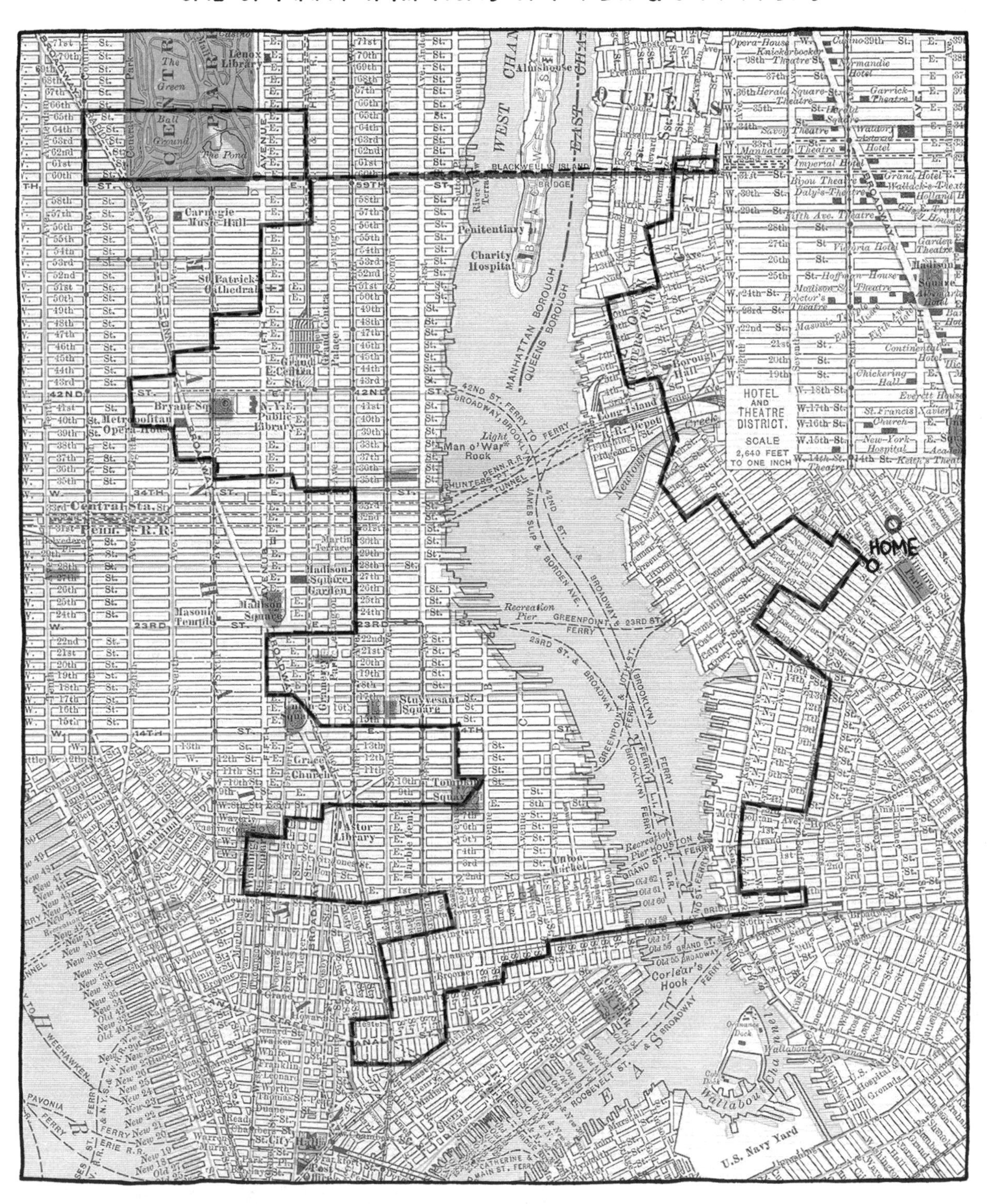

IF YOU WERE TO JOIN ME ON ONE OF MY LONG CITY WALKS, THIS IS WHAT YOU'D EXPERIENCE:

A DISCUSSION OF REAL-LIFE ISSUES THAT NEED ANALYZING AND/OR CRITICIZING.
AND THAT'S WHY I DON'T BOTHER CHECKING FACEBOOK EVENTS ANYMORE.
I ENJOY PERUSING THE EVENTS JUST FOR THE ENORMOUS SENSE OF RELIEF I GET KNOWING I DON'T HAVE TO SUFFER THROUGH ANY OF THEM.

EATING AT A CHEAP, UNCROWDED RESTAURANT THAT PLAYS MUSIC AT A REASONABLE VOLUME, OR GETTING STREET VENDOR FOOD OR PIZZA TO EAT IN THE PARK.

I DON'T KNOW WHY THERE AREN'T MASS RIOTS AGAINST LOUD MUSIC IN RESTAURANTS. WE DON'T HAVE TO TOLERATE LIVING LIKE THAT!! FUCKIN' SAVAGES.
NOT EVERYONE IS AS PASSIONATE AS YOU ARE.

LISTENING TO ME TELL YOU A BUNCH OF RANDOM FACTS FROM A BOOK I READ, A PODCAST I HEARD, OR A MOVIE/TV SHOW I WATCHED.

PINBALL WAS BANNED IN NYC UNTIL 1978! IT WAS A "PINBALL PROHIBITION," AND OFFICIALS WOULD SMASH THE MACHINES WITH SLEDGEHAMMERS, AND DUMP THEM IN THE RIVER. THEY'RE PROBABLY STILL DOWN THERE, JUST HANGING OUT...

BUT WHILE ALL THAT IS GOING ON, THIS IS WHAT I'M DOING UNBEKNOWNST TO YOU:

OGLING THE ARCHITECTURE AND DETAILS OF HISTORIC BUILDINGS.

IF ONLY I KNEW HOW TO SCUBA DI...
OOOOH, THAT DETAILED CROWN MOLDING ON THAT BROWNSTONE!

SCANNING THE GROUND FOR IRON WORKS–STAMPED BRASS NAMEPLATES ON BASEMENT SIDEWALK HATCHES.

LOOKING FOR ORNATE ANTIQUE DOOR HARDWARE ON OLDER APARTMENTS AND BUILDINGS.

LOOKING FOR OLD ARCHITECTURE PARTIALLY OBSCURED BY NEW ARCHITECTURE.

IT LOOKS LIKE THE NEW BUILDING IS EATING THE OLD ONE. MY CARTOONIST PAL TOM K. CALLS THAT "SHARKITECTURE."

MAKING A MENTAL NOTE OF EVERY TYPE OF FIRE ALARM ON THE STREET CORNERS.

SPOTTING PATCHES OF OLD SLATE SIDEWALK, OR HIDDEN COBBLESTONES PEEKING THROUGH A POTHOLE IN THE ROAD.

BASICALLY, I SPEND THE WHOLE WALK IN CURRENT NEW YORK CITY LOOKING FOR EVIDENCE OF THE PAST NEW YORK CITY.

AND ALL THE WHILE, I'M LOOKING AT APARTMENTS AND IMAGINING WHAT IT'D BE LIKE TO LIVE IN THEM, AND TO SIT ON THE FIRE ESCAPE OVER A SMALL STORE ON A CROWDED STREET AND PEOPLE-WATCH ALL DAY.

I'M PERPETUALLY FANTASIZING ABOUT A TIME I NEVER EXPERIENCED, AND IMAGINING A LIFE I'LL NEVER LIVE.

THE LONG WALK STARTS IN GREENPOINT, BROOKLYN, ALONG MANHATTAN AVE.

MARCO POLO
729 MANHATTAN AVE
ITALIAN LEATHER SHOES
Green Point
WE BUY
GREENPOINT
VISION CARE
ASSOC.
718/ 389-6234
PAIR of GLASSES $99
SALE 20-50% OFF
EYE EXAMS
CONTACTS
LABORATORY
DMV TEST
DESIGNER FRAMES
LASIK
GREENPOINT
złotko
BACKSTAGE BOUTIQUE
OPEN

BEDFORD AVE. NEAR N.7TH ST. IN WILLIAMSBURG

spikeHill
spikeHill
NORTHSIDE PHARMAC
HAPPY HOUR 4-7
NEW YORK CITY
Coca Cola ZERO
am

BEDFORD AVE. NEAR N.6TH ST.

S&B
194 BEDFORD
STELLA ARTOIS
CLOSED
SIERRA NEVADA
LUNCH
A
Happy Hour 3~6
P
水
MIZU
EXCEPT SUNDAY
EXCEPT SUNDAY
A
194
OPEN

新婚世界
RENTALS & SALES
BRIDAL GOWNS · TUXEDOS
WEDDING SPECIALIST
PHOTOGRAPHY & VIDEOGRAPHY
囍嫁
Manhattan Bridal
Wedding Center
212-219-8338
126
WEDDING
SPECIALIST
PHOTOGRAPHY
& VIDEOGRAPHY
ESPECIALES VENDEMOS AL DETALLE. TRAJES DE NOVIA PARA TODOS LOS TAUAÑOS PRECIOS DE FACTORIA. PEQUEÑOS MEDIANOS GRANDES
QUYNH PHARMACY
ATM
PLAY HERE
$2
50¢
$4
ATM
EBT
Gay City
THE BOWERY
CAPITALE
SAFE DEPOSIT VAULT

BOWERY AND GRAND ST. IN LITTLE ITALY/CHINATOWN

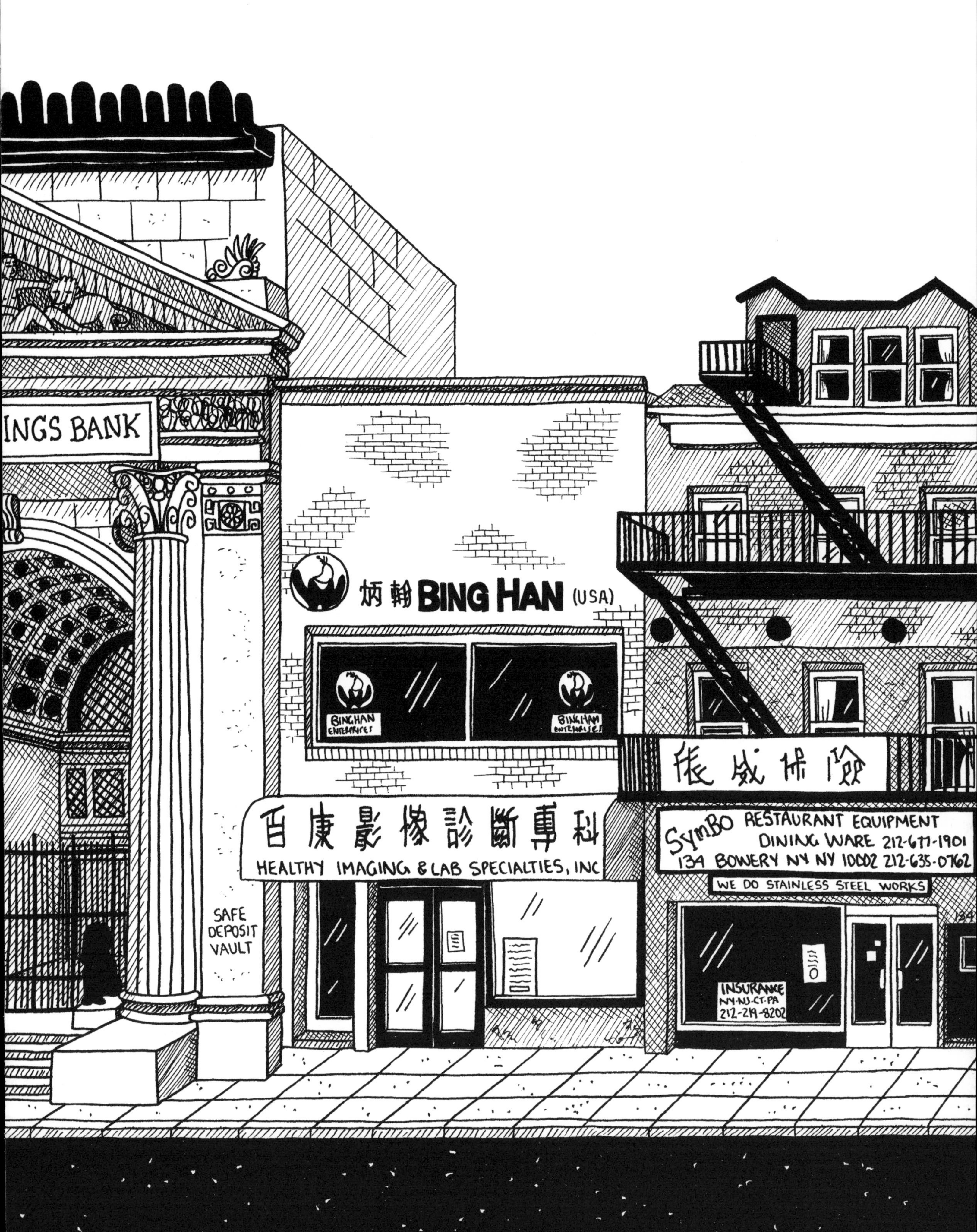

BOWERY NEAR BROOME ST.

TING
ING
Tel: 941-8482
FOR RENT
STOREFRONT
New Generation Lighting
20%
50%
New Generation Lighting
20%
50%
New Generation Lighting

BOWERY BETWEEN PRINCE ST. AND STANTON ST. IN THE LOWER EAST SIDE

NEW MUSEUM
NEW MUSEUM
NEW MUSEUM
BOWERY
PRINCE ST

LUDLOW ST. BETWEEN STANTON ST. AND RIVINGTON ST. IN THE LOWER EAST SIDE

livingroom
152 Ludlow
Gotham COURT
CAKESHOP
TONIGHT
WILL SHEFF
8 PM
FRIDAY
Shannon & The Clams

MACDOUGAL ST. BETWEEN MINETTA LN.
AND BLEECKER ST. IN GREENWICH VILLAGE
restaurant
A
the GRISLY PEAR
Closed
OFF THE
HAPPY HOUR 3-6
OPEN
TWO FOR ONE WELL DRINK!

OFF THE WAGON
BAR & GRILL
open until 4AM
HAPPY HOUR MON-FRI 2-8pm
ATM INSIDE
Artichoke
PIZZA
N BAR & GRILL
PITCHERS & SHOTS
NYC NIGHTS
Artichoke
DRAFT BEER
A
PIZZA
ARTICHOKE BASTILLE'S
Minettas
TAVERN
A

8TH AVE. BETWEEN W.40TH ST. AND W.39TH ST IN MIDTOWN/HELL'S KITCHEN

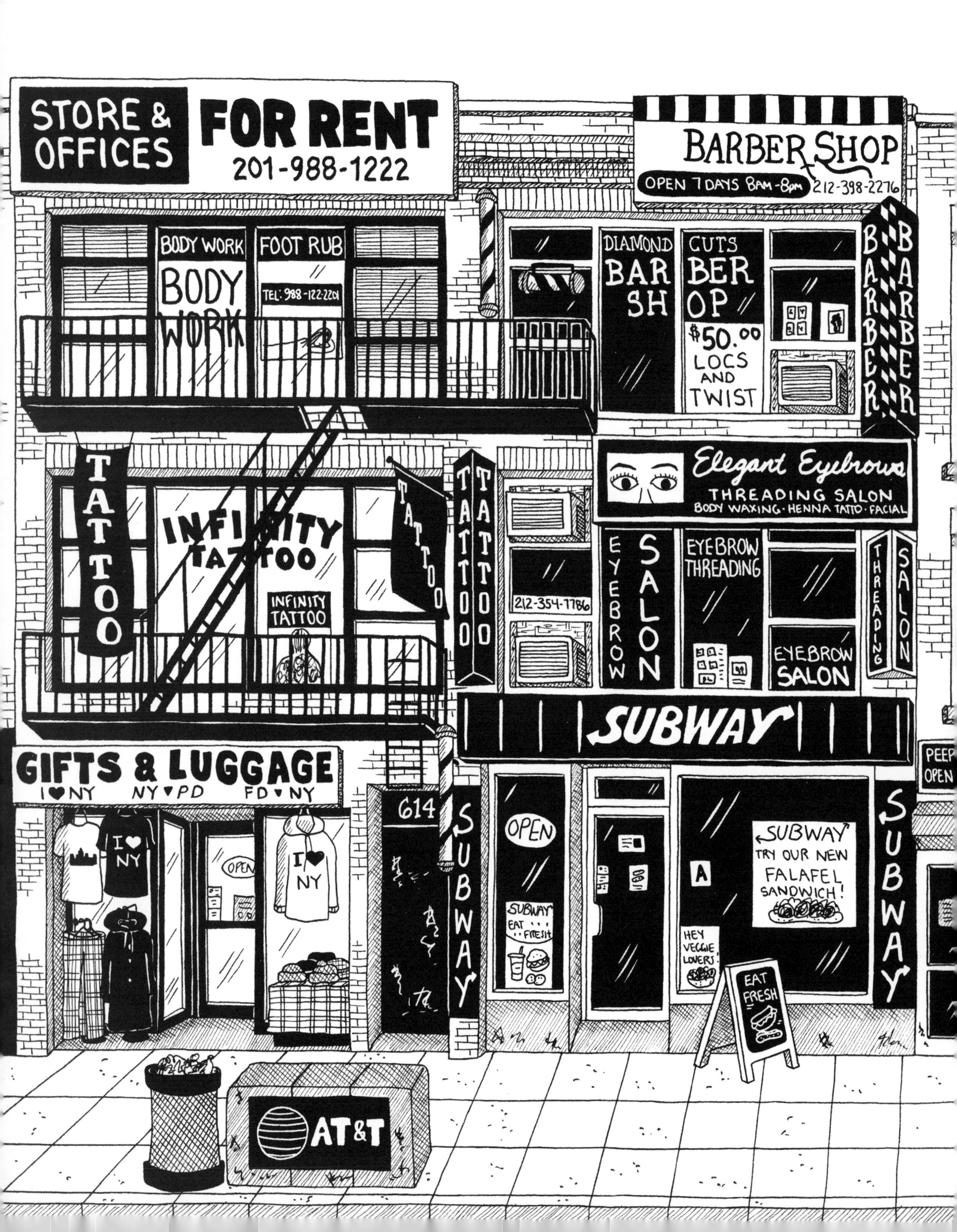

WE BU
GOLD & DIAMON
GEM
PAWNBROKERS
718 - CALL - GEM
SHOW
XXX
MOVIES
88 SPA
PAWN SHOP
PAWN SHOP
TAROT CARDS
PSYCIC READINGS
ALL MALE PEEP SHOW
BACHELOR PARTY
ADULT VIDEOS · XXX TOYS · LINGERIE
610 N.Y. TOYS 8TH AVE.
CITY GADGETS
CAMERAS · COMPUTERS · FAX
WE REPAIR ALL PHONES
· GOLD
· JEWELRY
· DIAMONDS
GEM
Pawnbrokers
TOYS
XXX
LINGERIE
ADULT TOYS
PEEP SHOW
XXX DVD
OPEN
ADULT DVDS
WE FIX ALL PHONES
2-6
NO STANDING 7AM-7PM
TAROT CARDS
PSYCIC READINGS
PSYCHIC
WE BUY DIAMONDS &
GOLD WATCHES
DIAMOND JEWELRY
FABULOUS DISCOUNTS
ON WATCHES, JEWELRY & GOLD

21ST ST. NEAR 43RD AVE. IN LONG ISLAND CITY

LIC
WELCOME TO QUEENS
SILVER CUP
SHOW SP PALACE
gentlemen's club
& restaurant
TOTALLY NUDE
42-50
ALL NUDE
GIRLS GIRLS
GIRLS GIRLS
GIRLS
GIRLS
GIRLS
ALL NUDE
PORN STAR NIGHT

The

End

RECOMMENDED READING & ONLINE SOURCES

I HAVE READ DOZENS OF BOOKS ABOUT NEW YORK CITY OVER THE YEARS, HERE IS A LIST OF SOME OF MY FAVORITES. NOT ALL OF THESE BOOKS ARE NON-FICTION HISTORY BOOKS, BUT SOMETIMES FICTION IS ESSENTIAL IN CAPTURING UP THE ESSENCE OF A CITY. I WILL UNDOUBTEDLY ACCIDENTALLY OMIT SOME BOOKS I ENJOYED, MY APOLOGIES TO ANY AUTHOR WHOSE BOOK I READ BUT DID NOT MENTION HERE.

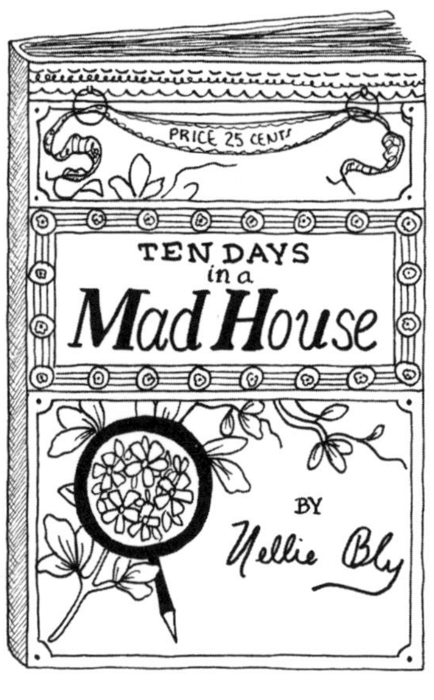

HELLO NY: AN ILLUSTRATED LOVE LETTER TO THE FIVE BOROUGHS. BY JULIA ROTHMAN
RATS: OBSERVATIONS ON THE HISTORY & HABITAT OF THE CITY'S MOST UNWANTED INHABITANTS. BY ROBERT SULLIVAN
THE GILDED AGE IN NEW YORK. BY ESTHER CRAIN
LET THE GREAT WORLD SPIN. BY COLUM MCCANN
FIVE HUNDRED BUILDINGS OF NEW YORK. BY BILL HARRIS (AUTHOR) AND JORG BROCKMANN (PHOTOGRAPHER)
NEW YORK DRAWINGS. BY ADRIAN TOMINE
BROOKLYN'S HISTORIC GREENPOINT. BY BRIAN MERLIS AND RICCARDO GOMES
JUST KIDS. BY PATTI SMITH
INSIDE THE APPLE: A STREETWISE HISTORY OF NEW YORK CITY. BY MICHELLE NEVIUS AND JAMES NEVIUS
NEW YORK: THE NOVEL. BY EDWARD RUTHERFURD
WILL EISNER'S NEW YORK: LIFE IN THE BIG CITY. BY WILL EISNER
MY NEW YORK DIARY. BY JULIE DOUCET
ALL THE BUILDINGS IN NEW YORK: THAT I'VE DRAWN SO FAR. BY JAMES GULLIVER HANCOCK
I NEVER KNEW THAT ABOUT NEW YORK. BY CHRISTOPHER WINN
THE NEW YORK TRILOGY. BY PAUL AUSTER
THE WORKS: ANATOMY OF A CITY. BY KATE ASCHER
EVERY PERSON IN NEW YORK. BY JASON POLAN
A HISTORY OF NEW YORK IN 101 OBJECTS. BY SAM ROBERTS
THE BATTLE WITH THE SLUM. BY JACOB A. RIIS

ONLINE RESEARCH SOURCES & ENTERTAINING SITES:

THE BOWERY BOYS—BOWERYBOYSHISTORY.COM
SCOUTING NEW YORK—SCOUTINGNY.COM
OLD NYC—OLDNYC.ORG
CINEMA TREASURES—CINEMATREASURES.ORG
CURBED NEW YORK—NY.CURBED.COM
MUSEUM OF THE CITY OF NEW YORK—MCNY.ORG
BKLYNR—BKLYNR.COM
THE TENEMENT MUSEUM—TENEMENT.ORG
GREENPOINTERS—GREENPOINTERS.COM
ATLAS OBSCURA—ATLASOBSCURA.COM
NEW YORK PUBLIC LIBRARY—NYPL.ORG
BROOKLYN PIX—BROOKLYNPIX.COM
UNTAPPED CITIES—UNTAPPEDCITIES.COM
NYC MUNICIPAL ARCHIVES—NYC.GOV/HTML/RECORDS/
AFTER THE FINAL CURTAIN—AFTERTHEFINALCURTAIN.NET
EPHEMERAL NEW YORK—EPHEMERALNEWYORK.WORDPRESS.COM
JEREMIAH'S VANISHING NEW YORK—VANISHINGNEWYORK.BLOGSPOT.COM

THANK YOU SECTION

MY UTMOST GRATITUDE FOR MAKING THIS BOOK HAPPEN GOES TO MY EDITOR, BECKY KOH, AND THE WHOLE BLACK DOG & LEVENTHAL TEAM, AS WELL AS MY AGENT, MICHELLE BROWER. MANY THANKS TO BOB MANKOFF AT *THE NEW YORKER* FOR TAKING A CHANCE ON ME, AND TO ROZ CHAST, WITHOUT WHOM NONE OF THIS WOULD HAVE HAPPENED.

THANK YOU TO THE WONDERFUL PEOPLE IN MY DAILY LIFE WHO KEPT ME SANE DURING MY TIME IN NYC, ESPECIALLY JEN PHIPPEN, SARAH GLIDDEN, LISA HANAWALT, DOMITILLE COLLARDEY, TOM BOLGER, AND DYLAN JONES. A PROFUSE THANK YOU TO OLIVER TRIXL FOR BEING A PATIENT PARTNER AND HELPING ME WITH TEDIOUS EDITING WORK. MANY THANKS TO MY HARDWORKING INTERNS, ERIKA JOHNSON, AARON SNOW, AND KARR ANTUNES. AS ALWAYS, THANK YOU TO MY FAMILY, WHO HAVE ALWAYS SUPPORTED ME, EVEN WHEN THEY MAYBE SHOULDN'T HAVE.

I WORKED ON THIS BOOK DURING MY LAST YEARS IN NYC, SPECIFICALLY IN MY GREENPOINT STUDIO, AND AT PROPELLER COFFEE (RIP) IN BROOKLYN, BUT OTHER PARTS OF THE BOOK WERE WORKED ON IN THE MANSFIELD CABIN AT THE MACDOWELL COLONY IN NEW HAMPSHIRE, IN A RENOVATED SHED IN COLORADO, IN AN OLD FARMHOUSE AT THE SOU'WESTER IN WASHINGTON, AND IN MY MOM'S GARAGE ATTIC IN CALIFORNIA. THANK YOU SO MUCH TO EVERYONE WHO PROVIDED SHELTER/FOOD/COMPANY/ISOLATION IN THOSE LOCATIONS. I'M EVEN THANKFUL TO MY ASSHOLE LANDLORD WHO ILLEGALLY EVICTED ME. HAD HE NOT GIVEN ME CHEAP RENT FOR SUSPECT REASONS, I WOULD HAVE NEVER HAVE BEEN ABLE TO STAY IN BROOKLYN FOR AS LONG AS I DID. AND LAST BUT NOT LEAST, THANK YOU TO NEW YORK CITY FOR EVERYTHING.

ABOUT THE AUTHOR

JULIA WERTZ WAS BORN IN 1982 IN THE SAN FRANCISCO BAY AREA. SHE LIVED IN BROOKLYN, NEW YORK FROM 2006-2016. SHE IS A PROFESSIONAL CARTOONIST AND AMATEUR HISTORIAN WHO DABBLES IN EXPLORING AND PHOTOGRAPHING ABANDONED PLACES, WEIRD TOWNS, AND OLD STUFF. HER AUTOBIOGRAPHICAL COMICS INCLUDE *DRINKING AT THE MOVIES*, *THE INFINITE WAIT AND OTHER STORIES*, AND *MUSEUM OF MISTAKES: THE FART PARTY COLLECTION*. HER WORK HAS APPEARED IN *THE NEW YORK TIMES*, *HARPER'S MAGAZINE*, *THE BELIEVER*, *MEDIUM*, *THE BEST AMERICAN COMICS*, AND OTHER PLACES. HER COMICS APPEAR REGULARLY IN *THE NEW YORKER*.